*This book is dedicated, with much love,
to my amazing wife Janet and my children Ariel and Xander.
The adventure continues…*

Tribute to Lisa Jane Gray (1959–2009)

As an additional dedication for this book on stop-motion animation, I am honored to present a photo tribute to Lisa Jane Gray, a very talented artist and contributor to the stop-motion community who passed away very suddenly on July 10, 2009. Lisa Jane was a great talent and a sweet lady whom I had the privilege to meet and talk with on a few occasions, before she left us all too soon. Her career as an animator and director spanned nearly 30 years, including feature films, television series, and commercials. She also taught animation students at the New Brunswick Community College's Miramichi Campus in Canada, and she worked for Cosgrove Hall in the U.K., Egmont Imagination in Denmark, various studios in New Zealand, and several studios across Canada, including several years as an animator and associate of Bowes Production in Vancouver. She is greatly missed by all who knew and worked with her.

(Various production photos courtesy of Bowes Production, Inc. Thanks to Paul Moldovanos and David Bowes for providing these images.)

Table of Contents

Foreword

By Henry Selick, director of *Coraline, The Nightmare Before Christmas, James and the Giant Peach,* and *Slow Bob in the Lower Dimensions*

There are many ways to make movies a frame at a time: drawing them by hand like Walt Disney's *Pinocchio* and Hayao Miyazaki's *Spirited Away*, computer graphics like Pixar's *Toy Story* and *The Incredibles*, 2D cut-outs like the cult feature *Twice Upon a Time*, animating sand or paint on glass, scratching film emulsion, moving pins on a screen, slicing wax and clay, and no doubt other techniques I've never witnessed. But I happen to love stop-motion best.

So much of animation's history has been about the pursuit of making things move smoothly, to hide the artist's hand. When CG animation hit the big time, first as special effects and then with the Pixar features, it delivered on this goal in spades. The animation was perfectly smooth, without a single, unintended bump or jerk. It was sexy and shiny, and audiences ate it up . . . and they still are.

CG can do anything, but it can't do easily what is inherent in stop-motion: give proof of the artist's hand through the inescapable mistakes made and communicate to the audience that what they are watching really, truly exists. It was this part that grabbed and haunted me when I first saw Ray Harryhausen's work at age 5—I knew his Cyclops actually existed!

Why does even crude stop-motion animation have an effect on us? Ken Priebe, the author of this great book, and I share a similar theory: stop-motion connects us to the time when our toys came to life through the power of our imaginations.

My Journey

I didn't plan on becoming a stop-motion director; it just happened. I was going to art school when I was first bitten. I'd made a life-sized figure for a sculpting class and couldn't decide on just one pose. It had simple joints, so I started to change the pose, looking for something better. In photography class, I began to shoot little series of pictures, changing things in the frame. I desperately needed my artwork to *move*. So, I made the journey west to study animation at CalArts, where I saw a Jan Svankmajer short called *Jabberwocky*. It was a life-changer for me, with powerful images inspired by Lewis Carroll and stop-motion that grabbed hold of you.

While working at Disney, I made a short film called *Seepage*, which featured both hand-drawn animation and stop-motion figures sitting around a real swimming pool. I was hooked and left Disney to work on a cut-out feature, the next-best thing to stop-mo. Having made several short films on my own, they made me a sequence director, and I storyboarded several sequences and pitched in doing some animation.

As my life-without-a-plan unfolded, I did feature storyboard drawings and designs for the claymation sequences on Walter Murch's feature *Return to Oz*. I next did more storyboard work for director Carol Ballard, who had me shoot some second-unit miniatures where I realized I barely knew anything about lighting real stuff. More lessons learned.

I eventually got going with a bunch of stop-motion MTV spots I wrote and directed, which I'm still proud of to this day. I built stuff, lit and shot some, and animated a few, but it was here that I started to put together a small crew—people who were better than I was at a given task. I hired better animators than me, like Eric Leighton, Anthony Scott, and Tim Hittle from the revived *Gumby* series. And when I landed nine Pillsbury Doughboy commercials, the team grew again. I got the go-ahead for my animated pilot, *Slow Bob in the Lower Dimensions*, hired Pete Kozachik to light and shoot it, and the team grew once more. And when Tim Burton, an old friend from my Disney days, called to ask if I wanted to direct *The Nightmare Before Christmas*, we were all ready to step up and make that movie.

We worked for three and a half years on *Nightmare* in some old warehouse space in San Francisco, and when the film was released in 1993, my extraordinary team of artists and I felt we'd done Tim's tale proud. That same year, though, CG beat out Phil Tippett's stop-mo dinosaurs for *Jurassic Park*. And in 1995, a year before our second film, *James and the Giant Peach*, came out, *Toy Story* was released, and stop-motion features were over. Except, they weren't.

Your Journey and This Book

Here it is, 2010, and stop-motion, the most ancient and magical form of animation, is more popular than it's ever been. There are TV series like *Robot Chicken*, three or four feature films are going into production at once, more students at art and film schools are taking up stop-motion, and, from the amount of new stop-motion bits on YouTube, more kids of all ages are wrestling toys, clay, dolls, and puppets to life than at any time in history. *And* there are now multiple books on stop-motion where none existed before, including the one in your hands. Ken Priebe's *The Advanced Art of Stop-Motion Animation* is the best book on the subject available. Ken has incredible knowledge of stop-motion history (I thought George Pal invented replacement animation, and I was certain *Mad Monster Party* was the first U.S. stop-motion feature . . . Ken knows better). He shares great how-to info for all the steps and many of the choices in making your own stop-motion film, from making puppets to rack-focusing your camera lens to types of lip sync. He includes wonderful interviews (including one each with my friends and comrades-in-arms, Pete Kozachik and Trey Thomas, who both worked with me on all my features). He covers stop-motion education, stop-motion blogs, and festivals. Ken seems to cover it all, and he covers it well. I'm both hurt and a little angry that Ken didn't have the decency to have been born 20 years earlier so that we could have copies of his book when we first started *The Nightmare Before Christmas*.

I stand on the shoulders of Willis O'Brien, Ray Harryhausen, George Pal, and Jan Svankmajer, and I owe my name in stop-motion to my brilliant crew members like Anthony Scott, Eric Leighton, Paul Berry, Trey Thomas, Pete Kozachik, and Joe Ranft. Let *The Advanced Art of Stop-Motion Animation* be your leg up, and good luck with the great films you're going to make.

Henry Selick, April 2010

Acknowledgments

Once again, going through another several months of late nights and caffeinated beverages working on another book, I could not possibly have conceived it without the generous help and support of so many people, who deserve all the thanks in the world. First and foremost, thanks to my Lord and God Jesus Christ for "animating" the whole process, sustaining me, and making all the connections to bring it together in one piece. Extra-special thanks to my amazing wife, Janet, for her assistance, patience, and encouragement, and to our little ones, Ariel and Xander, who rock my world and keep making me smile. Special thanks to my extended family in the U.S. and Canada and my church family at Cedar Park for their encouragement, prayer, and support. Thanks also to the students and staff of VanArts and Academy of Art University, to my friends from the Vancouver chapter of the Association for Computing Machinery's Special Interest Group on Graphics and Interactive Techniques (ACM SIGGRAPH), and to my friend Steve Stanchfield for his continued support after initially getting me started and hooked on animation many years ago.

Extra thanks to my special interview subjects—Seamus Walsh, Mark Caballero, and Chris Finnegan at Screen Novelties, Pete Kozachik, Trey Thomas, Bronwen Kyffin, Larry Bafia, Webster Colcord, Marc Spess, Ryan McCulloch, and Justin and Shel Rasch—for the gift of their time and wisdom, and the images they shared to complement their words. Also, a second helping of thanks to Justin, Shel, and Bronwen for the extensive contributions they made in other parts of this book, in particular the sections on puppets and stereoscopic photography. This book is that much richer with your contributions, and I definitely could not have written these sections without your generous assistance!

The first chapter on the history of stop-motion features alone has a huge list of people to thank for providing permission and access to images, research, and detailed information about the films: L.B. Martin-Starewitch, Dan Goodsell, Jerry Beck, Rick Catizone, Michael Sporn, Rick Goldschmidt, Mark and Seamus at Screen Novelties, Yoram Gross and Mimi Intal at Yoram Gross

Films, Mario Caprino at Caprino Studios, Will Vinton and Gillian Frances at Freewill Entertainment, Barry Purves, Jurgen Kling, Mike Belzer, Derek Hayes, Naomi Jones, Christiane Cegavske, Brian Demoskoff, Marjolaine Parot, Dean English, Marc Stephenson, Tatia Rosenthal, Jason Vanderhill, Adam Elliot and Samantha Fitzgerald at Adam Elliot Pictures, Adriana Piasek-Wanski at La Parti Productions, Carrie Filler and Chris Woolston at Premavision Studios, Mark Shapiro and Maggie Begley with Laika, Howard Cohen at Animaking Studios, and Emily Harris, Heidi Leigh, and Whitney Morris at the Animazing Gallery. Extra special thanks to Stephen Chiodo, Richard Kent Burton, and John Ellis for the extensive information and photo archives from *I Go Pogo*, and to the extensive chain of e-mail connections that unraveled the obscure history behind *Bino Fabule*, which began with Jason Vanderhill and led me to the kind assistance of Tamu Townsend, Erik Goulet, Denis Roy, Andre A. Belanger, Louis-Philippe Rondeau, and Elaine Bigras at CinéGroupe. Thank you all for this unique documentation of stop-motion history!

For their contributions, assistance, advice, support, and sharing of images for chapters and sections on puppets, digital cinematography, visual effects, education, and animation festivals, I would also like to extend special thanks to Melanie Vachon, Don Carlson, Dave Hettmer, Ron Cole, Frida Ramirez, Emi Gonzalez, Lucas Wareing, Chayse Irvin, Henrique Moser, Gary Welch, Shawn Tilling, Brett Foxwell, Anthony Scott and K Ishibashi, Patrick Boivin, Steve Stanchfield, Nick Hilligoss, Rich Johnson, Richard Svensson, Carlo Vogele, Gautam Modkar, Jason Walker, Pete and Sue Tait, Talon Toth at Protodemon Studios, Roni Lubliner at Universal, Patricia Dillon and Sophie Quevillon at the National Film Board of Canada, Chris Walsh at Sheridan College, Stephen Chiodo and Max Winston at CalArts, Beth Sousa and Matt Ellsworth at Academy of Art University, Jurgen Kling of Weirdoughmationfilms, Elizabeth Seavey at Bendle High School, Lee Skinner of Little Scholar Productions, Peter Lord and Amy Wood at Aardman, Galen Fott of Bigfott Studios, Erik Goulet of the Montreal Stop-Motion Film Festival, and Jeff Bell, James Emler, and Christa LeCraw from the VanArts Digital Photography Department. Thank you all!

And to all who contributed to the appendix on the stop-motion community, (on the companion CD), this book is a gift to all of you for the way you encourage and support all of us in pursuing this mysterious craft: Marc Spess, Mike Brent, Shelley Noble, Yasemin Sayibas Akyez, Ron Cole, Santino Vitale, Season Mustful, Jeffrey Roche, Sven Bonnichsen, Don Carlson, Jeremy Spake,

Jesse Broadkey, Chuck Duke, John Ikuma, Ethan Marak, John Hankins, Emily Baxter, Rich Johnson, Chris Walsh, Paul McConnochie, Ceri Watling, Ben Whitehouse, Guillaume Lenel, Richard Svensson, Adrian Encinas Salamanca, Julie Pitts, Miles Blow, and Nick Hilligoss.

If this was like a verbal acceptance speech, I'm sure the band leader would be starting the music and rushing me off the stage by now, so last but not least, I have to say an extra-special thanks to Colin Gray, David Bowes, and Paul Moldovanos for helping me honor the memory of Lisa Jane Gray in this book, Anthony Scott for his kind assistance, Henry Selick for the gift of his amazing foreword, the entire staff of Course Technology, editors Dan Foster and Lionel I. Orozco, and especially Heather Hurley for initially asking me to write another book!

Thank you *all*…and to Ray Harryhausen, Happy 90th Birthday!

See you in the movies!

Introduction

Stop-motion animation is in the hands of the people. I say this as a pun. As a craft, the act of animating in stop-motion requires a person to literally place a puppet in their hands and bring it to life, frame by frame. The other meaning is that in the past few years, the art of stop-motion has experienced a renaissance that has not only brought it more prominently into the big film studios, but also brought it into the hands of regular people worldwide. It is happening in cramped suburban garages and spacious studio soundstages. It is also making its way to more homes, schools, websites, and mobile devices in a manner that is unprecedented in our time.

When stop-motion first started as an art form, it seemed to be kept as a mysterious and closely guarded magic trick. The publicity of the time behind films like *King Kong* (1933) and the feature film *Hansel and Gretel: An Opera Fantasy* (1954) revealed false information to the masses about just how stop-motion was really done. For decades following, fans of stop-motion films had to rely on stamp-sized photographs in science-fiction magazines to try and guess how they were made, and then take a stab at it with a Super 8 camera. Once they had completed their films, there were very limited venues for showing them to anyone other than themselves. It's a different world now, and the secret is out, so today's filmmakers are gladly faced more with questions about how to tell a captivating story than about with the technique itself. In addition to the tools becoming more accessible, the Internet now provides a free platform for everything from simple experiments to full-fledged films. In the online universe, artists not only can share their films, but also can connect with other artists who can offer advice and support to make them even better.

What is also amazing about this growth for stop-motion animation is how fast it has recently happened. In 2006, I wrote my first book, *The Art of Stop-Motion Animation* (Figure I.1), as a practical guide for how stop-motion films were made.

Figure I.1

The Art of Stop-Motion Animation (2006) by Ken A. Priebe.

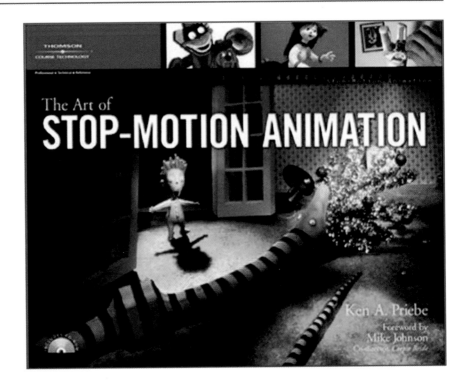

At that time, we were just starting to see the advent of digital SLR cameras and their use for stop-motion photography, both in feature films and independent projects. Blogs and online journals for documenting productions had been around for a few years, but they were really just beginning to become more popular. Facebook, Twitter, and Livestream did not exist, and YouTube was brand new—no one was really sure how long it would last. And now, look at what has happened. Just a few years later, and stop-motion is everywhere—online, on television, and in theaters. People still love it as much today as they did when Kong first emerged from behind the trees on Skull Island. At its heart, the basic techniques behind stop-motion have not changed, but we now have the capacity to present it in the sharpest resolution possible, combine it seamlessly with computer graphics, and even shoot it in 3D. Just imagine what the next 4 years could bring!

My own experiences with stop-motion animation and other life adventures have also evolved since I last published my first book. A month after the book was released, my daughter Ariel was born, so the summer of 2006 kind of felt like having two babies at once. That fall, my friend Leslie Bishko, who was involved with the Vancouver chapter for the Association for Computing Machinery's Special Interest Group on Graphics and Interactive Techniques (ACM SIGGRAPH), asked if I would be interested in being part of a stop-motion event to help promote my book. I was delighted for the opportunity and was able to participate in an evening of presentations and panel discussion with none other than Anthony Scott (animation supervisor, *Corpse Bride*), Peter Muyzers (visual effects artist, *Corpse Bride*), and Larry Bafia (animator from Will Vinton Studios and PDI). I was asked back to speak for various Vancouver SIGGRAPH events related to stop-motion, and became an active member and volunteer with the chapter, helping to organize their annual Spark FX and Spark Animation festivals and bring inspiration and innovation to the community (http://www.siggraph.ca).

Another opportunity that came my way was being asked to develop an online stop-motion course for the Academy of Art University's Cyber Campus, an online version of the degree programs offered through their school in San Francisco. Using my book as a required text, I got the chance to expand on the instructional sections through two online courses, ANM 380 (Stop Motion Animation 1) and ANM 382 (Stop Motion Animation 2). Subsequently, I have taught these courses online and helped more students improve their skills in the stop-motion craft. The process of building these courses also involved flying down to San Francisco to shoot animation and puppet-building demos in their production studio, which was hard work but a great deal of fun. On one of these visits, I had the opportunity to meet in person the technical editor for my first book (and this one), Lionel I. Orozco of Stop Motion Works (Figure I.2).

Figure I.2

Author Ken Priebe (left) and technical editor Lionel I. Orozco (right) at the Academy of Art University's Cyber Campus studio, proud to welcome you to another book!

As 2009 dawned, I continued my work as a mild-mannered admissions advisor for VanArts (Vancouver Institute of Media Arts) by day and a crime-fighting stop-motion instructor by night, both for students at VanArts and online for the Academy of Art University. Another addition to my family was also preparing for his debut; my son Xander was born that summer. Meanwhile, the stop-motion universe was generating a lot of buzz from the release of the feature film *Coraline*, which had advanced the art form into new territories of innovative storytelling, and many other independent films were being noticed as well. Riding the crest of this wave, I was approached by Course Technology with the idea of writing another book that would go into more up-to-date detail on the art form. Several months later, you are holding that book in your hands.

My first book, *The Art of Stop-Motion Animation*, was written as a practical guide to the basic principles of stop-motion filmmaking, providing a solid introduction for anyone new to the medium. The focus of this new volume is to take a closer look at the techniques of stop-motion that were touched on only briefly in the first book and to cover some advances in the art form that have only come into fruition since 2006. You will find new techniques for building puppets, including the technology behind rapid prototyping of computer models for stop-motion production. You will read more detailed information on camera rigs, effects, and shooting stop-motion with a digital SLR camera, including stereoscopic photography (to make your films in eye-popping 3D). The basic principles of animation covered in the first volume are expanded into specific applications for character performance, and there is more material covered on visual effect compositing techniques. The history of the medium, this time around, puts more focus on stop-motion films made in feature-length format, including several obscure films that have never been documented to this extent. Also, whereas the first volume featured six interviews with other stop-motion artists, this new book presents eight new interviews with some of the best and brightest in the field, spanning everything from big studio productions to low-budget indie filmmaking.

If you are a fan of stop-motion or any other kind of animation, I trust you will find plenty of good reading material in this book. However, because it's an advanced volume, if you are new to learning animation and want a book for guidance on how stop-motion is done, I would recommend my first book. The basic principles covered in *The Art of Stop-Motion Animation* are important to grasp before moving on to the more advanced techniques covered in this book. All things considered, there is only so much a book can accomplish in covering the vast array of skills required for stop-motion, but my hope is that both volumes together will provide you with a good launching pad for your own creations. The vast resources for stop-motion available online and the help of other enthusiasts should also be continually tapped so that we can all continue to find new ways for telling stories in this medium.

Tools and technology will always continue to change and become more advanced. However, in his essay "What Is Cinema?" the noted French film critic Andre Bazin reminds us, "The dream of creating a living human being by means other than natural reproduction has been a preoccupation of man from time immemorial: hence such myths as Pygmalion and Galatea." We may be able to digitally remove the strings and rigs from our modern-day puppets, but deep inside ourselves we are simply fulfilling the dreams of those who graced the Greek amphitheaters and medieval marionette stages with that simple vision: to create the illusion of life.

Welcome, read on, and enjoy this magic between the frames.

On the CD

The companion CD for this book contains QuickTime videos of various animation exercises and clips that are referenced within the text for your own enjoyment, study, and analysis. The CD also contains two special appendices in pdf format, which represent the growth of stop-motion education and the online stop-motion community, celebrating the work of several artists who share their work through their websites and production blogs.

CD-ROM Downloads

If you purchased an ebook version of this book, and the book had a companion CD-ROM, we will mail you a copy of the disc. Please send ptrsupplements@cengage.com the title of the book, the ISBN, your name, address, and phone number.

Thank you.

1

History of Stop-Motion Feature Films

Most of the stop-motion animation produced in the past century, of which most audiences are aware, has been done for either short formats or special effects. The earliest stop-motion films were merely experiments in moving objects before the camera, like *Bewitched Matches* (1913) and *The Automatic Moving Company* (1912). The former was actually a stop-motion sequence for a live-action short. American puppet films lasting only 7 to 12 minutes were produced by Kinex Studios for home viewing and by George Pal for theatrical distribution, while the Czech movement of puppet film shorts began overseas in Eastern Europe. At the same time, stop-motion effects for creature sequences in live-action fantasy films began with the innovations of Willis O'Brien and Ray Harryhausen, moving onto *Star Wars* and countless other films of the 1980s. Independent short films such as Will Vinton's *Closed Mondays* and Co Hoedeman's *Sandcastle* would also gain recognition in festivals and win Best Animated Short Film at the Academy Awards. Another vessel for stop-motion in short format worldwide was television, which brought us Gumby, Morph, Colargol, the California Raisins, and many other characters, series, parodies, and commercials.

Whether it was for a short film or a brief fantasy sequence in a feature, these stop-motion efforts were designed to hold the audience's attention only for a brief moment, a mere bridge getting them from one feature of entertainment to another. The short format for stop-motion is a double-edged sword in the opportunity it has lavished on the medium. For the most well-executed stop-motion sequences, such as Harryhausen's 5-minute skeleton fight in 1963's *Jason and the Argonauts*, the shorter format provided a solid frame to place as much quality as possible into them. Often there was not enough time or budget to create the same amount of animation for more than what any feature film required, so all available resources were applied to creating these short moments of beautiful entertainment.

At the same time, the jerky quality inherent in many of the early examples of stop-motion photography made it difficult for audiences to sit through more than a few minutes. If the technique distracted the audience from the story or character development, stop-motion could not be utilized as much more than a novelty.

Combining quality stop-motion animation with a format long enough to truly involve an audience on an emotional level, through a longer story arc of about 70 to 120 minutes, proved to be a very difficult task to pull off in its early development. The number of stop-motion features produced would often have several years of dormancy between them, depending on the country. The time-consuming nature of stop-motion in general, combined with the extra effort needed to produce more than one hour of it, has partly contributed to this sporadic output. The commercial success or failure of these films would also have an impact on how often they would arrive, since it was also difficult to finance projects of this magnitude.

Feature-length projects, which are simultaneously the most expensive and profitable form of filmmaking, often set the bar for success of any medium in the animation field, regardless of their popularity in shorter formats. In 1937, Walt Disney took the world by storm with the phenomenal success of *Snow White and the Seven Dwarfs*. It was not the first animated feature ever made (chronologically), but it was the first to set the standard for what the animation medium could achieve in a feature-length format. For decades afterward, the Disney studio was far ahead of what others tried to achieve in producing animated features, in terms of artistic innovation and commercial success. For a time, there were other features such as *Yellow Submarine* (1968), Ralph Bakshi's *Fritz the Cat* (1972), and Don Bluth's *The Secret of NIMH* (1982), which went into artistic directions that Disney was failing to delve into at the time. However, few of these films, as fun as they are, reached the same level of mass commercial appeal as the timeless classics of Disney animation's golden age.

It would be company branches owned by Disney that would help to bring the animated feature back in vogue, through landmarks like *Who Framed Roger Rabbit* (1988), Pixar's *Toy Story* (1995), and even Tim Burton's *The Nightmare Before Christmas* (1993). *Nightmare*, of course, was a major turning point for stop-motion as the medium's first feature-length project to receive worldwide distribution and a huge following for years after its initial release. Meanwhile, in the years following, CG features by Disney/Pixar (*Finding Nemo*, *WALL-E*), DreamWorks SKG (*Shrek*, *Madagascar*), Blue Sky (*Ice Age*, *Horton Hears a Who!*), and others grew to dominate and saturate the feature market. The CG boom of the past decade expanded to the point of prompting rumors of the extinction of more traditional techniques of hand-drawn and stop-motion, partly fueled by Disney's misguided decision to abandon the hand-drawn medium for features. Yet this rumored extinction was not necessarily the case; these traditional features were simply coming from different places. Hayao Miyazaki's Studio Ghibli kept hand-drawn features alive in Japan, and the critically acclaimed *Persepolis* took the medium into a much more personal realm of expression. In 2005, two stop-motion features, *Wallace & Gromit: The Curse of the Were-Rabbit* and Tim Burton's *Corpse Bride*, were brought to the screen within two weeks of each other.

The year 2009 provided a unique renaissance for all media of feature animation, including successful CG releases like *Up* and *Ice Age: Dawn of the Dinosaurs,* Disney's return to hand-drawn animation with *The Princess and the Frog*, and a fresh approach to the medium by the brilliant *The Secret of Kells* from Ireland. Also having an equally strong voice in 2009 was an unprecedented run of five stop-motion features to be released, each differing greatly in style, technique, and distribution. The two mainstream releases were Henry Selick's *Coraline* and Wes Anderson's *Fantastic Mr. Fox*, both appealing to family audiences. The festival circuit welcomed the more adult sensibilities of Adam Elliott's *Mary and Max*, Tatia Rosenthal's *$9.99*, and *A Town Called Panic* by Stéphane Aubier and Vincent Patar. The variety in personal styles within these films and the timing of their releases within the same year are unprecedented for the medium of stop-motion. The fact that more features using stop-motion are already following in their wake indicates an exciting trend that the stop-motion feature film has truly come of age. It could be that the art form finally has an opportunity for the presence it deserves, amidst the vast canon of cinema that is brought to audiences worldwide each year.

Features made with two-dimensional cut-outs or that use stop-motion as a special effect within live action have a history of their own, and their influence is still felt by today's filmmakers. *King Kong* alone inspired an entire genre of fantasy filmmaking and has rightly had several books and articles written about its influence. The history of the feature-length stop-motion puppet film is also an interesting story to unravel, and it is worth investigating to see exactly why it has taken nearly a full century for this format to reach the potential it is now enjoying. To clarify the focus of the films I am referring to, this is specifically a look at films that fit into the following categories:

- A running time of anywhere from approximately 61 to 120 minutes

- A theatrical release (actual or intended) into festivals or cinemas

- The exclusive use of three-dimensional puppets, models, or clay figures throughout the entire film

A few films are also included that combine puppets and live action but focus on a whole cast of puppets through most of the film's running time. For the sake of beginning to document this history in the limited space of a single chapter, here is a look at how these puppet features have evolved.

The history of the puppet feature begins with the pioneering puppet animator from Russia, Ladislas Starewitch. Starewitch was a filmmaker and entomologist who got started in animation making short stop-motion films with embalmed insects rigged with wires. He is credited with producing the first known narrative shorts using the medium, most notably *The Cameraman's Revenge* in 1912. After moving to Paris he continued making short puppet films throughout the 1920s. From 1929 to 1930, he produced his first feature-length stop-motion puppet film, *Le Roman de Renard* (*The Tale of the Fox*). The story for the film was based on the 11th-century tales of Reynard the Fox, an anthropomorphic fox famous for his cruel trickery. The French version of the story from this time period was derived from even older stories about Reynard dating back to medieval times. Variations of the tale spanned several countries; around this time, in the 1930s, even Walt Disney in America was exploring the idea of adapting it into animation. The idea was dropped because of the inherent nastiness of the title character, but many decades later Disney would resurrect some of the story ideas for its 1973 animated version of *Robin Hood*. While Disney's Robin Hood was also portrayed as a fox, Starewitch's version of the original Reynard tale was truer to form in capturing the cruelty and craftiness of the main character. After outsmarting a wolf and several other characters, Reynard the Fox is summoned to appear before the Lion King to answer for his crimes. The conflict escalates into an epic battle sequence as the finale of the film.

The level of detail and subtlety in *The Tale of the Fox* (Figures 1.1 and 1.2) is outstanding, especially for the time it was made, and the story is filled with humor, action, and a great deal of well-crafted entertainment. The puppets, which Starewitch called "ciné marionettes," were capable of fantastic facial expressions and varied greatly in size. The smallest puppets were a little more

Figure 1.1

A scene from Ladislas Starewitch's *The Tale of the Fox*. (© Collection Martin-Starewitch.)

than 1 inch tall, and the Lion King was the tallest puppet in the film, standing nearly 3.5 feet. As many as 75 individual puppet characters were featured in the film, and in many scenes they shared the screen in very elaborate battle scenes, reported to have involved 273,000 different movements. This is even more impressive when considered that it took Starewitch only 18 months to complete the film (from script and scenery to shooting) and that his crew was simply his family. He worked alone with his daughter Irene, who was his lifelong collaborator, and his wife Anna and younger daughter Nina helped when necessary. This is unique considering most features take more time and people to create, even with more technology than what was available at the time. In terms of chronology, *The Tale of the Fox* was indeed the first fully animated puppet feature to be produced, and technically the first to be released as well, although it was delayed by several years because of technical problems with the soundtrack. Although the animation was complete by 1930, it would not

Figure 1.2

The Lion King and Reynard the Fox from *The Tale of the Fox*. (© Collection Martin-Starewitch.)

be shown to audiences until 1937 in Germany and 1941 in France. In the meantime, during these delays, Starewitch continued making shorter puppet films.

Another puppet feature would be produced in Russia during this time, although this one included a live actor interacting with a large cast of puppets. It was likely the first film to be directly inspired by *King Kong*, which director Alexsandr Ptushko saw in 1934 and decided to apply the same pioneering effects to his own film. The film was *The New Gulliver*, released in 1935, based on Jonathan Swift's *Gulliver's Travels*, but with a decidedly more Communist bent to the plot. A reported 1,500 puppets were constructed for the film and featured extensive use of clay replacement heads for dialogue and facial expressions. The faces of the puppets were extremely exaggerated, and they spoke and sang in squeaky voices created by changing the pitch of the soundtrack. Most of the matte shots combining the live actor with the puppets were done in camera, as opposed to optically in post-production. All of these techniques for the puppets, sound mixing, and matting effects with live action were breakthroughs for Russia, and Ptushko was hailed for it. The film was a big success for its time, even catching the attention of Hollywood legends like Charlie Chaplin, and it had an influence on many other filmmakers in the decades to come. Ptushko followed up his success with a series of short films and a few other features combining live action with stop-motion and live puppetry, such as *The Golden Key* in 1939.

Starewitch's *The Tale of the Fox* finally premiered in Berlin in April 1937, now with a fully funded German soundtrack, and it was a big success. Months later, on December 2, 1937, Germany would see another stop-motion feature released called *Die Sieben Raben* (*The Seven Ravens*), made by brothers Ferdinand and Hermann Diehl. Based on a Brothers Grimm fairy tale, it told the story of a young maiden whose brothers have been turned into ravens by a curse. The girl tries to break the spell and ends up being sentenced to burning at the stake for witchcraft. The film mostly featured human puppets, and lots of dialogue (in German, of course) was used to tell the story. The craftsmanship of the extremely realistic replacement mouths, which appear to be done in clay blended into the faces, is stunning for the time it was made. The animation and lip sync are brilliantly done and complement the acting of the puppets for a very naturalistic effect. Aside from a few minor fantasy sequences, the film is mostly simple dialogue scenes with human puppets and has a live-action feeling to the staging, even to the point of matte shots that combine live-action flames next to the puppets. However, an interesting prelude to the film shows a live actor taking a jester puppet out of a box and assembling it, before the jester comes to life through stop-motion and begins narrating the story. It was a common theme of the Diehl brothers to show the process of stop-motion in this manner, as if signaling to the audience right away that they were watching a puppet film. They also used the technique in their short films featuring Mecki the Hedgehog, who would come to life after being sculpted right on his workshop table. Because most films exist only within themselves and would not show the actual process, this was a unique approach to the puppet film. It seemed to suggest to the audience right away what they were actually watching, while at the same time creating a very realistic and believable world in miniature.

The 1940s brought very little to the screen in the format of full-length puppet features, possibly because of World War II dominating at least half the decade in many countries. Ironically the war did play a part in the first stop-motion Technicolor feature to be made in Britain, which was a training film for the Admiralty called *Handling Ships* in 1945. The film was made by the newly founded Halas and Batchelor studio, which was primarily making propaganda and training films at that time. *Handling Ships* used stop-motion animation of model ships to demonstrate their proper piloting and navigation. Although never released to theaters and not exactly a "puppet feature," the film was a landmark for introducing a technique to a country that would become one of the leaders in stop-motion animation.

Another stop-motion feature made in the 1940s that barely had a screen release was a Belgian puppet version of *The Crab with the Golden Claws*, based on a comic book of the same name, featuring a young reporter named Tintin and produced by Wilfried Bouchery. The film faithfully follows the story of Tintin's run-in with a group of drug cartels, the introduction of Captain Haddock, and a crime-fighting adventure through the Sahara Desert. The comic characters were realized as very simple puppets that appear to be made of wood or plastic with real fabric clothing; tiny paper mouth shapes appear to have been used for their dialogue. The low production values for the film are obvious—several shots are barely animated at all, with characters simply frozen into poses or sitting still in boats that were shot floating in live-action water. The editing and screen direction were equally crude, with camera angles changing and rarely cut together properly. All the same, the film was screened to a special group of guests at Brussels' ABC Cinema on January 11, 1947. Another public screening followed in December 1947, but then Bouchery declared bankruptcy and fled the country. The Cinematheque Royale de Belgique archived a copy of the film, and it was recently released on DVD in France.

The story behind producing the first stop-motion feature in America is particularly unique. It began in the late 1930s with a Broadway producer named Michael Myerberg, who had gained a reputation for lavish showmanship to get his projects off the ground. He had become business manager for conductor Leopold Stokowski and was responsible for getting him involved with Hollywood films, including Disney's *Fantasia* (1940). Excited by the creative potential for combining music with animation, he approached puppet animator Lou Bunin to develop an incredibly ambitious animated feature. Starting in 1942, Stokowski, Myerberg, and Bunin would spend three years planning a feature film that would adapt Richard Wagner's 14-hour opera *The Ring of the Nibelungen* into four hours of puppet animation. The project called for extremely elaborate puppets of gnomes, trolls, dragons, Valhalla warriors, mermaid-like creatures called "Rhinemaidens," and several epic battle scenes. They got as far as a full operatic voice cast, storyboards, sets, several puppets built by Bunin, and a completed animation sequence. Universal was prepared to produce the project until one of its executives raised concerns over the association to Adolf Hitler's admiration for Wagner's music. With the country ever deeper in the war effort, the ambitious project was abandoned, and Myerberg and Bunin parted ways.

Myerberg began plans for another stop-motion feature called *Aladdin and the Wonderful Lamp*, based on the classic Aladdin tales. With his associates Peter Lanucci and Herb Schaeffer designing the armatures, Myerberg developed intricate puppets that employed magnetic feet that would adhere them to metal sets. The armatures also had a unique switch built into the limbs to help the animator lock them into position after moving them. Clay sculpting and character design by James Summers and foam latex casting by George Butler completed the puppets, which Myerberg called "Kinemans." Myerberg, in true showman fashion, began embellishing false information for potential film distributors about how the Kinemans were manipulated by a mysterious electronic process that cost thousands of dollars, used secret formulas, and could achieve more than 800,000 human expressions.

After six months of work on *Aladdin* and signing a British actor named John Paul as director, Myerberg abandoned the project and decided to move forward with adapting the story of the Brothers Grimm fairy tale *Hansel and Gretel*, which he felt was more marketable. Rather than being based solely on the original tale, it would be an English translation of the 1892 opera version written by Engelbert Humperdink. His crew set up a studio in a synagogue in New York's Lower East Side, partly because it had a balcony that allowed the directors to oversee all the sets from high above. *Hansel and Gretel: An Opera Fantasy* (Figure 1.3) would become not only the first American stop-motion feature film, but also the first animated feature produced in New York and the first to be based on an opera. Professional Broadway and opera singers would contribute their voice talents, including Anna Russell as the evil witch Rosina Rubylips.

Figure 1.3

Production still from *Hansel and Gretel: An Opera Fantasy.* (© 1954, Michael Myerberg Productions.)

Production of the film was unusual in that nobody on the crew had any experience in animation. Since animation was essentially a series of still images strung together, Myerberg hired noted fashion still photographer Martin Munkasci as director of photography. Munkasci had never used a movie camera before, and he found the lighting style required for animation to be a severe departure from what he was accustomed to. Sets were built by Latvian immigrant Evalds Dajevskis, who was likely hired for his experience as a scenographer for the Liepaja Opera and Ballet Theater and his knowledge of the European landscape. The sets were constructed from papier-mâché and were so large they required trap doors built in for the animators to access the puppets. The animators themselves had never done stop-motion before, but some of them had experience working with puppets. Don Sahlin and Teddy Shepard had apprenticed on *The Howdy Doody Show*, and Kermit Love had experience in puppetry, ballet, and costume design. The other animators were actors Joe Horstman and his wife Inez Anderson (who was the key animator on Gretel), ballet dancer Danny Diamond, sculptor Sky Highchief, and Roger Caras. Out of these mentioned, only Horstman, Anderson, Diamond, and Shepard received a credit on the film, along with other animators Ralph Emory, Hobart Rosen, and Nathalie Schulz. The crew of new animators was given a three-week training period and then went straight into production, often being interrupted by knocks on the studio door from people wanting to book the synagogue for weddings and other events. The magnetic puppet feet and electrified sets caused another faux pas when a crew member shut the power down one night, and the puppets fell over while in poses for the middle of a shot. Another unusual facet of *Hansel and Gretel*'s production was that the entire film was shot in sequence. As the release date grew closer and money was running out, the animation in the final scenes became rushed and jerkier than earlier sequences. There were two major group scenes: one involving a choir of angel children in a dream sequence, and another with a group of children released from the witch's spell at the end of the film. The crew ran out of time and money to create original sculpts for these puppets, so they simply re-cast copies of the character designs for Hansel and Gretel. The completed film is a strange but entertaining piece of stop-motion history, and an interesting experiment in trying to adapt classical opera into an animated film. There is something inherently creepy about the puppets and their facial expressions and some jarring cuts in the screen direction, but the film is a good showcase for the lovely detail of the sets, and the witch's performance is a delight to watch.

Myerberg's showmanship continued into the publicity behind the film's release (Figure 1.4). He continued the myths about his mysterious Kinemans, even creating a promotional film suggesting the puppets were controlled entirely by an electronic box with a series of turning dials. (In reality, a similar device was designed only for manual cable-controlled facial animation in some close-ups.) Myerberg premiered *Hansel and Gretel* himself in October 1954 at New York's Broadway Theatre, and RKO, soon to be ending its contract with Disney, enthusiastically picked it up for distribution. The official release was accompanied by an extensive marketing campaign that included such items as figurines, toys, candy, and Nabisco cookies (Figure 1.5). Despite modest success and fond nostalgic memories for those who saw it, *Hansel and Gretel: An Opera Fantasy* did not exactly start a hot trend for stop-motion in America, but it

Figure 1.4

Newspaper ad for *Hansel and Gretel: An Opera Fantasy.*

does have a unique place in the grand history of many art forms at once, combining opera, technology, and puppet animation. Production of the Kineman puppets continued into television commercials, including the original Jolly Green Giant, which was apparently banned from the airwaves for frightening too many children. (It has since surfaced on YouTube and truly is quite disturbing.) Later, a studio break-in by vandals caused all the Kinemans to be destroyed, and Myerberg returned to Broadway, passing away in 1974.

Figure 1.5

A sample of the *Hansel and Gretel* marketing campaign with Nabisco.

Some who had worked on various stages of *Hansel and Gretel* continued into other stop-motion ventures. Don Sahlin and Kermit Love tried getting a live-action/puppet feature version of Beatrix Potter's *The Tailor of Gloucester* produced in London, with animated mice puppets. It was never realized, but Sahlin continued into more stop-motion on George Pal's *tom thumb* (1958) and *The Wonderful World of the Brothers Grimm* (1963) and would later become a puppet designer for Jim Henson's Muppets. Lou Bunin, after parting ways with Myerberg, ended up producing his own stop-motion/live-action version of *Alice in Wonderland* in France in 1949 (Figure 1.6). Although framed by completely live-action bookend scenes, most of the film taking place in Wonderland was made in puppet animation, with actress Carol Marsh as Alice matted or cut into the scenery. The film was funded by the J. Arthur Rank Organization, directed by British radio/TV pioneer Dallas Bower, and shot by noted French cinematographer Claude Renoir. Bunin animated many of the puppet scenes himself and also had the help of former Disney animator Art Babbitt, who designed several walk cycles for the puppet animators to use for reference.

Figure 1.6

Newspaper ad for Lou Bunin's *Alice in Wonderland*. (Lou Bunin, 1951.)

Ironically, a cartoon version of Alice was simultaneously being made by Disney. A much-publicized conflict ensued over the release of both versions throughout its production. Disney was favored for exclusive right to the use of Technicolor, which Bunin's film was originally being shot in, so Bunin was forced to process the original negative using the Ansco color process. Ansco used a blue dye that changed the colors and muddied up the soundtrack so that it could not be heard properly without a blue-tinted exciter bulb when projected. Disney tried to delay the release of Bunin's film in 1951, but Bunin released it anyway, two weeks before the release of Disney's version. Disney went after him in court but lost the case because of the conclusion that *Alice in Wonderland* was public-domain material and had been adapted to film previously.

Neither film fared very well at the box office originally, although Disney's version has become the more popular version over time. However, many, including Bunin himself, felt that the stop-motion version was truer to Lewis Carroll's original book, capturing the famous illustrations by John Tenniel and showing a clear contrast between the real world and Wonderland. The sets were wonderfully surreal and abstract, with curved shapes and open compositions similar to the cartoons of Warner Bros., likely because they were designed by Gene Fleury and Bernice Polifka, who had worked for Chuck Jones at Warner Bros. One particularly clever special effect involved a row of mirrors to re-create the Lobster Quadrille dance sequence, which made two lobster puppets reflected in the mirrors appear like a whole crowd of them on screen. Overall, the film has a strange, dreamlike quality and is certainly one of the most visually inventive film versions of the classic book. Bunin later began developing an ambitious stop-motion feature based on the book *High Water at Catfish Bend* that would never be realized. Despite these setbacks to his feature-length projects, Bunin made a big name for himself in New York producing stop-motion commercials and shorts, and he is still remembered as a unique contributor to the medium.

Around this same time that puppet animation was trying to find its voice in America, on the other side of the globe it was on its way to being much more strongly established. Czechoslovakia and other parts of Eastern Europe had a long history of traditional puppet theater; it naturally found its way into stop-motion filmmaking while retaining its same lyrical essence. The master of the Czech puppet movement would undoubtedly be Jiri Trnka, who produced some feature-length films along with his many influential shorts. After starting his studio in 1946, he ended up embarking on what would become his first feature, *Spalicek* (*The Czech Year*), released in 1947. The film is divided into six segments that illustrate a full year of seasonal Czech customs: Shrovetide, Spring, the Legend of St. Prokop, the Fair, the Feast, and Bethlehem. Traditional Czech folk songs enliven the animation. The final film was a huge success that put Trnka on the map as the country's leading puppet animator. This success led to the possibility for another feature, *Cisaruv Slavik* (*The Emperor's Nightingale*), in 1949. This film was based on the Hans Christian Andersen tale of a Chinese emperor with a toy nightingale who forgets about the real nightingale who would comfort him with his song. The significance of this film was that it introduced Trnka to America through theatrical distribution there, with an English narration by Boris Karloff (Figure 1.7). In both versions, a beautiful musical score by Vaclav Trojan blended perfectly with the puppets and scenery. Critics worldwide hailed the film as a masterpiece of the medium.

Figure 1.7

Newspaper ad for the U.S. release of *The Emperor's Nightingale*. (Trnka Studios, 1949.)

"*A wondrous and magical picture.*" -N.Y. TIMES

...A MAGIC NIGHTINGALE · A FARAWAY LAND · A WORLD OF ENCHANTMENT...

HANS CHRISTIAN ANDERSEN'S

THE EMPEROR'S NIGHTINGALE

—IN GLORIOUS COLOR

A SMALL BOY AND A MIGHTY EMPEROR DISCOVER THAT ALL THEIR RICHES AREN'T WORTH AS MUCH AS ONE FRIEND!

PRODUCED BY WILLIAM L. SNYDER   DISTRIBUTED BY NEW TRENDS ASSOC., INC.

Another feature, *Bajaja* (*Prince Bayaya*), followed in 1950. This was a medieval tale of a young peasant who overcomes many odds to win the heart of a princess. Trnka used *Bajaja* as a platform to push the envelope in terms of the rich detail and complexity that could be achieved with puppet animation, creating a scope of effects much more epic than his earlier works. What is most interesting about Trnka's work is the tension between what the Czech government agreed to fund and preferred he create, and what Trnka himself wanted to create. Some of his films directly reflect Czech culture and ideals, into which he put just as much pride and care, but he also wanted to explore stories from other cultures. His other features were *Staré pov sti eské* (*Old Czech Legends*) in 1953, which is a collection of Czech hero epics, and *Sen Noci Svatojanske* (*A Midsummer Night's Dream*) in 1959, based on William Shakespeare's play. *A Midsummer Night's Dream* was shot in widescreen and was certainly Trnka's most exquisite and ambitious production to date. It expressed Trnka's style and personal views of puppet animation, which did not rely on any lip sync or facial expression to tell the story. He was more concerned with the music and picture working together to achieve a lyrical effect that brought the essence of traditional puppet theater to the screen. As beautiful and artistic as his epic film was, many common audiences did not connect with it on the same emotional level, which can be said of many "art films" done in feature length. (Ironically, the same year, Disney released *Sleeping Beauty*, which had many similarities to *A Midsummer Night's Dream* in its ambition, scope, and focus on beautiful art direction over direct emotional engagement for the audience, as many critics felt.) All the same, when it comes to treating the art of stop-motion puppet animation to a high level of grace, beauty, and respect, Trnka set the bar and inspired a whole legion of animators in his wake.

The 1960s and 1970s were an interesting time for cross-cultural pollination between different countries producing stop-motion features, particularly Czechoslovakia and Japan with North America. Japanese animator Kihachiro Kawamoto, after working briefly with one of Japan's leading puppet animators, Tad Mochinaga, went to Czechoslovakia to work with Trnka at his studio in 1963. Trnka encouraged him to respect the puppet film as an art form and embrace the lyrical style of his culture, so Kawamoto brought this influence back to Japan and inspired the puppet movement there. Meanwhile, the films of Mochinaga inspired an entirely new partnership that would bring the Japanese animation style to America. Back in America, through commercials, series, and specials, stop-motion animation began to find a voice on television as early as the 1950s. In the 1960s, the medium found a new leader through the studio of Rankin/Bass. Originally under the name Videocraft International, founders Arthur Rankin, Jr., and Jules Bass joined forces with Mochinaga's studio in Japan in 1958 and made a name for themselves through their Animagic TV specials. They also created some features for the big screen. Throughout the production of these features, Rankin was very hands on at the Japanese studio, while Bass oversaw much of the music and script writing from his head office in New York. Rankin took up residence in Japan for months at a time, working alongside the animators, costume builders, and storyboard and fabrication departments.

Their first feature, *Willy McBean and His Magic Machine*, was produced around the same time as their famous *Rudolph the Red-Nosed Reindeer* TV special and was released in 1965 (Figure 1.8). The origins of the film came about through a time-traveling character named Willy Nilly, who was featured in a few episodes of their *The New Adventures of Pinocchio* series for television. Ideas for a spin-off series grew into a feature-length script about Willy McBean, his monkey sidekick Pablo, and their adventures traveling through time to stop the mad Professor Von Rotten from altering the course of history. The original story and characters were designed by *Rudolph*'s designer Tony Peters, who was rooted in the style of the UPA studio that was popular in the '50s. The following year, 1966, brought a musical feature, *The Daydreamer* (Figure 1.9), to the screen, which was part of a three-picture deal with producer Joseph E. Levine that combined the Animagic puppets with an all-star cast of live actors. Noted illustrator Al Hirschfeld designed the poster and credit sequence for the film, in which Paul O'Keefe plays a young Hans Christian Andersen who dreams about four of his well-known stories, told in stop-motion.

Figure 1.8

Tad Mochinaga animates a
scene from *Willy McBean
and His Magic Machine.*
(© 1965, Rankin/Bass
Productions/Rick Goldschmidt
Archives.)

Figure 1.9

Hiroshi Tabata works on
the Thumbelina sequence
of *The Daydreamer.* (© 1966,
Rankin/Bass Productions/
Rick Goldschmidt Archives.)

While these early features had minimal impact with most audiences,
Rankin/Bass hit its stride with one of its best productions, the feature *Mad
Monster Party* (Figure 1.10), released in 1967. Baron Von Frankenstein, voiced
by Boris Karloff, creates a destructive formula and invites a full cast of classic
monsters to share in his discovery. Frankenstein, Dracula, the Wolfman, the

Mummy, the Creature, the Invisible Man, and Dr. Jekyll/Mr. Hyde are all there, including a Peter Lorre–inspired lackey named Yetch and the Monster's Mate, modeled after and voiced by Phyllis Diller. The plot unfolds as the monsters conspire against the baron's nephew and successor Felix, who also becomes romantically entangled with his sexy assistant Francesca. The film was co-written by Harvey Kurtzman, creator of *Mad* magazine, and the characters were designed by another *Mad* contributor, Jack Davis. The work of these artists gave the film a fresh look that differentiated it from the designs of earlier shows, but it still maintained the classic Rankin/Bass feel. The film, full of witty puns, sight gags, and a jazzy '60s score, became a cult classic, a regular staple for Halloween screenings, and an inspiration for many stop-motion artists, including Henry Selick and Tim Burton.

Figure 1.10

Boris and Monster's Mate puppets from *Mad Monster Party.* (© 1967, Rankin/Bass Productions/Rick Goldschmidt Archives.)

Rankin/Bass continued producing both cel and puppet animation well into the 1980s, but it would be several years until the studio attempted one more stop-motion feature: *Rudolph and Frosty's Christmas in July*, released in the summer of 1979. The film brought some of its classic characters together for a story with many plot twists, surrounding an evil king named Winterbolt. Despite an impressive voice cast, songs by Johnny Marks, and strong production design (Figure 1.11), the film was not very successful; it is likely that a Christmas film in the middle of summer was a hard sell for audiences.

Figure 1.11

Kyoko Kita works on Animagic puppets for *Rudolph and Frosty's Christmas in July*. (© 1979 Rankin/Bass Productions/ Rick Goldschmidt Archives.)

Nevertheless, Rankin/Bass had plenty of other successes that would inspire dozens of other stop-motion feature projects for decades to come. Mark Caballero and Seamus Walsh of the stop-motion film collective Screen Novelties are very inspired by the work of Rankin/Bass. They both feel (and I quite agree) that the history and traditions of Japanese kabuki theater and bunraku puppetry come through quite strongly in the animation itself. Looking at the timing and posing of the puppets of Japanese stop-motion (such as Kawamoto's *The Demon* or even earlier works), a similarity can be noticed. Rankin/Bass' background in theater also meshed well with the style of their Japanese production team to produce a unique playfulness to the look of these films. It is important to look for the connections between traditional art forms and modern stop-motion, especially in a feature-length format where it can be easy for an audience to get lost in the technique itself.

Elsewhere in the world, stop-motion features continued to make appearances and impacts on the medium. The first full-length puppet feature to come out of Israel was *Joseph the Dreamer* (Figure 1.12) in 1961, based on the biblical story from Genesis about Joseph and his brothers. The film was directed by Yoram Gross, who began making experimental films based on Joseph's dream sequences, and the results inspired him to make a feature version. He issued a press release announcing his intentions for the project, which drew the attention of puppet-maker John Byle and illustrator John Burningham. They agreed to collaborate and fashioned stylized puppets out of rubber with wire armatures. Actors from Israel's Habima National Theatre provided the voices, and the film was primarily photographed and animated by Gross and his wife Alina, working mostly during the cooler nighttime hours over a period of two years. *Joseph the Dreamer* was scored by Eddie Halperin and the Kol Radio Orchestra, and its premiere was opened by Israeli President Yitzhak Ben-Zvi. It went on to screen at Cannes and won several international film prizes. Today, Yoram Gross still produces animated entertainment and has released *Joseph the Dreamer* on DVD for new generations to enjoy (http://www. yoramgrossfilms.com.au).

Figure 1.12

Production still from *Joseph the Dreamer.* (© 1961, Yoram Gross Films.)

The Magic Roundabout was a French TV series by Serge Danot that gained great popularity in the late '60s, even more so in the U.K. In 1970 a feature based on the series was released in France called *Pollux et le Chat Bleu* (with the English version, *Dougal and the Blue Cat*, released in the U.K. in 1972). Written and directed by Eric Johnson, the film tells about an evil blue cat named Buxton, who enters the ruins of an old treacle factory, crowns himself king, and unleashes an epidemic of blueness upon the land. It becomes up to Dougal and his friends from the Magic Garden to defeat Buxton's plans and restore color to their world. *The Magic Roundabout* and its subsequent feature version had long since gained a reputation for its rumored underlying subtexts related to political, societal, and drug-related references. The epidemic of blueness was read as a metaphor for conservatism by some, and many people have mulled over the meaning behind scenes involving magic mushrooms and other hallucinatory images. Whether or not this was all intentional, *Dougal and the Blue Cat* is certainly a product of its time and is still enjoyable for its strangeness, surrealism, quirky animation, and appealing designs.

The 1970s also brought a very significant original stop-motion feature to Norway called *Flaklypa Grand Prix* (known as *Pinchcliffe Grand Prix* in its U.K. release version), which has become a national treasure with a huge cult following. Director Ivo Caprino had begun making short films and commercials with both live-action and stop-motion puppets in 1948. He had much support from his artistic parents; his mother would end up helping him build puppets and sets. Caprino continued making films into the '50s and '60s that captured elements of European folk tales and short stories with delightful puppet characters. His first feature film, produced in 1959, *Ugler i Mosen* (*Owls in the Marsh*), was mostly live action, with some stop-motion sequences. His second feature project, about the Norwegian writer Peter Christen Asbjornsen, was never realized because of a lack of funds. Instead, it was adapted into a series of short films through the 1960s. Caprino began working on a half-hour television special in 1970 that was based on the books of cartoonist Kjell Aukrust. The special was ultimately abandoned because of difficulties in adapting the material into a short format, but many of the sets and puppets were used for what became a full-length feature. The feature took more than three years to make and had a very small crew of set builders and cameramen, with Caprino directing and animating (Figures 1.13 and 1.14).

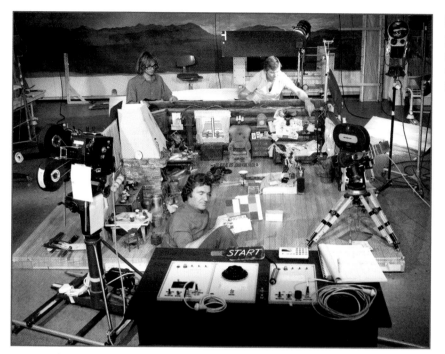

Figure 1.13

Ivo Caprino (center) and crew on the set of *Flaklypa Grand Prix*. (© 1975, Caprino Studios.)

Figure 1.14

Ivo Caprino and crew on the exterior set of *Flaklypa Grand Prix*. (©1975, Caprino Studios.)

Flaklypa Grand Prix tells the story of an inventor named Reodor Felgen (U.K. version: Theodore Rimspoke), who lives quietly on a hilltop with his assistants: a bird named Solan Gundersen (U.K. version: Sonny Duckworth) and a hedgehog named Ludvig (U.K. version: Lambert). The trio (Figure 1.15) teams up with an Arab sheik to build an amazing race car named "Il Tempo Gigante" to compete in a Grand Prix race against their rival, the villainous Rudolf Blodstrupmoen. Highlights of the film include the complex Rube Goldberg–type contraptions in Felgen's house, a delightful ragtime band number at the race's opening ceremony, and the Grand Prix race itself. The race is incredibly exciting and beautifully edited, as the camera speeds along behind the cars through the elaborate miniature sets of the winding country-side race track (Figure 1.16). On many levels, the film is fun to watch and works brilliantly in terms of the set design and characterizations of the puppets.

Figure 1.15

Reodor Felgen, Solan Gundersen, and Ludvig of *Flaklypa Grand Prix*. (©1975, Caprino Studios.)

Flaklypa Grand Prix was released on August 28, 1975, and became the most successful Norwegian film ever made, selling more than 5.5 million tickets in a country with a population of only 4.5 million. It has enjoyed similar success in Denmark, Russia, Japan, the U.K., and elsewhere. It has been translated into 14 languages and traditionally runs on Norwegian television every Christmas Eve. The feature continues to inspire a devoted fan base, and after Ivo Caprino's death in 2001, a PC video game based on the film was produced

Figure 1.16

Shooting the race scenes from *Flaklypa Grand Prix.* (©1975, Caprino Studios.)

by Caprino's son Remo and grandson Mario. The family maintains a website for Caprino Studios (http://www.caprino.no) and has released these wonderful puppet films on DVD.

The late '70s was a tumultuous time for the animation industry in general—many of the old studios had shut down, and most of the work being done was cheap Saturday morning fare for television. The most significant film to come out during this time was unquestionably *Star Wars* in 1977, which inspired a new revolution in using stop-motion for special effects into the next decade. Amidst the science-fiction spectacle of the time, cartoony puppet features did not have much chance to stand out and were faced with limited commercial success. As a precursor to a trend that became very popular throughout the 1980s, in some cases TV series were adapted into big-screen feature versions. A popular European stop-motion TV star from the late '60s and early '70s who appeared on the big screen was Colargol, a little bear who wants to sing and travel around the world. *The Adventures of Colargol* was a Polish/French series animated by Tadeusz Wilkosz at the Se-Ma-For Studio; it became known as *Barnaby* in the U.K. and *Jeremy the Bear* in Canada. Unlike *Dougal and the Blue Cat*, which was an original feature based on a series, the *Colargol* features were simply episodes from the TV series strung together as one story. Three of these adapted features were released in Poland: *Colargol na Dzikim*

Zachodzie (*Colargol in the Wild West*, 1976), *Colargol Zdobywc Kosmosu* (*Colargol, Conqueror of Space*, 1978; Figure 1.17), and *Colargol i Cudowna Walizka* (*Colargol and the Magic Suitcase*, 1979).

Figure 1.17

Polish movie poster for *Colargol, Conqueror of Space,* Se-Ma-For Studio, 1978.

In 1979, there was also a very limited theatrical run of another extremely bizarre puppet feature from Japan. Takeo Nakamura, an animator on Rankin/Bass' TV special *Santa Claus Is Coming to Town* (1970) afterward partnered with the Sanrio Studio (creators of Hello Kitty) in 1975. He spent the next four years directing a feature called *Nutcracker Fantasy*, which was loosely based on the famous Peter Tchaikovsky ballet and a story by E.T.A. Hoffmann. The influence from working with Rankin/Bass was certainly not lost on Nakamura; the puppet designs were similar enough to make many people mistake it for a Rankin/Bass production, although it certainly was not. The film opens with a terrifying sequence telling the bedside story of the "Ragman," who creeps into children's beds at night and turns them into mice. This leads into the story of a young girl named Clara (voiced by Melissa Gilbert in the English dub), who is given a nutcracker doll by her strange Uncle Drosselmeyer (voiced by Christopher Lee). She then slips into a fever-induced dream state where she goes into battle against the evil Queen Morphia, a giant two-headed mouse, and the queen's entire mouse army. The various plot twists involving a king, a spooky fortune teller, and a heroic warrior named Franz are mixed with live-action ballet scenes, more incredibly disturbing mice sequences, and an extremely trippy "land of happy times" sequence that defies all description. After its very brief run in theaters, *Nutcracker Fantasy* was released to video and a few cable television airings, which was enough to traumatize plenty of children throughout the early '80s. The opening "Ragman" sequence surfaced on YouTube and prompted a few nostalgic viewer comments about how it had scarred them for life.

The puppets in all of these early feature films were typically crafted out of foam latex, plastic, wood, fabric, or other rubber materials. The use of modeling clay as a material for creating puppets and sets began in several experimental stop-motion films in the 1910s and 1920s then faded into obscurity for several decades. It would not be explored again until Art Clokey brought his iconic Gumby character to television in the 1950s, and it was further brought into popularity by Aardman Animations and Will Vinton in the 1970s. Nobody had attempted to use clay animation in a feature-length format until a company named Stowmar Enterprises embarked on an animated version of Walt Kelly's popular comic strip *Pogo*. The production rights for *Pogo* were arranged in partnership with Walt Kelly's widow, Selby, by executive producer Kerry Stowell and screenwriter/director Marc Paul Chinoy. Armed with a $2 million budget, they went into production on a clay-animation feature called *I Go Pogo* from 1979 to 1980. Also involved in the early stages of the company were Charlie and Stephen Chiodo, a team of brothers from New York who had grown up making their own animated films. *I Go Pogo* was produced in Arlington, Virginia, right outside Washington, D.C., and production was set up in an office space in the Crystal City's Crystal Underground shopping mall. At one point, they had a storefront area where the character-fabrication department was situated; although the windows were covered in paper for the sake of privacy, one face-sized hole was cut into the door. Crew members called this storefront area "the fish tank," and mall shoppers would discover on their own that an animated feature was secretly being made inside.

The *Pogo* production was a starting point for many animators still working in the industry today, including Steve Oakes, who would become head of Curious Pictures in New York, and Justin Kohn, Kim Blanchette, and Kent Burton (Figure 1.18), who all worked most recently on *Coraline*. Blanchette was a university student at the time, and the rest of the crew was largely made up of other local artists, students, and amateur animators. Stephen Chiodo served as director of animation, designed the clay puppets, and supervised the many aspects of production. All of the scenery was made of Polyform Sculpey, and the puppets were a sophisticated combination of malleable plasticine clay for flexibility and painted ridged Sculpey parts for non-moving accessories. Press molds were made for creating the basic shape of the clay character, which would then be finessed with smoothing tools and texture stamps. Albert the Alligator, for instance, had a stomach plate pressed from a rubber mold that maintained the fine detail while the clay body was flexed. A genuine attempt was made to keep the surfaces of the characters smooth and hide the lumpy texture and fingerprints made by the animator; the sets were kept severely air conditioned to help keep the clay from softening too much. An attempt was made to market the film's technique as "Flexiform," but it was actually nothing more than clay combined with other standard sculpting materials. For the sets, trees were made of plaster casts from rubber molds, foliage from plastic craft-store arrangements, and reeds made of sheet copper. The sky backdrops were made of giant milked Plexiglas sheets covered with blue gels that were illuminated from behind and had shapes cut out of them for clouds. The characters' plain white eyeballs were cast in resin and steel wool, and the pupils were separate pieces of rubber strip magnets. These magnetized pupils would stick to the steel wool in the eyes just forcefully enough that they could be lightly pushed around the surface of the eyes for movement. Another innovative technique used in the film was wax replacement cycles built for walking sequences, some of which were shot as silhouettes against the back-lit sky backgrounds.

Figure 1.18

Animator Kent Burton working on a scene from *I Go Pogo.* (© Possum Productions/Walt Kelly Estate.)

The film's story consisted of the comic strip's regular cast of characters preparing for the Okefenokee Swamp's election and conspiring to nominate the reluctant Pogo Possum as a presidential candidate. The voice cast was an impressive line-up of popular comedic talent, including Jonathan Winters, Ruth Buzzi, Vincent Price, and Stan Freberg. The film itself was very heavy on dialogue, but the animation team tried to enliven the screenplay with some visual gags. Stephen Chiodo recalls:

> In an opening sequence featuring Mr. Mole and the Deacon chatting in a cave, I animated a great scene of the Deacon leaping off a table onto a stalactite (Figure 1.19), which then crashed down onto the table. I also did a 20-second shot of Albert the Alligator (Figure 1.20), who gets his finger stuck in a knothole, and then his entire head, with his head squishing and popping through. But the director, Marc Chinoy, cut out those visual gags and left in all the heavy dialogue scenes.

After *Pogo* wrapped in 1980, the Chiodo brothers packed up and moved to California, eventually working on Tim Burton's early films and starting their own studio. The rest of the crew scattered as well to further make their mark on the filmmaking world.

Despite a modest marketing campaign in the papers and on television, *I Go Pogo* did not get the proper theatrical release that was intended through 21st Century Distribution. It was instead quietly released directly to VHS and Betamax videotape as an exclusive title for Fotomat (Figure 1.21), and the tapes were sold through their photo pick-up shacks in parking lots. It was picked up for another video release as *Pogo for President* by Walt Disney Home Video in the early '80s and aired a few times on HBO. (A few edits were made to different video and television releases—for example, Chiodo's knothole sequence was added back into the Disney version.) Despite these brief appearances, the film has since faded into obscurity. Although it was well animated and had some very funny sequences, many fans of the original *Pogo* strip feel that the film did not capture the essence of the characters or the political satire to its full potential and that it was largely bogged down by too much dialogue. The Stowmar producers did not continue into other animation ventures, but their *Pogo* feature did at least provide a launching pad for many in the creative department and provided an interesting footnote in the canon of Kelly's beloved creations.

Figure 1.19

Deacon Mushrat in a cut scene from *I Go Pogo*. (© Possum Productions/ Walt Kelly Estate.)

Figure 1.20

A production still of puppets from *I Go Pogo*. (© Possum Productions/ Walt Kelly Estate.)

Figure 1.21

Promotional material for the Fotomat video release of *I Go Pogo*. (©Possum Productions/Walt Kelly Estate.)

Clay animation finally made its way to movie screens a few years later, in 1985, when Oscar-winning animator (and founder of the term "Claymation") Will Vinton created his first Claymation feature film, *The Adventures of Mark Twain* (entitled *Comet Quest* in the U.K.). Vinton's studio in Portland, Oregon, had already made a big name for itself producing award-winning short films that pushed clay animation to a level of filmmaking. The Vinton style was that everything on screen was made of clay, from puppets to props and sets. Animator Barry Bruce had refined Vinton's signature style for fluid lip sync and clay morphing, and techniques for clay painting on glass were developed by Joan Gratz. These animated methods were all brought to fruition and further development in their first feature, which told the story of Mark Twain himself (Figure 1.22) traveling in a magical zeppelin to meet his destiny with the arrival of Halley's Comet in 1910. Tagging along with him on his journey were his own characters Tom Sawyer, Huck Finn, and Becky Thatcher, who explore the many secret passages of his flying machine and encounter many surreal adventures. Most surreal of these is a terrifying sequence based on Twain's *The Mysterious Stranger*, where Satan appears to the children in a morphing Noh theater mask. As Twain recounts some of his other works like "The Diaries of Adam & Eve" and "The Celebrated Jumping Frog of Calaveras County," the film switches gears to illustrate these particular tales with more inspired Claymation. Many of the techniques used on previous short films needed to be streamlined to be more efficient because of the feature-length format. Multiple copies of characters were cast out of molds, stronger armatures were developed, and replacement systems were developed for lip sync, including the mustache of Twain himself. *The Adventures of Mark Twain* was praised by many animation enthusiasts for its inventive visuals and was an important step toward bringing the clay medium from its familiar short formats into a more epic scope for the big screen.

Elsewhere in the world, other stop-motion features were released to small audiences and festivals for limited releases throughout the 1980s. *Rennyo and His Mother* was the first feature-length film by Kihachiro Kawamoto in Japan, released in October 1981. It captured in puppet animation an ancient legend of the figure of Rennyo, who restored Shin Buddhism to Japan as a promise to his mother, who had disappeared when he was a child. In 1982, Otto Fotky in Hungary produced a stop-motion feature called *The Adventures of Sam the Squirrel*, and the same year saw a Czech puppet feature of *Robinson Crusoe* and a stop-motion mixed-media feature from France called *Chronopolis*, a surreal science-fiction epic.

Figure 1.22

A scene from *The Adventures of Mark Twain.* (© Will Vinton Productions.)

In the U.K., Cosgrove Hall Studios was making a strong name for itself in creating animated content, mostly for television. Amidst the many shows the studio produced, it scored one of its biggest hits with the stop-motion feature adaptation of *The Wind in the Willows* in 1983, based on Kenneth Grahame's classic book. The film followed the book's adventures of the characters Mole, Rat, and Badger in their attempts to rein in the wild antics of Mr. Toad. A highlight of the feature was the incredible amount of detail that was crafted into the miniature sets and puppets. Patterns for kitchen crockery and magazines were created in miniscule scale to create the atmosphere described in the original book. Each puppet was constructed in latex over delicately constructed ball-and-socket armatures, including mechanisms for very subtle facial expressions. Part of the team behind *The Wind in the Willows* would be the first collaboration between Peter Saunders and Ian MacKinnon, who teamed up to eventually form the world's premier puppet-fabrication studio for countless other productions. Also part of the small animation team was Barry Purves (Figure 1.23), who would later go on to be an award-winning key player in British animation himself. *The Wind in the Willows* was a huge critical success and went on to win a BAFTA, an Emmy, and many other awards. A stop-motion TV series based on the film continued from 1984 to 1987, as well as a spin-off series and TV feature centered more on the adventures of Mr. Toad.

Figure 1.23

Animator Barry Purves on the set of *The Wind in the Willows* series. (© Cosgrove Hall Films.)

Although the original *Willows* film was the only feature production meant for theaters, Cosgrove Hall also created a stop-motion movie for television called *The Fool of the World and the Flying Ship* in 1990. This exquisite film won another Emmy and many other awards for the studio. Another stop-motion production from the same time period was *Truckers*, which originated as an episodic TV serial but was later re-edited and packaged as a feature version. *Truckers* was based on a popular novel by fantasy writer Terry Pratchett, about a race of tiny people called Nomes and their journey of survival through stowing away on humans' trucks. One of the lead animators for the series was Paul Berry, who later directed the short film *The Sandman* and would go on to work on *The Nightmare Before Christmas*.

In the former East Germany, a couple of stop-motion features (and many more shorts) were produced in the 1980s by a studio named DEFA, with direction by Gunter Ratz. A feature called *Die Fliegende Windmühle* (*The Flying Windmill*), based on a book by Guenther Feustel, was released in 1982. This colorful film is about a little girl named Olli who receives a bad grade in school and runs away from home, ending up going on an adventure in a flying windmill with a dog, a horse, and a mad scientist. The film was interpreted by some as socialist propaganda disguised as a children's film. Whether this is valid or not, the film has a cult following among those who remembered it from childhood. Ratz directed another feature to East German theaters called *Die Spur Führt Zum Silbersee* (*The Trace Leads to the Silver Lake*). It was essentially in the style of an American western and based on a book by Karl May, who was famous for western stories written in the 1890s. This animated version was closer to the original book than a live-action version that had been produced in the 1960s. Like typical Hollywood western films, the historical elements of the stop-motion *Silbersee* feature were not completely accurate, given that May had never visited the U.S., and East Germany did not receive exposure to these westerns for several decades. Following a limited East German theatrical run in 1989, the film was aired on public television to all of Germany following the Berlin Wall collapse in 1990. It was first aired as five episodes over the Christmas season and would be shown a year later in one piece. The poor box office for its initial release scrapped Ratz's plans for another feature called *The Ghost of Llano Estacado.*

Czechoslovakia brought one of its most notorious feature films to the screen in 1988, directed by another one of the country's most famous directors, Jan Svankmajer. It was a stop-motion/live-action adaptation of *Alice in Wonderland,* simply titled *Alice.* While still based on the classic Lewis Carroll story, it is decidedly more surreal even than Lou Bunin's version and the polar opposite of Disney's. Svankmajer's vision was to adapt the tale with nightmarish imagery, including puppets made of socks, living animal skulls, taxidermy specimens, and animated meat. One of the most disturbing and iconic images from the film is the introduction of the White Rabbit, made from a real stuffed rabbit, who pulls his pocketwatch out of his chest cavity and leaks sawdust. *Alice* became a cult classic and inspired a whole genre of surrealist stop-motion with dark themes and found object animation.

Also in 1988, there was a bizarre stop-motion/live-action science-fiction feature that came out of Montreal. It was called *Bino Fabule,* named after the title character (played by Italian actor Pietro Pizzuti), who was the only live actor within a cast of stop-motion puppets. Bino is a scientist from the planet Karmagor who lives with his astrophysicist turtle sidekick, Torticoli. He dreams of being able to fly and discovers a magical crescent-shaped character named Claire de Lune (Figure 1.24) who flies in a crystal spaceship. Claire de Lune escapes from Bino when he tries to steal her flying powers, and she crash lands on another planet inhabited by a cast of living pots, pans, and weird alien creatures (Figures 1.25 and 1.26). One of the alien leaders, Potassium, becomes jealous of Claire de Lune's powers and attempts to destroy her. Meanwhile, Bino and Torticoli follow the activities on the planet with their video radar system, and through a series of other adventures ultimately end up saving Claire de Lune and the alien planet from destruction.

Figure 1.24

Claire de Lune, a main character from *Bino Fabule*. (© CineGroupe.)

Figure 1.25

One of the large stop-motion sets for *Bino Fabule*. (© CineGroupe.)

Bino Fabule was originally conceived as a possible television series by director Rejeanne Tailon, but the project eventually landed enough funding to develop it into a feature film. It took nearly two years of persuasion by producer Jacque Pettigrew to finance the project, which was finally made through the CineGroupe production house in Montreal, with co-production by studios in Belgium and France. The live-action sequences were all shot in Belgium, along with a live-action Torticoli puppet that came from the French studio.

Figure 1.26

A cast of characters from *Bino Fabule.* (© CineGroupe.)

The crude live-action puppet was used in the background or edges of the frame whenever he shared the screen with Bino, but when Torticoli was on screen by himself, he was a stop-motion puppet. Line producer Andre A. Belanger (now head of Spectra Animation Studios) organized the flow of studio production in Montreal, where all of the stop-motion sequences were shot. Bill Maylone was in charge of making lead wire armatures and molding the puppets, which were made of silicone rubber with replacement eyes and mouths. Most of the fabricators and animators had very little experience with stop-motion, but a unique feature of the production was the camera they used to shoot it. Technician Andre de Tonnancour created a custom-made movie camera out of a Nikon 35mm still camera with a film magazine attachment that could hold 100 feet of film. This camera was small enough to be placed on a large boom dolly for sweeping camera moves through the miniature sets, very much like today's frequent use of digital SLR cameras to achieve the same effect. Ironically, with this technical innovation, the production of this futuristic science-fiction film provided a glimpse into the future of using small still cameras for stop-motion. Unfortunately, it did not do much for the film itself, which did not perform well in its theatrical release. The film was later broadcast on television in its full length and also broken up into three episodic half-hours, but it has since faded into obscurity. It is definitely a strange film in the vein of many other science-fiction cult movies of the '80s era, and the designs and effects have a very interesting quality to them.

Up to this point, original full-length puppet features were a mixed bag of limited commercial successes, failures, and experiments that did not make much impact outside of a few enthusiasts and were otherwise virtually unknown or unreleased outside their countries of origin. But the 1980s to early 1990s was an interesting time for stop-motion, where many elements were coming together to set the stage for a major breakthrough in the puppet feature. The generation who grew up as kids in the 1950s and 1960s, being hooked on *Rudolph*, *Gumby*, re-issues of *King Kong*, and the Harryhausen film releases, began making their mark well into the 1970s and 1980s. Of the stop-motion enthusiasts who blazed trails in the 1980s, Phil Tippett would revolutionize the art of stop-motion creature effects, particularly through perfecting techniques for motion blur on *The Empire Strikes Back* (1980) and *Dragonslayer* (1981).

It was during this same time period that Tim Burton and Henry Selick were both working at Disney, clearly disillusioned about the idea of "drawing cute foxes" for the 1981 feature *The Fox and the Hound*. The atmosphere at the studio was one of trying to move forward into new territories, but lacking the chemistry and confidence to push them far enough. After Selick left to pursue stop-motion films in the San Francisco Bay Area, Burton managed to make his stop-motion short *Vincent* (1982) at Disney and created concept art for a story titled *The Nightmare Before Christmas*, which remained owned by the studio and tucked away in its archives. As ground-breaking as *Vincent* was, circumstances caused Burton to leave the studio and go forth to change the face of filmmaking elsewhere (through *Batman* and other early features).

Meanwhile, Will Vinton's Claymation specials and commercials helped create a boom of popularity in stop-motion clay animation in the late '80s, and many clay animators honed their talent on the Saturday-morning show *Pee-Wee's Playhouse*. These popular shows helped set the stage for the original clay superstar Gumby to make his comeback in a new TV series. Art Clokey brought together a unique cross section of talent for his new show, and for many it was their first big break in the stop-motion world. The team of animators who came together on this show included Mike Belzer, Stephen Buckley, Angie Glocka, Tim Hittle, Eric Leighton, Lionel I. Orozco, Anthony Scott, Trey Thomas, and Richard Zimmerman.

This band of new talent would ultimately join forces with others on *The Nightmare Before Christmas* (Figure 1.27), which was given the green light by Disney's Touchstone Pictures in 1990. Tim Burton chose his former Disney comrade Henry Selick to direct the film, based on his experience in stop-motion and brilliant attention to detail. It was a deeply personal project for Burton—a culmination of his love for the stop-motion specials he loved as a

Figure 1.27

Concept sketch of characters from *The Nightmare Before Christmas*. (Courtesy of the Animazing Gallery/Touchstone Pictures.)

child and his story about Jack Skellington (Figure 1.28), the king of Halloween Town who decides to replace Santa Claus on Christmas Eve. At the heart of all the creepiness and nostalgic vibe to the film was a poignant love story between Jack and his admirer, Sally.

Nightmare was produced in 40,000 square feet of warehouse space in the San Francisco Bay Area over a span of three years. This was the first time a stop-motion feature was produced with a high-level budget and a wide range of experienced talent in the medium. Disney was back on top, animation was cool again, and stop-motion had been riding the wave of its first major golden age in all of its facets: clay, puppets, and creature effects. *Nightmare* combined nearly every puppet and filmmaking technique that had ever been used for stop-motion, including front/rear projection, double exposure effects, casting in foam latex, ball-and-socket armatures, replacement animation, and strong character performance. The production design was incredibly strong, and another unique feature was the extensive use of modern motion control to make the camera a moving part of the story. Topping it all off perfectly was an unforgettable score and songs by Danny Elfman, a regular collaborator on Tim Burton's films.

Figure 1.28

Concept sketch of Jack Skellington from *The Nightmare Before Christmas.* (Courtesy of the Animazing Gallery/Touchstone Pictures.)

At the same time as production was occurring on *Nightmare*, the film *Jurassic Park* was being produced with the intention of including the highest level of stop-motion dinosaur effects ever used. Tests in new breakthrough computer animation technology would ultimately nullify the use of stop-motion for the film and put the nail in the coffin for the creature-effects technique when released in the summer of 1993. However, *The Nightmare Before Christmas*, released later that year, proved that the idea of moving puppets frame by frame could finally work for a feature and that it would still have a bright future ahead of it. Director of photography Pete Kozachik (see full interview with Pete in Chapter 5, "Interview with Pete Kozachik, ASC") describes the significance of the film:

> *Nightmare* came along at just the right time, and it was the show that managed to keep stop-motion from completely going away. There was a popular wisdom among the stop-motion effects geek community that we all wanted to do a full stop-motion feature, but nobody would take out a loan to finance it. The interest would mount up too much in this slow-moving process, whereas you can just do it much faster in live action and not go broke paying back the loan. But in this case, Disney put out enough money to produce what was initially supposed to be a low-budget stop-motion feature. A bunch of us got together and threw everything we had at it, figuring it would never happen again, so let's make it something special. We spent six weeks just on the first shot (which was of Jack skiing down the snowy hills and onto a train in Christmas Town) and didn't know how we were going to produce hundreds more shots to finish it, but we got there.

The success of *Nightmare* was strong in its initial release and only continued to grow in the coming years on DVD and beyond. It was unique for the time it was made and remains unique by today's standards. Based on the unique vision and great pool of talent that were displayed in the film, Disney had instilled confidence in Henry Selick to direct a follow-up feature in stop-motion, *James and the Giant Peach*, based on the famous book by Roald Dahl. Many of the same crew members from *Nightmare* regrouped to work on the new feature, including British animator Paul Berry as animation supervisor. Tim Burton was also involved as a producer, but *James* was a film that brought the design and personal style of Selick more to the forefront. Much like Selick's earlier work for MTV, *James* combined elements of puppet animation with cut-outs, computer animation, and live action. From the outset, it seemed intended to be an experimental mix of media; the original idea was to combine a live actor as James throughout the whole film. This led to consideration of a completely stop-motion film, and it ended up being stop-motion framed by opening and closing live-action segments.

James and the Giant Peach is a delightful film with some outstanding visuals and inspired animation (including a cameo appearance by Jack Skellington), although it did not match the same level of success as *Nightmare*. Also, by the time of its release in 1996, audiences were still reeling from the new CG innovations by Pixar's *Toy Story* and the wave of films inspired by *Jurassic Park*'s ground-breaking effects. Even Disney's other traditional features of the time, *Pocahontas* (1995) and *The Hunchback of Notre Dame* (1996), were coming off as formulaic to most, and audiences were beginning to drift into new areas of interest. The relationship between Disney's company Miramax and Henry Selick also became strained, as plans for another feature called *Toots and the Upside Down House* were abandoned. Selick moved forward on a new stop-motion project based on a graphic novel called *Dark Town*, which was eventually renamed *Monkeybone*. Although that film contained some amazing stop-motion character sequences, the end result released in 2001 became more of a strange live-action film that did not fare well at the box office.

Amid this renaissance of computer-generated visuals and new ways to make movies, the stop-motion puppet feature continued its mixed bag of popular hits and other limited release obscurities. *The Secret Adventures of Tom Thumb* was a 1993 release from the U.K. directed by Dave Borthwick of bolexbrothers that mixed puppet animation with pixilation of live actors. Tom Thumb himself is a sickly little puppet figure who escapes from an experimental science lab and embarks on a journey to return to his parents. The style of the film is gritty, surreal, and reminiscent of Svankmajer, the Brothers Quay, and the darkest Czech films.

Back in America, 1995 saw a limited theatrical run of *Gumby: The Movie*, the first feature film starring Art Clokey's clay icon (Figure 1.29). The story featured Gumby and his pals in a rock band planning a benefit concert, which is threatened by the Blockheads' attempt to replace them with robots. The feature was actually produced during the wake of the *New Adventures of Gumby* series, riding the coattails of the show's newfound success and the fledgling talent who started on the show. Art Clokey financed the $3 million feature himself and stuck with the same level of simplistic charm that had existed in the series. In fact, he simplified it so much that he narrowed his animation team to a third of its original size and took about 30 months to shoot it. The animators who stayed to work on the feature ended up moving on to work on *The Nightmare Before Christmas* shortly afterward. Production on *Gumby: The Movie* had wrapped up around 1992, with intention of a fall 1993 release. However, there were significant delays in distribution, and even when the film was distributed, nobody heard about it because there was virtually no advertising or marketing. It was relegated to a director's cut on video not long after its lackluster release, but it managed to find an audience among die-hard fans of the show.

Figure 1.29

Gumby and Pokey, stars of *Gumby: The Movie*. (Courtesy of Premavision Studios.)

Clay animation in a feature-length film would finally have its shot at worldwide commercial success by 2000. The 1990s had seen the rise of another stop-motion superstar with the genius of animator/director Nick Park. Park had put the British Aardman Animation, founded by Peter Lord and David Sproxton in the 1970s, on the map with his Oscar-winning short *Creature Comforts*. This was followed by further Oscar wins for *The Wrong Trousers* and *A Close Shave*, starring Wallace and Gromit. Expansion of the latter film to feature-length was pondered at one point, but certain restrictions kept it at the half-hour length of its prequels.

A feature film was the logical next step for Aardman, and several Hollywood studios were knocking on their door. The bridge between the two studios would be found in producer Jake Eberts and his affiliation with Pathe Films, which agreed to finance development for a feature. Several ideas based on popular stories were considered, but Aardman felt that an original idea was best. Some drawings of chickens in Nick Park's sketchbook led to the idea of an escape movie with chickens. Upon pitching this idea to Eberts, the Aardman team found itself in front of Steven Spielberg, Jeffrey Katzenberg, and David Geffen, founders of the new DreamWorks Animation SKG.

Before long, a co-financing and distribution agreement between DreamWorks and Pathe proclaimed that Aardman's first feature would be *Chicken Run* (Figure 1.30), directed by Nick Park and Peter Lord. American screenwriter Karey Kirkpatrick was brought on board to help Park and Lord crystallize their story, which told of a group of British chickens on a farm ruled by the evil Mr. and Mrs. Tweedy. A chicken named Ginger (voiced by Julia Sawalha) dreams of flying to freedom with her friends, who come to believe an American rooster named Rocky (Mel Gibson) is the answer to their prayers. Scenes of mystery, suspense, and adventure ensue as the chickens develop their master plan to escape their fate of being turned into pies by their captors.

Figure 1.30

Promotional still for
Chicken Run. (DreamWorks/
Pathe/Aardman/The Kobal
Collection.)

The film drew much of its inspiration from the 1963 film *The Great Escape* and other POW films from the same era and mixed it with great design, funny characters, and (of course) outstanding animation. *Chicken Run* was shot in standard 35mm film, but it was the first feature film in Europe to use frame grabbers for digitally storing frames to register the animation. Computer animation was also used for shooting rough animatics of their storyboards to get a better sense of the cutting and motion between scenes. Very little computer animation was used in the film itself, except for a huge gravy explosion near the end. Five years in the making, *Chicken Run* was a big success for the Aardman/DreamWorks partnership; it became one of the most entertaining films of the year and was loved by audiences and critics alike.

The year 2000 also brought to the screen a stop-motion feature called *The Miracle Maker*, based on the life of Jesus Christ, a significant story to tell at the dawn of the new millennium. Directed by Derek Hayes, it was a co-production between Wales and Russia, and took five years to produce. While the Welsh studio produced some cel animation sequences and overall production, all the puppet animation was developed and shot by Russian animators at Christmas Films, which had a long tradition of adapting Biblical stories to stop-motion through their *Testament* film series.

With Russian animation director Stanislav Sokolov leading the stop-motion production, great attention to detail was paid to capturing the customs, attire, architecture, and landscape of first-century Israel with perfect historical accuracy. Puppet animation, which in its very essence is created from scratch with a great sense of purity, lent itself perfectly to taking on this momentous task, and it was taken very seriously by the entire crew. The image of Jesus himself (Figure 1.31) was a culmination of many different representations of him through the ages and was ultimately inspired by photos of people from the region where he had lived. The puppets' heads were cast in dental acrylic with sculpted replacement mouths and their bodies in a rubber material called Fastflex. The results were stunning in their realism and were made even more powerful by a moving musical score and unique script that told the story through the eyes of a young girl named Tamar, based on the Biblical Jairus' daughter, whom Jesus raised from the dead in the New Testament (Figure 1.32). Although the story of Jesus had been told across centuries through classical art and also on film, it had never been done quite like this. The film received praise from audiences in theater and television screenings worldwide.

Figure 1.31

Puppet of Jesus Christ from *The Miracle Maker.* (© 1999 SAF and Christmas Films.)

The years surrounding the new millennium saw more stop-motion features that were largely unknown and obscure to most of the world, including *The Magic Pipe* (1998) from Russia and *Prop and Berta* (2000) from Denmark. In Czechoslovakia, two feature-length anthologies called *Jan Werich's Fimfarum* (2002) and *Fimfarum 2* (2006) delighted audiences with a menagerie of short stories directed by noted stop-motion filmmakers Aurel Klimt, Vlasta Posposilova, Jan Balej, and Bretislav Pojar. South Africa also produced its first animated stop-motion feature film in 2003, called *Legend of the Sky Kingdom.*

Figure 1.32

A scene from *The Miracle Maker.* (© 1999 SAF and Christmas Films.)

It was based on a children's book by producer Phil Cunningham and employed puppets and sets built from found objects of junk (therefore, the film was referred to as "junkmation" by the filmmakers). This was not only a budgetary restriction, but also an homage to the folk art of Africa, which is often made from discarded objects. In 2005, *Colargol* animator Tadeusz Wilkosz brought a new puppet feature to Polish cinemas called *Tajemnica Kwiatu Paproci* (*The Secret of the Fern Flower*), and Kihachiro Kawamoto completed a new feature called *Shisha No Sho* (*The Book of the Dead*).

The year 2006 saw completion of the 13-year production of an independent stop-motion feature called *Blood Tea and Red String* (Figure 1.33), directed by American filmmaker Christiane Cegavske. Cegavske was an art student who was inspired upon seeing Jan Svankmajer's *Alice*, and she began animating short films while studying at the San Francisco Art Institute. Her short-film projects began to grow into what would become her feature, which was financed mostly by working as a lead animator and sculptor for various studios in Los Angeles. *Blood Tea and Red String*, described as "a handmade fairy tale for adults," tells the story of two groups of creatures, the White Mice and the Creatures Who Dwell Under the Oak, and their conflict over gaining possession of a beautiful doll. The story is filled with surreal, dream-like imagery, is told entirely without dialogue, and features a haunting musical score by Mark Growden. The award-winning film played in several film festivals and was the first of an eventual trilogy by Cegavske, who is now working on her second feature, *Seed in the Sand*. (Cegavske's production stills and other artwork can be found at http://www.christianecegavske.com.)

Figure 1.33

A scene from *Blood Tea and Red String*. (© 2006 Christiane Cegavske.)

Meanwhile, as independent rarities of puppet features spawned across the globe, Aardman was busy moving forward on its multi-picture deal with DreamWorks. As *Chicken Run* wrapped, pre-production moved forward on a re-telling of the Aesop fable *The Tortoise and the Hare*, but story problems prevented the feature from going any further. There had been talk of making a feature-length film with Wallace and Gromit, so it was finally decided to pursue it as the next project, entitled *Curse of the Were-Rabbit* (Figure 1.34). This time, Nick Park would co-direct with Steve Box, who he had also worked with on the last two Wallace and Gromit short films. The story told of the classic man-and-dog duo and their adventures rescuing their local village from a giant mutant rabbit that threatens to ruin the annual Giant Vegetable Competition.

The filmmaking techniques used for the new film were mostly the same as had been used before, although there were some new uses for computer animation employed for certain effects. CG was used to animate the bunnies floating around in the Bun-Vac 6000 machine used by Wallace and Gromit to capture an entire brood of bunnies; it would have been difficult to animate this in stop-motion. The clay texture of the bunnies was scanned onto the CG models to keep the same appearance, and the effect is seamless. The film also employed some creative use of green-screen compositing and fog effects to aid in creating certain shots for the horror film atmosphere. Overall, the film retained the hand-crafted quality, humor, and classic British flavor of the original short films while becoming more epic in scope to appeal to a mass audience. It is a movie made by and for people who love movies, filled with nods to *Metropolis*, *King Kong*, *Beauty and the Beast*, *The Wolfman*, *An American Werewolf in London*, and the Hammer horror films of the 1960s, all put together for a smashing good ride.

Figure 1.34

Production still from *Wallace and Gromit: The Curse of the Were-Rabbit.* (DreamWorks/Aardman/The Kobal Collection.)

While Aardman was producing its feature in Bristol, another stop-motion feature was being produced at Three Mills Studios in London: Tim Burton's *Corpse Bride*. The genesis of the film can be attributed to the late Joe Ranft, who was a storyboard supervisor on *The Nightmare Before Christmas*. Always one to recognize a good story, he came across a European folk tale about a man who unknowingly proposes to a dead woman. He told Tim Burton about the story, knowing it was "something he could really capture," and before too long Burton's sketchbook got some ideas brewing. Similar to *Nightmare*, Burton knew the project called to be done in animation, but he let the project gestate for several years until the time was right to bring it forward.

Following *Nightmare*, of course, there was a glut of CG films straddling the late 1990s and 2000s, including Burton's own *Mars Attacks!* (which was CG after being originally meant to feature stop-motion). When *Corpse Bride* figuratively rose from the grave of his sketchbooks, some thought was given to using CG. A few tests were done, but Burton knew that the project would have much more resonance if it was done in stop-motion.

At first, the film was considered to be produced at the former Will Vinton Studios in Portland, but the partnership was not meant to last. When the project was officially given the green light by Warner Bros., a crew of regular Burton collaborators combined with new talent was assembled in the U.K. Mike Johnson was chosen as co-director. Johnson had been an assistant animator on *Nightmare* and went on to direct a short film called *The Devil Went Down to Georgia* and several episodes of *The PJs* at Will Vinton Studios. The puppets (Figure 1.35) were designed by premier fabricators MacKinnon & Saunders and were the first to employ a new technique for facial animation. Rather than extensive use of replacement heads, as had been done in other films, the *Corpse Bride* puppet faces were manipulated by complex mechanisms of paddles and gears underneath a silicone skin. Animators would insert a tiny Allen key into holes positioned in the puppet's ear or the back of the head to make the jaw drop, the corners of the mouth twitch, and other kinds of subtle movements.

The other breakthrough for *Corpse Bride* was the first use of digital still cameras for shooting all the animation. This decision was made two weeks before production was to start, despite the fact that they had 30 classic Mitchell film cameras and piles of film stock on the shelves ready to be used. The entire film was shot with Canon EOS-1D Mark IIs and provided instant feedback of each scene, which made dailies easy to view and approve on the spot. All of the digital scenes were cut together using Apple's Final Cut Pro, which was another first for a stop-motion feature.

Corpse Bride opened just two weeks after *Curse of the Were-Rabbit* in October 2005, and both were nominated for Best Animated Feature at the Academy Awards (against *Howl's Moving Castle*). The simultaneous mainstream releases and nominations were unprecedented for stop-motion in general. On Oscar night 2006, Wallace and Gromit took home the prize, which was the third time for Nick Park's beloved dog and his owner, but a historical first for a stop-motion feature film. Despite this success, Aardman parted ways with DreamWorks after completing its third feature, *Flushed Away*, which was done in computer animation.

Figure 1.35

Puppets from Tim Burton's *Corpse Bride.* (Courtesy of the Animazing Gallery/Warner Bros.)

Riding on the popular success of these films, Switzerland's first major foray into stop-motion feature production (with co-production from France, Belgium, and the U.K.) came about with *Max & Co.* It was the first feature by directors Frederic and Samuel Guillaume, two brothers who had previously made a few short films. The story, incorporating detailed animalistic puppets designed by MacKinnon & Saunders, told of a teenager named Max on a search for his father. He is taken in to work at a fly-swatter factory called Bzzz & Co. and gets involved in a mission to save the local village from the plot of an evil scientist. With a budget of nearly $30 million, *Max & Co.* was the most expensive film project ever produced in Switzerland. Production set up in an old Tetra Pak factory in the small Swiss town of Romont, with a diverse international crew of stop-motion and live-action filmmakers. The animation director was Guionne Leroy from Belgium, who had experience working on *Toy Story*, *James and the Giant Peach*, and *Chicken Run*. Many of the other experienced stop-motion artists came from England, working with others from Canada and all across Europe (Figures 1.36 and 1.37). The director of photography, Renato Berta from Switzerland, had nearly 30 years of live-action credits to his name and was shooting his first stop-motion feature. Many unique techniques contributed to the dark urban atmosphere the directors were aiming for, including photography of real local skies and landscapes composited into the backgrounds.

Figure 1.36

Marjolaine Parot animates on *Max & Co.* (Photo courtesy Brian Demoskoff/ characters © Max-LeFilm.)

Figure 1.37

Brian Demoskoff animates on *Max & Co.* (Photo courtesy Brian Demoskoff/characters © Max-LeFilm.)

Despite critical raves and winning the Audience Award at the 2007 Annecy Animation Festival, the official European release of *Max & Co.* in February 2008 did not live up to expectations. It only sold 16,000 of the 110,000 tickets anticipated, and the production company formed to create the film declared bankruptcy. This turn of events obviously limited the potential for a wider release, and so far the DVD release has apparently been limited to France. The extremely high production values, fluid animation, sophisticated puppetry, and beautiful design that went into the film make *Max & Co.* an unfortunately lost gem that may simply slip into cult status.

A similar fate befell the final release of Canada's first stop-motion feature *Edison and Leo* (Figure 1.38), which had a smaller production budget of $10 million, funded by Vancouver's Perfect Circle Productions, Telefilm, and Infinity Features. Written by George Toles, the film was set in the late 19th-century Canadian prairies and centered on the exploits of shady inventor George T. Edison. When a failed experiment injures his wife, Edison's plea for help to a native tribe results in a series of murderous plot twists, including the electrification of his son, Leo.

Figure 1.38

A scene from *Edison and Leo*. (© Perfect Circle Productions.)

The "steampunk" tone of the film was decidedly not geared toward a family audience, and it featured scenes of graphic violence and sexual innuendo. The original director ended up leaving the production midway and was replaced by Neil Burns, who had stop-motion experience from working at Cuppa Coffee Studios in Toronto. Many of the animators also relocated from Cuppa to work on the feature, which was shot in the gymnasium of a former First Nations school in Mission, British Columbia. The location was also home to most of the puppet fabrication, set workshops, and post-production. Scenes were shot with digital still cameras, and the images traveled through a fiber-optic cable network straight to the editing suites in house. (I had the opportunity to visit the set during production and was pleased to find one of my former stop-motion students working in the puppet department.) For a relatively low-budget project, they attempted to put a good level of detail into the look of the film, in particular the beautiful set design. Unfortunately, the dark story and mean spirits of the characters were not enough to endear most audiences to the final product. The film played in the Vancouver International Film Festival in 2008 and the Ottawa Animation Festival in 2009, but it did not secure a standard theatrical release and went straight to DVD. Historically speaking, it is great that Canada has finally produced a fully animated stop-motion feature with a unique visual style, and hopefully it will happen again.

In production at the same time as *Edison and Leo* was another stop-motion feature with a very adult sensibility, an Israeli/Australian production called *$9.99* (Figure 1.39), directed by Tatia Rosenthal. Rosenthal was born in Israel and is now based in New York, where she studied animation at NYU's Tisch School for the Arts. (The influence of her studies definitely made its way into *$9.99*; she based the design of one of her puppet characters after the Tisch School's head of animation, Oscar-winning animator/historian John Canemaker.) Prior to her feature, Rosenthal had made two stop-motion shorts—*Crazy Glue* and *A Buck's Worth*—in collaboration with Israeli writer Etgar Keret. The latter film consisted of a tense dialogue scene between a businessman and a homeless man, which served as the basis for what would become *$9.99*.

Figure 1.39

A scene from Tatia Rosenthal's *$9.99*. (Courtesy Here Media/Regent Releasing.)

Armed with a low budget, five months of pre-production began in Australia in August 2006. Production began in 2007, shooting with digital still cameras and a small crew of animators for 40 weeks, and post-production was completed afterward in Israel. Using naturalistic puppets of humans made from silicone, the feature consists of several interweaving stories surrounding several tenants in a Sydney apartment complex. The thematic elements of the various characters' encounters are tied through the common thread of 28-year-old David Peck, who is reading through a book claiming to explain "the meaning of life, yours for only $9.99." The existential script walks a fine line between fantasy and reality, and although it has the feeling of a live-action film, it is presented in a fashion that has much more resonance through being animated.

Rosenthal referred to the style dictated by Keret's stories as "magical realism," which lent itself well to the stop-motion medium. Certain elements of the film, like a young boy dreaming up intricate shadow puppets on his bedroom wall and another character portrayed as a winged angel, would have stuck out as effects gimmicks in a live-action film, but through an entirely stop-motion universe, they fit much better, with a style all their own. The puppet characters are realistic in their movements but stylized enough to present themselves as more impressionistic and symbolic to the philosophical musings of the screenplay. Overall, the film is very unique, bringing a fresh, mature approach to stop-motion among the more caricatured mainstream offerings geared more toward kids. Several noted Australian actors, such as Geoffrey Rush, also lent their voice talents to the film. *$9.99* premiered at the Toronto International Film Festival in 2008, and the following year began to find its way into theaters and festivals, picking up positive reviews and awards along the way.

Australia was not only home to the production of *$9.99*, but also Adam Elliot's feature *Mary and Max* (Figure 1.40). Elliot was already established as a successful figure in the independent animation scene, with several short films and an Oscar to his credit. While studying animation at the Victoria College of the Arts in 1996, he made a strange six-minute biographical clay animation short called *Uncle*, which was a surprise hit at several festivals. Elliot's signature style brought forth in his film consisted of very limited animation of clay characters, who often stared blankly at the camera, and shooting in black and white. A low, deadpan narration told the story behind the tragic lives of these plasticine characters in a matter that is unsettling yet very touching. The power of Elliot's films lies in the brilliant writing, combined with funny character design and a blend of humor and melancholy. *Uncle* was followed by a series of short films executed in the same style of dark, dry wit: one called *Cousin*, another called *Brother*, and finally the 22-minute epic *Harvie Krumpet*, which would take home the Academy Award for Best Animated Short Film in 2003.

Riding the wave of this success, Elliot would spend the next five years crafting his first feature-length film. *Mary and Max* is recognizable as the same signature style of his previous films, but it is brought to a whole new level of beauty, storytelling, art, and technique. The story tells of a pen-pal relationship between Mary (voiced by Toni Collette), a young girl living in Australia, and Max (voiced by Philip Seymour Hoffman), an obese Jewish man with Asperger's syndrome living in New York. They continue writing letters back and forth as Mary grows into adulthood and Max goes through a series of personal trials, ultimately moving toward a beautiful, touching conclusion. Like his earlier shorts, the film is dark, sad, poignant, and hilarious, all at the same time. Elliot drew from many personal experiences writing and directing the

Figure 1.40

A scene from *Mary and Max*. (© 2009, Adam Elliot Pictures.)

film, basing it on a real pen-pal relationship he had and his thematic exploration of people who are different. The film was shot with Stop Motion Pro software interfacing with digital SLR cameras by a talented production crew that included six animators and about 120 other artists and technicians. Hundreds of tiny props, puppets, and sets were handcrafted for the film, and according to production facts from the U.S. press kit, more than 7,800 muffins were consumed (5,236 by the director). *Mary and Max* opened the Sundance Film Festival in 2009, which was a first for both Australia and feature animation, and really helped to push the animation medium to a higher level of acceptance by the film industry.

Panique au Village (*A Town Called Panic*) is yet another stop-motion feature that has recently toured festivals and theaters, premiering at the Cannes Film Festival. Based on the TV series of the same name by Stephane Auber and Vincent Patar in Belgium, the aesthetic of *A Town Called Panic* (Figure 1.41) deliberately resembles tiny, old-fashioned plastic toys moving crudely and erratically through miniature clay sets and typically features fast-paced gags and hilarious slapstick. The main characters of the series and the feature are housemates Cowboy, Indian, and Horse. In the feature, Horse falls in love with his music teacher, Madame Longray, and Cowboy and Indian wake up remembering that it is Horse's birthday. They frantically decide to make him a barbecue as a present, which results in the destruction of their house and a series of adventures involving a giant robotic penguin and a family of underwater sea creatures. The crude nature of *A Town Called Panic*, developed by the directors when they were art students, is completely at odds with the more carefully crafted films it shares the screen with, but that is half the point. The wacky French dialogue, jittery animation, and lightning-fast pacing of the film and its bizarre story make it a fun ride (and incredibly funny).

Figure 1.41

A scene from *A Town Called Panic*. (© 2009, La Parti Productions.)

While these independent features were hitting the festival circuit in 2009, the first big stop-motion feature event for mainstream theaters that year was *Coraline* (Figures 1.42), released in early February. The evolution behind the film began when famed horror/fantasy writer Neil Gaiman fell in love with *The Nightmare Before Christmas* and was inspired to work someday with director Henry Selick. He wrote *Coraline* as a novel, inspired by his own daughters, and sent the manuscript to Selick, who also fell in love with the story and wanted to make it into a film. The story was about a young girl named Coraline who discovers an alternate world through a door in her new house. Everything in this "other" world seems to be much more enticing than her life in the real world, but it soon unravels into a nightmare that Coraline must find a way to defeat.

The project went through many years of finding the right studio, distributor, and medium to bring it to the screen. Choices to make it live action, computer animation, stop-motion, or a combination of these finally came to a head in 2006, when production as a fully stop-motion feature finally began at Laika Studios in Portland, Oregon. Phil Knight had acquired Vinton Studios in 2003 and renamed the company Laika in 2005, and *Coraline* would be the first feature produced under this new regime. The crew was a unique combination of talent, combining many who had worked consistently with Selick since his MTV days with local Portland artists and others from around the globe.

Figure 1.42

A scene from *Coraline*.
(Courtesy Focus Features/
The Kobal Collection.)

The film was the first to use two new technologies for stop-motion filmmaking: rapid prototyping and stereoscopic photography. Rapid prototyping was a method for printing out 3D computer models of replacement animation and props into physical resin materials in order to combine the technical smoothness of CG into a stylized stop-motion set. Stereoscopic photography was a method for actually shooting the stop-motion sets in 3D by taking left- and right-eye images of each frame and aligning them for stereo 3D projection. (Both of these techniques are described in more detail in Chapter 3, "Building Projects" and Chapter 4, "Digital Cinematography," respectively.)

Even with this new technology and state-of-the-art compositing effects, every effort was made to keep *Coraline* as handcrafted as possible. Amazing miniature work was done in the puppet fabrication department, in the realms of posable hair, tiny knit sweaters, and innovative animated plants for a fantastic garden sequence. Along with Laika, Focus Features did an incredible job marketing the film through a creative website and effective advertising, and the anticipation paid off upon the film's release. Audiences and critics alike gave it glowing reviews, making it a great success. As a whole, the awesome vision of Gaiman and Selick made *Coraline* a masterpiece that set the bar much higher for what the art of stop-motion could accomplish, in its design, story, animation, and technical innovation.

It is fascinating to note that the nearly 80 years of history behind the theatrical puppet feature began with Starewitch's *Tale of the Fox* and has come full circle with Wes Anderson's *Fantastic Mr. Fox* (Figure 1.43). Anderson did admit that the Starewitch film inspired the look he wanted for his film. Based

Figure 1.43

A scene from *Fantastic Mr. Fox*. (20th Century Fox Film/The Kobal Collection.)

on the classic children's book by Roald Dahl, the film tells the story of Mr. Fox and his attempts to save his family from being captured by his human arch enemies. Anderson took great liberties with expanding the content of the book into enough story material for a feature in his own signature style of deadpan humor, flat compositions, and eccentric characters. The puppets were fabricated by MacKinnon & Saunders, with elaborate facial paddles for very detailed but subtle animation. Also, aesthetically, Anderson wanted to maintain the crawling fur that would occur when the animators touched them.

Several unique approaches were taken to the production itself, done at Three Mills Studios in London. The voices, done by George Clooney, Bill Murray, and other well-known talent, were recorded on location rather than in a studio. This made the characters feel more like they were living in their respective scenes, whether they were in a field or inside a cave. The animation director was former Will Vinton Studios animator/director Mark Gustafson, who coordinated production on the actual sets. Wes Anderson directed the film mostly by e-mail from his office in Paris, viewing and commenting on still pictures and motion tests for his crew members remotely on a regular basis. He wanted as much of the film's effects as possible to be done in front of the camera, utilizing cotton for smoke and large strips of cellophane for an iconic waterfall scene. The results were a very creative, hilarious film that caught audiences and critics by surprise with rave reviews in late 2009. It has a very adult sensibility in the vein of Anderson's other films but is still intelligent and entertaining enough for kids to enjoy. Both *Fantastic Mr. Fox* and *Coraline* were nominated for Best Animated Feature at the Academy Awards, a fitting tribute to the long-overdue recognition of the stop-motion feature film and its history.

As 2010 is upon us (at the time of this initial book printing), the future looks bright for feature films made in stop-motion animation. What is also fascinating is just how international the spectrum is for these films. Animaking Studios, the largest animation studio in Brazil, has been working for the past several years on its first stop-motion feature, *Worms* (Figure 1.44), based on its award-winning short film of the same name. The new feature film is made for all ages, with a focus on children, following the adventures of a pre-teen worm named Junior. The film is slated for release in Brazil and Latin America very soon, and it appears to be receiving much support from distributors, media, and followers of their production blog (http://www.minhocasofilme.com.br).

Figure 1.44

Production still from *Worms*. (Courtesy of Animaking Studios.)

Elsewhere, a stop-motion feature called *O Apostolo* is being produced in Spain, a feature version of the TV series *Sandmunchenn* in Germany, and in Poland a stereoscopic stop-motion feature is being produced called *The Flying Piano*. Back in the U.S., Screen Novelties is moving forward with the Jim Henson Company on a feature version of their short film *Monster Safari* (which you can read more about in Chapter 2, "An Interview with Screen Novelties"). There is also an independent feature by Julie Pitts and Miles Blow in Australia called *Wombok Forest* still in production, and indie stop-motion filmmakers Justin and Shel Rasch (see Chapter 13, "An Interview with Justin and Shel Rasch") have dreams and plans for a feature project in the years to come.

In addition to independent features, the larger studios are moving forward on more stop-motion feature productions. Aardman Animation is producing *Pirates* under its new partnership with Sony Imageworks, and Tim Burton has officially joined forces again with Disney to create a feature-length stop-motion version of *Frankenweenie*, the live-action short he made for Disney back in 1984. Meanwhile, stop-motion fans are waiting with anticipation as plans come together for future projects at Laika Studios and the next venture for Henry Selick. As the future unfolds, we can certainly look forward to the advanced art of stop-motion animation continuing its history on the big screen, with infinite possibilities and new stories to enchant us.

Author's Note: This history chapter is dedicated to the memory of Art Clokey (Figure 1.45), whose work was the inspiration behind many of these stop-motion features.

Figure 1.45

Art Clokey (1921–2010). (Courtesy of Premavision Studios.)

2

An Interview with Screen Novelties

Figure 2.1

(Left to right) Chris Finnegan, Mark Caballero, Seamus Walsh.

Screen Novelties is a special stop-motion film collective in Los Angeles, formed in 2003 by Seamus Walsh, Mark Caballero, and Chris Finnegan (Figure 2.1). Their style of filmmaking, which combines puppetry and stop-motion with a classic cartoon feel, can be seen in numerous short films, commercials, and sequences for TV specials shown on Cartoon Network, on Nickelodeon, and at several festivals. They are also well known for helping stop-motion master Ray Harryhausen in 2002 to complete his short puppet film *The Tortoise and the Hare*, which had been left unfinished 50 years earlier. I first enjoyed their film *Mysterious Mose* at the Spike and Mike's Festival of Animation several years ago; I have since enjoyed their unique approach to animation and puppetry and greatly appreciate their passion for preserving stop-motion's history. Naturally I wanted to acknowledge their work and invited them to have their thoughts contributed to this book.

Website: www.screen-novelties.com

KEN: *How did you all meet each other and get started with stop-motion?*

SEAMUS WALSH: Mark and I were in a class together at UCLA Extension, a series of night classes they offered for hands-on camera instruction, and we were paired up together on a project by chance. We started talking about stop-motion films like Rankin/Bass' *Mad Monster Party* and other stuff that we liked, and we were both saying, "Wow, you're the only other person I've met who has even heard of that movie!" So we just started helping each other out on our projects for a few years.

MARK CABALLERO: Then we figured that rather than spend more money on our own education through the school system, we'd take whatever little money we had left and use it to buy a Bolex and make films on our own. We made two short films. The first one we did, *Old Man and the Goblins*, got us into MTV Animation to work on *Celebrity Deathmatch* out in New York. That's where we met Chris.

CHRIS FINNEGAN: I had gone to college in Chicago and was doing some freelance work there before getting the call to move to New York. Mark and Seamus also created their short film *Mysterious Mose* right before coming out to work on *Deathmatch* and completed the post-production there. At that time, around 1998, *The PJs* from Will Vinton Studios was also gearing up on the west coast, but on the east coast, anyone who was into stop-motion animation was getting hired to work for *Deathmatch*. We saw it as a great opportunity to be able to animate every day, sort of like a stop-motion boot camp, and we still work with many of the animators and fabricators who we worked with on that show.

MARK: The other great thing about that show was that there wasn't a whole lot of direction, so we were able to pretty much direct ourselves. That led to a lot of unique animation styles, so rather than stick with the standard Vinton style or what have you, we were able to find voices for ourselves in doing the animation.

SEAMUS: It was really grueling, but a lot of really nice people worked on it and banded together in the face of all the pressure. You had to get the shows done really fast, but we kind of liked the looseness and anarchy of it, which was fun.

KEN: *After that, what led to Screen Novelties being set up back in Los Angeles?*

SEAMUS: Afterwards, Mark and I ended up coming back to L.A. because we had a cheap living situation here, and we started making films again, including helping Ray Harryhausen restore his film *The Tortoise and the Hare* (Figure 2.2). We also started the Web shows that eventually became *Robot Chicken*. Back then it was called *Sweet J Presents*; it was a webseries of 13 episodes done for Sony's website.

Figure 2.2

Mark Caballero animates the tortoise for Ray Harryhausen's short film. (Courtesy of Screen Novelties.)

CHRIS: I stayed in New York a while longer doing freelance work then came out to L.A. to work on *Sweet J* with Mark and Seamus, which went on for about four or five months. After that project wrapped, we all started talking about starting a studio. Part of it was fulfilling a dream of ours, but part of it was also trying to generate work for ourselves since freelance work was dying down a bit.

MARK: We never really thought of Screen Novelties as a stop-motion studio for hire, but more like a production company for our own films. Of course, it's rare that you get to sell your own projects, so we like to take on bigger freelance projects, and it does end up being like a small business. It's really just the three of us, plus a few assistants and a small stable of people we can bring in whenever there is a big budget on a project.

CHRIS: After Mark and Seamus worked on *The Tortoise and the Hare*, it got some attention and led to our first major work-for-hire job. Nike wanted to do a Harryhausen-inspired spot with a minotaur and a hydra, based on the association we had with Ray. That was our first commercial, and the first big project like that is always the hardest one for directors to land. Once we got that, it really helped get the ball rolling with the company.

MARK: Around that time we also got the call from Seth Green to help them start *Robot Chicken* for Adult Swim, so we worked with them on that for the first couple seasons. We also felt that we wanted to branch off and do our own thing so that we didn't lose what we really wanted to do. Between commercials or spots for Cartoon Network, we're still developing our own projects. We have a *Monster Safari* feature in development and another short featuring our witch doctor character, which has been in our heads for a long time.

SEAMUS: It's a constant struggle because we're always getting caught up in the freelance work, and we left *Robot Chicken* so we could do our own shorts but started running out of money. So right now our work on *Chowder* and *The Marvelous Misadventures of Flapjack* for Cartoon Network (Figures 2.3) has replaced what we were doing before. It's still a lot of work, but it doesn't require as much of a commitment. *Robot Chicken* had 16 stages producing an episode a week, so it was very much all consuming.

MARK: Plus on both of those shows, they still give us a bit of artistic freedom, but more so with *Chowder* and *Flapjack*, we're able to experiment more. That helps us because any experimental stuff we do we can work into our archives and hopefully work into bigger projects.

KEN: *What specific roles do each of you normally play when working on these projects?*

SEAMUS: For the most part, we try our best to trade off projects, so that each of us is the creative head of whatever new project comes in, whether it's a commercial or any kind of freelance work.

MARK: Chris does a lot of the producer-type work, and Seamus leans more towards design, but we all have creative input and will look towards whoever is the head of any particular project.

Figure 2.3

Seamus Walsh animating (left) and Chris Finnegan dressing a set (right) for production. (© Screen Novelties and Cartoon Network.)

CHRIS: A typical arrangement for a studio would be that one person does all the business and another person does the creative, but we're all animators who have made our own films. We will bring in other producers or coordinators at times to help with the bigger projects so that we can focus on the creative side, but we all pitch in and do whatever is possible to make it work.

MARK: It's more like a collective, where sometimes all three of us will take credit for directing, or if somebody has more of a say in something, then they will do it.

KEN: *What is your studio facility like?*

SEAMUS: We have a 1,800-square-foot studio space in a warehouse behind some stores on Melrose Avenue and Fairfax, kind of in a back-alley area. It's just enough space to keep the rent paid, with one larger stage and a few smaller stages.

CHRIS: When we do need more space, there are a few extra garages across the way where we can store our power tools, saws, spraying booths, and chemicals.

KEN: *What kind of camera equipment and software do you typically use, and have they changed at all over the years?*

SEAMUS: There haven't been too many changes. It's only been in the past 10 years or so that we started shooting everything digitally. Back on *Celebrity Deathmatch*, we used digital cameras and Adobe Premiere 4.2, which had a stop-motion capture function. Then when we did the *Robot Chicken* pilots for the Web, it was our first time using digital SLR cameras and patching the frames together in After Effects or Final Cut Pro. Since then we've just been using After Effects to put everything together.

MARK: As far as cameras go, we've just evolved with the times, so every couple of years we'll invest in new ones, like the Sony R1 we're still using currently.

CHRIS: There are also so many more digital camera options now for stop-motion compared to even five or six years ago. SLR cameras now have a live video feed option, so we got a couple of those, and we still enjoy using the Video LunchBox tools since they're simple to use. We've also started using Dragon Stop Motion on a few projects, but for post-production on our own projects seen all the way through, it's still After Effects that we will typically use for digital rig or flicker removal. Or sometimes the post, editing, and color correction will be done elsewhere by the commercial client we're providing the animation for.

SEAMUS: The camera that's used also depends on the project. If it's a fast-paced project, it's nice to not have to deal with an SLR and the interchangeable lenses. On *Robot Chicken* we just had fixed-lens cameras because you could go quickly and never had to clean the sensors or other things like that. But on other projects, like our recent *SpongeBob SquarePants* project (Figures 2.4), we used a higher-end Nikon D300. For Nickelodeon, we just re-did the opening sequence of *SpongeBob* in stop-motion for the 10th anniversary of the show, which was a lot of fun.

Figure 2.4
Puppets and set for Spongebob SquarePants 10th anniversary. (© Screen Novelties and Nickelodeon.)

KEN: *What materials do you commonly use for your puppets?*

SEAMUS: The methods we use are mostly like how Rankin/Bass made their puppets back in the day; that part hasn't changed very much. We're usually more drawn to fabric and fur textures than clay or silicone puppets. We try to use build-up as much as possible and usually just use wire armatures because they are more loose and flexible.

Unless you're going to spend lots of money making your ball-and-socket armature really nice, they end up having many limitations and being rather clunky. Plus our style is much more on the cartoony side, and wire allows you to do rubber-hose limbs and animation easily.

MARK: If we knew that we were going to do animation with more repetitive actions, or if the puppets have to last a long time, then we'll go with ball and socket, but we've rarely needed to go there. For that matter, even with foam latex puppets, we don't go there if we don't need to. We like the look of build-up puppets, and there's a lot to play with—for instance, using found objects and stuff like that. One of these days we'd like to try a replacement walk cycle, like the old George Pal Puppetoon style.

CHRIS: One thing technically that's been an innovation over the last few years that we've used in building props, sets, and puppets is the availability of laser cutting. If a character has stick-on replacement mouth shapes, we can set those up as vectors in Illustrator and get them laser cut on card stock or vinyl. This saves a lot of time cutting things out with X-Acto knives. Especially on a project like *Robot Chicken* or similar series where you need so many of those mouths, laser cutting is a great tool to have access to.

KEN: *Have you been looking into the rapid prototyping technology as well?*

CHRIS: We haven't done it yet, but we're kind of itching to try it out because it's a very intriguing technique.

MARK: Yeah, we're looking for a juicy-enough project to try it out on since it can get a little pricey.

KEN: *Do you guys have a collective or personal favorite project, or any that you are most proud of?*

SEAMUS: Well, everything you do, you like something about it. To do it in stop-motion, you have to really throw everything you have behind it.

CHRIS: Before we officially started the company, Mark and Seamus did a stop-motion dream sequence for a Cartoon Network *Flintstones* 2D feature called *Flintstones on the Rocks* (Figure 2.5), and that's one of the things that people keep mentioning over the years.

SEAMUS: Yeah, that was really fun because they wanted that real Ed Benedict style to everything. We sculpted everything with that in mind, keeping that real 1960s feel. The puppets turned out really nice on that one, mimicking the Hanna-Barbera style, but in stop-motion. It was strange because we had to find a nice balance between moving it or not moving it and having it look dead but just alive enough to make it feel like limited animation. We were pretty proud of how that one came out.

Figure 2.5

Puppets from *Flintstones on the Rocks*. (© Screen Novelties and Cartoon Network.)

MARK: I guess the bias would be definitely with our own stuff as well because we have a lot more fun with the freedom it provides. We get excited about it since we don't have to match another style or run it through someone else. Also, working with Ray Harryhausen was really exciting.

SEAMUS: Yeah, I don't know how we could ever top working with Ray. The fun of getting to rework all that footage was a great challenge. It was just one of those labor-of-love projects that didn't have any money involved and was done in our garage off hours. It took forever, but it was so much fun.

CHRIS: The *Monster Safari* short we did for Nickelodeon (Figures 2.6) had a lot of blood, sweat, and tears put into it. Unfortunately, it didn't go forward with the network, but it did get the Jim Henson Company interested, so we're going forward on a feature with them.

MARK: The feature is in the very early stages at this moment; we're working with the writers on a second draft of the script. Our plan at this point is to go with Henson to get some financing together. It's going to be one of those things where we are pushing the idea of an independent animated feature with a low budget so that we can try to have as much freedom on it as we can.

SEAMUS: You want a project like this to have a high enough budget that you can pay people well, but low enough that you can still not have every decision being made or questioned by the big people. Henson seems confident they can find the money to get it made, so we're keeping a positive outlook on it, and the script is coming together really well.

Figure 2.6

Seamus Walsh (left) and Mark Caballero (right) animating on *Monster Safari*. (© Screen Novelties.)

CHRIS: The movie business is funny that way; we could be working on it in either six months or six years.

MARK: Yeah, I'd say we're hoping the current popularity of stop-motion will justify our cause.

SEAMUS: And the *Monster Safari* short we did is something we're particularly proud of because it is the current best example of where we are headed, both visually and story-wise.

KEN: *Has making a feature always been a dream or major goal of Screen Novelties?*

CHRIS: Doing work for television in stop-motion is always fun and has been for a while, but it's also exhausting because there is never the budget or time really to do exactly what you want to do with it. You're always making compromises; doing features gives you more opportunity. You can spend days just lighting a shot and finessing more details to get exactly what you want.

MARK: Plus with TV work, of course we would never turn down any offers to do a series, but after a while, when you've inundated a few episodes with one character, it doesn't feel as special anymore. That's the thing about stop-motion—there's still not enough of it out there to make it not special, so we want to make sure we don't contribute to that. Instead of creating a series of multiple episodes with the same characters each time, we'd rather tell one good story with those characters and then perhaps move on to the next story.

KEN: *What advice do you guys have for someone doing stop-motion production in a creative studio team environment?*

CHRIS: One thing for us, since we're a small studio, is that we tend to hire people who are jacks of all trades. We can't always afford to hire people who only animate, composite, or build puppets. People who can do more of those things at once are a good fit for us because that's our background, and we all like to animate, build, produce, and direct. That may not fit at a bigger studio, where things are more specialized, but even beyond that, we've found that some students and others who can do everything tend to shine in every part. Some animators who can also build puppets can end up being better animators for it.

MARK: It's always attractive for us to bring somebody in who knows multiple parts of the process. For any freelance animator who goes in, whether it's for a feature or a TV series, it's still valuable if you know everything because when you're animating you understand where the lights are and how to treat a puppet. The more knowledge you have about what you do, it makes it better and easier for you, so we do encourage that. For us as a studio, it works to keep things small, set a goal and stick to it, and not get too big too fast. Also it's vital to bring in people who know business and don't want to work in the creative side of things so that the artists can focus on that completely.

SEAMUS: When we were on *Robot Chicken*, people would send in reels; since we were the animation directors, we'd have to evaluate them. When you meet people, you can tell who can roll with the punches and not get too focused on the technical details. With stop-motion you do have to pay attention to things like that, but there would sometimes be animators who got so wrapped up in the technical side that they couldn't produce the daily animation quota. If you're talking about students who want to become animators, there are not many stop-motion jobs out there, and you'll be competing with others who have lots of experience. You have to compare your work to the best stuff out there and push yourself to achieve that. It's much more competitive to get on a show like *Robot Chicken* now than when the show was just starting out. You have to find your unique style and know as many different aspects of the craft as possible so that you have other skills to fall back on. If animation jobs are not open, you can find work building sets or something like that.

KEN: *You guys seem to be very interested in preserving the history of stop-motion animation, whether it's finishing Ray Harryhausen's short film or restoring the original Rankin/Bass puppets from their* Rudolph *special (Figure 2.7). What comments do you have on your motivation behind this?*

SEAMUS: We got into this because of a love for the art form itself. We never took that many actual animation classes, so a lot of it has to do with an attempt to see as much stop-motion that's been produced as possible. There was a video store called Eddie Brandt's, where the owners took a bunch of their 16-millimeter films and transferred them to video, which gave you the chance to see tons of stuff that's never been released.

Figure 2.7

Restoring the original Rankin/Bass *Rudolph* puppets. (Courtesy of Screen Novelties.)

Mark and I used to go there on the weekends and rent five or six videos at a time; that's where we discovered Ladislas Starewitch, George Pal's Puppetoons, Fleischer, and stuff like that. We had an appetite for seeing as much stuff as possible that has been produced out there, and that just kind of snowballed.

MARK: It's important to know your history, and stop-motion is such a small facet of filmmaking that it's really not that difficult to know a little bit about your predecessors and what they accomplished. I always get attracted to the people who know that kind of stuff because that means they are drawing their knowledge from that and applying it to what they're doing right now.

SEAMUS: You know someone is passionate about the art form when they've taken the trouble to seek out things like Karel Zeman films. We're often surprised to meet stop-motion people who don't seem to know or care much about Zeman's *Adventures of Baron Munchausen*, for example. We know it's obscure, so we would enjoy having people over to our apartment and showing them this esoteric stuff, and they would always appreciate it.

CHRIS: It's getting easier to find these films now with many of them being released to DVD, like the Japanese market, for instance, putting out more obscure stuff. It's still striking how much stop-motion has been produced over the years that nobody has ever seen, like Bretislav Pojar, Zeman, and so on. When you actually see it, a lot of the design and animation is better than anything that's been done, even in recent years.

SEAMUS: The Internet is definitely helping that. Even back in the mid to late '90s, it was impossible to see anything. I remember as a kid looking in Ray Harryhausen's *Film Fantasy Scrapbook*, seeing images from the fairy tale films, and feeling frustrated that there was no possible way to see the actual films. Now, luckily, these have been released, and you can also go onto YouTube and find things like Joop Geesink. Especially with stop-motion, I think you have to know the history of it in order to find out what your little contribution to the art form is going to be. We were just watching some of the Puppetoons recently, and we saw a double-bounce horse walk done with replacement cycles! This was done about 70 years ago, and even as good as modern films like *The Nightmare Before Christmas* and *Coraline* are, nobody has ever topped this double-bounce horse walk. You need these things to set your bar high.

MARK: It's just like if you study 2D animation; you have to know your predecessors like Disney, Warner Bros., and Fleischer, so why not make that apply to stop-motion as well? For that matter, when we were renting all of these videos and going through everything frame by frame, both with 2D and puppet films, we found that you can learn something from all of it.

SEAMUS: I would still count Rod Scribner and Ward Kimball as much of an inspiration as Jiri Trnka because all the principles of 2D animation apply directly to stop-motion as well.

CHRIS: It's definitely something we try to keep in the front of our minds with everything we do; a lot of stop-motion tends to default to realism or very dark, heavy themes. We like to apply more of these elastic 2D principles to the medium because you don't see as much of it. Aardman Animations has done some of that as well, so they are a big inspiration.

MARK: We don't have anything against the darker material, like Jan Svankmeyer and stuff. But we get a lot of reels from people who use imagery inspired by that genre but don't bother to take it a step further and learn more about those films. They could do more research and find other filmmakers, like Kihachiro Kawamoto in Japan, who did stuff like that, too.

CHRIS: So much of the student work seems to default to that Brothers Quay/Jan Svankmeyer look for some reason. I'm not sure why that is; perhaps it's what people see more of.

SEAMUS: It could be because with that material, you don't have to adhere directly to character animation. A film like *The Nightmare Before Christmas* has a very high level of character animation going on, and that's something that people take years to achieve, whereas on the surface of the Svankmeyer stuff, it's more about atmosphere and tone, not so much about a tangible walk cycle.

MARK: We have been seeing a slight change in that because we've hired a couple of guys out of CalArts who do work outside of the dark, drippy stuff, which is nice to see. I think they're trying to change that in the schools as well; some of our peers are teaching there, applying what they've learned in the outside world to teaching the students. I know that at CalArts and USC, they like to have a fine line between character animation and experimental; stop-motion was always just experimental before, which is a shame. We would go there to give presentations and often see such a line dividing the two. We feel that even if you're doing experimental animation, you need a character in order to convey what you're trying to express. Now that our friends are in there, we're starting to see a change in that, which is great.

SEAMUS: It could have something to do with the technology, too. In the past 10 years or so, as LunchBox systems and software like Dragon have become more available, they allow you to take risks that you couldn't have taken before, when you were shooting on film and couldn't snip frames out of the negative. I think back then, people would just play it safe, whereas now, being able to flip and roll your stop-motion frames like you would for 2D animation, you can push stuff and take chances, knowing you can always cut back. That wasn't possible before, so I think that has a lot to do with the increase of 2D-style stop-motion happening now.

CHRIS: Plus with digital rig removal tools, if you want to make a character jump in the air, in the past that was a real challenge. Now it's easier.

KEN: *Do you think these tools are helping stop-motion find more of a place in the industry as a whole?*

MARK: Yeah, stop-motion is carving more of a niche out there now, whereas in the early '90s we would see an animated puppet film only about as often as you used to see it as a special effect in the old days. Now that CG has trumped that for dinosaurs and effects, stop-motion has become more of a preference, based on what the director wants to do. If a director like Wes Anderson decides to do his next movie in stop-motion, then he can, and nobody is objecting, saying it's too expensive or whatever, because it's not anymore. It can cost just as much as any other film, so I think it's becoming more accepted as just another way to make a movie that people will want to see.

CHRIS: Also, in the past 10 years or so, we've seen a massive advance in CG with the rendering becoming slicker and smoother, and the general audience ate it up and followed it. But it has gotten to the point where CG has saturated, where it's not an attraction in itself just to see a computer film. We'd love to see stop-motion in the mix with CG and also with 2D because there's no reason 2D should be dead. If it suits your story, it should be a viable option.

SEAMUS: All the techniques have a different look, so why not have them all on the table, unless one of them is extremely cost prohibitive compared to the others? At feature-level work, they are all now pretty much the same; it just depends on which medium you like to work in. I think people tend to gravitate towards the low-fi stop-motion work because it doesn't look like CG. Many average people who saw

Corpse Bride probably thought it was done with computers. It's weird because the audience probably doesn't care whether something is done in stop-motion. We're not kidding ourselves that there are tons of average people thinking, "I wish there was more stop-motion being done"; I think people just want to see something that looks fun or is interesting to them at that time.

CHRIS: I think it's important to stress that there is CG animation out there that deliberately tries to look like stop-motion and is very convincing in the way it's rendered out to look that way. You have to ask whether it's worth it to do CG and create a stop-motion look, but I think the process of actually building physical objects and having animators move things in real space affects the way the animation comes out. A bunch of people sitting at computers are never going to produce the same kind of vibe as people creating real miniature environments.

SEAMUS: From anyone I've talked to who has tried to mimic the stop-motion process in CG, they all say it takes so much time to put the imperfections in that you could almost do it faster in stop-motion to begin with.

CHRIS: We often speculate about how people feel about stop-motion in the industry—that perhaps if the films flop, people will stop making them. Fortunately, *Coraline* found an audience, and we hope that trend continues.

MARK: It will be interesting to see what Aardman's next feature is like, since some people speculate that *The Curse of the Were-Rabbit* didn't make as much money as they thought it would, perhaps due to some strife with DreamWorks. The general assumption is that the big moneymakers are CG, but *Chicken Run* also did really well, so if their next film with Sony does well, it's good for those of us in stop-motion.

CHRIS: It's tough going month to month in the business sometimes, but you really can't ask for more. There are quite a few pockets of stop-motion going on in L.A. right now between the crew at Shadow, Chiodo Bros., and so on. And up in Portland, there's a network of people who do it, plus a handful in New York.

MARK: It's nice having that network because if you do stop-motion, chances are you know about 80% of the others who do it as well. We adapt our crew to each job we get, so if we need more people, we just tap into that. We feel really fortunate to be doing stop-motion. There are not many people in the world who actually get to do what they want for a living and get paid for it.

SEAMUS: Yeah, it's weird that we've managed to survive this long! As a kid I never thought I'd be able to make a living doing stop-motion. There are only a few studios that do it, and many more do it as a hobby. It's just fun.

3

Building Puppets

A t the 2006 Ottawa Animation Festival, I had the rare privilege to meet stop-motion filmmaker Kihachiro Kawamoto and hear him speak on a panel. Knowing that he had studied the craft under the legendary Jiri Trnka, I asked him which lessons were the most important he had learned from Trnka. His reply was that Trnka had told him, "A puppet is not a miniature human. He has his own world." In my first book, *The Art of Stop-Motion Animation*, Chapter 7, "Building Puppets," there was a basic overview of character design, doll armatures, ball-and-socket armatures, wire armatures, foam latex molding, latex build-up, and clay puppets. This volume's chapter will go into a bit more detail about some of these methods and introduce some new ones, from plug-in wire armatures, face armatures, and silicone molding/casting to cable controls, rapid prototyping, and replacement puppets. The end goal of these methods is the same when the cameras start clicking: to bring these carefully crafted figures to life in that other world on the screen.

Let me reiterate one of the most important principles to follow: *design your puppet based on what is required of it,* in terms of its character and movement. Which parts are hard, flexible, replaceable, heavy, or light will have a direct impact on the animation of your puppet, so design everything with this in mind. Also remember that your puppet will be touched continually throughout the animation process and will need to be strong enough to hold each position between frames. The decisions you make regarding which methods or materials you use will also depend on your budget, skill level, available space, and time allotted. Often, the simplest solutions work best. Other times, things can get more complicated, but if you build with the end goal in mind, things will fall into place with a little practice.

You may find that whatever related art forms you have experience with will influence which puppet-building techniques you prefer to use. If you have a sculpting or painting background, you may find latex build-up a satisfying technique to work in. If you are very technical and like building things out of metal, wood, or hardware materials, you may gravitate toward wanting to machine ball-and-socket armatures. The possibilities for making puppets are as infinite as everything else in the universe; there is really no wrong way to sculpt a face, build an armature, or design a way to combine different materials together (although some materials don't tend to mix well). You just find whatever works for you and go crazy with it!

When building puppets, a universal rule is to have a table-top space to work with that can be dedicated to the process for a considerable length of time. If all you have is your dining room table, go with that, but it helps to cover it with cardboard, sheets of brown paper, or wax paper to help materials from sliding around, getting lost, or damaging any of your furniture. Be aware of the mess that can and will be created and which items close to your workspace, including your clothes, can be permanently soiled by the materials you're using. Take this from someone who has spilled latex everywhere and ruined his clothes on a few occasions. But hey, it's all in the name of art, right?

If you build your own puppets, some of the methods described in this chapter are written in a tutorial fashion that allows you to treat the text and pictures as a guide. You should feel free to deviate from the text once you become more confident and come up with your own ideas based on the foundations provided here. In other cases, some of these methods are merely an overview of the process and can be complemented by other sources of guidance. One additional disclaimer: When dealing with chemicals like epoxy glue or putty, silicone, plastic, or other toxic substances, this chapter will describe the process for you, but *always* read the safety instructions that come with these materials. These advanced puppet-building methods should be done in a controlled environment with plenty of ventilation and kept isolated from situations where pets or small children could get into them. Good art often involves pain, but it's nice to avoid trips to the hospital if you can. Materials never behave the same way twice, and you will always be fighting with them, but this is all part of the process. Above all, do your research, ask for help, let yourself make mistakes, and enjoy it!

Plug-In Wire and Sockets

Wire armatures are great for producing simple characters at relatively small sizes and provide a good range of movement at a relatively low cost. A simple wire armature is typically built of 1/16-inch aluminum wire that has been twisted into double strands and is held together with epoxy putty for any rigid parts. The biggest disadvantage to wire armatures, of course, is that they will snap and break eventually, even if they are built really well. If your wire armature is covered with detailed latex build-up or has a casted foam latex body, it doesn't have much of a future once it breaks. This can be frustrating, especially if it happens in the middle of a long stop-motion scene that takes you several days to shoot. By whatever methods are in your means, it is in your best interest as both a puppet-builder and an animator to prolong the life of your puppet as long as you possibly can. As you plan everything else, plan for eventual breakage of your puppet and balance this with how much animation you need to shoot.

One way to create a wire armature that hopefully will last longer is to design it with sockets that allow you to remove and replace certain body parts if and when they do break. Being able to remove an arm or leg and replace it with a new one can save you from scrapping an entire puppet or hours of animation. The following pages will show some very simple and more advanced methods for building your own armature from scratch, implementing wire and sockets. Some people refer to these types of armature designs as "plug-in" armatures, meaning the replaceable parts are plugged into their corresponding sockets.

As always, you should start your puppet's design and its corresponding armature on paper. On a regular sheet of 8½ by 11 paper, draw a diagram of your puppet standing in a generic standing pose. You can use larger paper, depending on the size of your puppet, but keep in mind that the larger the puppet, the more important the issue of top-heaviness becomes. Depending on the design and materials used, the size of your puppet can easily move it beyond the point where a wire armature will support it, and you may need to consider other methods. For a simple wire-and-socket armature, a small to medium size is best and will typically work for any puppet ranging from 6 to 10 inches in height. Draw your character diagram in a generic pose with arms slightly fanned out from its sides to give you plenty of space to work around. In the example shown in Figure 3.1, I've designed a basic human figure. The diagram shows some additional movement I wanted to incorporate in the shoulders, using the sockets to give him the option of shrugging by shifting them upward. Some added sketches of the shrugging arms help me visualize this a little bit for scale purposes. For the spine, I used a piece of plastic beaded doll armature, and cut some pieces of brass square K&S tubing, which will be used for the sockets (Figure 3.1).

Figure 3.1

A diagram to follow for the puppet design, with doll armature piece and K&S tubes.

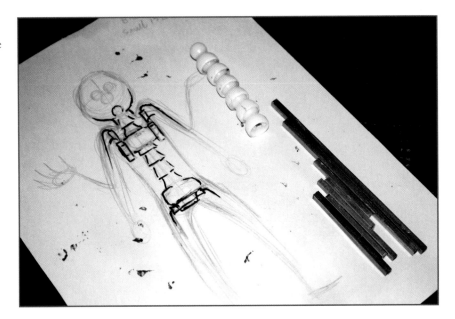

For the K&S tubing, you should purchase at least two different sizes from your local hobby shop. (If you don't have a hobby shop or hardware store in your neighborhood that sells K&S tubing, try ordering from http://www.ksmetals. com.) The idea behind the two different sizes is that the smaller size will slide into the larger size and fit together. In this case, I used K&S stock number 153 for the larger tube, which is the 3/16 size, and K&S stock number 152 for the smaller tube, which is the 5/32 size. A twisted strand of 1/16 armature wire is meant to slide into the 5/32 tube, so this is the right size for it to slide in snugly without wiggling around.

For the two shoulder sockets, the large tubes are attached to the armature, so the small tubes can plug in from the top. For the hip sockets, one tube is attached to the armature horizontally on the bottom, so the small tubes can plug in on each side. The small tubes should not go all the way through to the edges of the large tubes, but should have a tiny bit of space sticking out. To help keep the tubes in place, not pushing too far in, you can plan for punching a dent in the large tube at the point you want the small tube to stop and essentially lock into position. With this configuration in mind, lay the K&S tubes over the diagram and make marks with a felt-tip marker to determine the sizes to which they should be cut (see Figure 3.2 for a closer look at the measured marks).

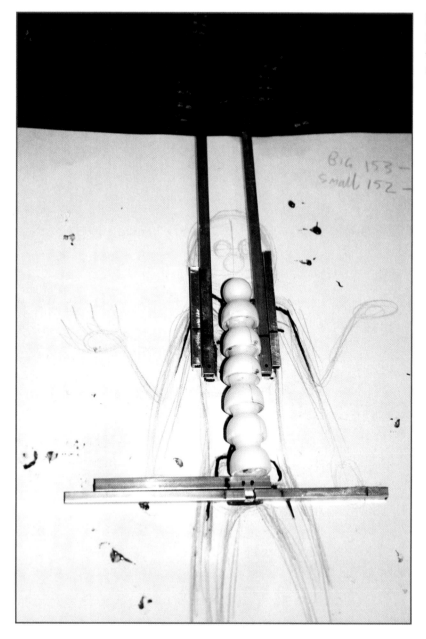

Figure 3.2

K&S tubes lined up with the diagram for measurement purposes.

To make the dents in the tubes, simply line them up in a mitre box, place a small Phillips screwdriver, a nail, or a center punch on the exact spot, and give a few small taps with a hammer (Figure 3.3). Then, cut the large tube pieces and slide the small tubes in to make sure they lock into position properly. An alternate step to this process is to slide the tubes into each other and then punch a small dent into both of them. This will provide a notch for the smaller tube to fit into and lock strongly into position. The double dents will keep the plug from slipping out, but it also might make it harder to pull out if needed, so experiment to see what works best for your design.

Next, you can cut the small pieces. As you progress, keep lining things up with your diagram to make sure you are staying on track with things in terms of size (Figure 3.4). To get the small pieces out of the larger sockets, simply use a small Allen key to push them out from the other side (Figure 3.5).

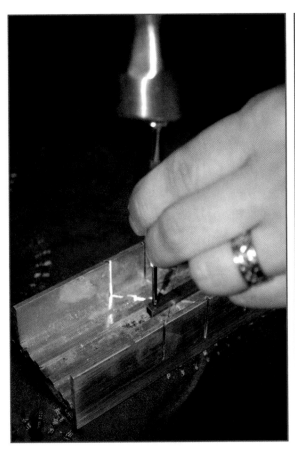

Figure 3.3

Hammering a dent into the K&S tubes.

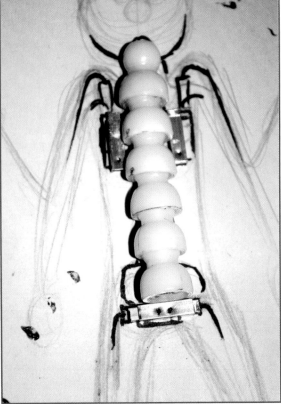

Figure 3.4

Lining up the tubes with the diagram.

Once all of your pieces are cut, attach the large socket tubes to the armature in the proper place with hot glue (Figure 3.6). This will not be the ultimate solution for keeping them affixed because it's not strong enough for all the pressure you'll eventually put on the puppet. It's just a temporary measure for keeping the pieces in the right place. Next, for the arms and legs, cut and twist some aluminum wire pieces and slot them into the small tubes. Continue measuring against your diagram, and put the whole figure together to make sure it's working for you in terms of proportions (Figure 3.7).

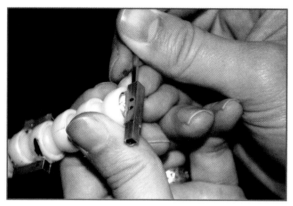

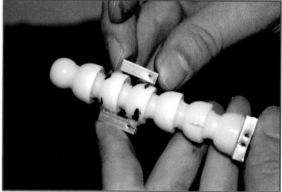

Figure 3.5

Pushing the tubes out with a small Allen key.

Figure 3.6

Hot gluing the socket tubes to the armature.

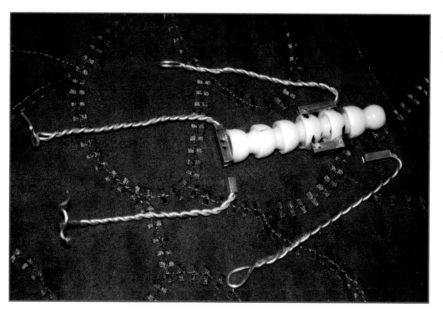

Figure 3.7

The various pieces and limbs slotting together.

The next step is to permanently glue the wires into the small tube pieces. Use a tube of two-part steel epoxy glue, squeezing out equal amounts and mixing them together on a piece of cardboard with a Popsicle stick until they are an even color (Figure 3.8). You only have a few minutes to work with the epoxy until it sets, so dip the wires into it right away (Figure 3.9) and then slot them into the tubes (Figure 3.10). Let them sit for at least 45 minutes to an hour to ensure that they are firmly set inside. While that's going on, you can affix the large socket tubes to the doll armature with some epoxy putty (Figure 3.11). When everything is dry, you have the essential elements in place for a simple plug-in armature with removable arms and legs (Figure 3.12).

Figure 3.8

Mixing the two-part epoxy glue.

Figure 3.9

Dipping wires into the epoxy glue.

Figure 3.10

Gluing wires into the K&S tubes.

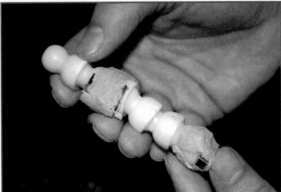

Figure 3.11

Affixing the socket tubes to the armature with epoxy putty.

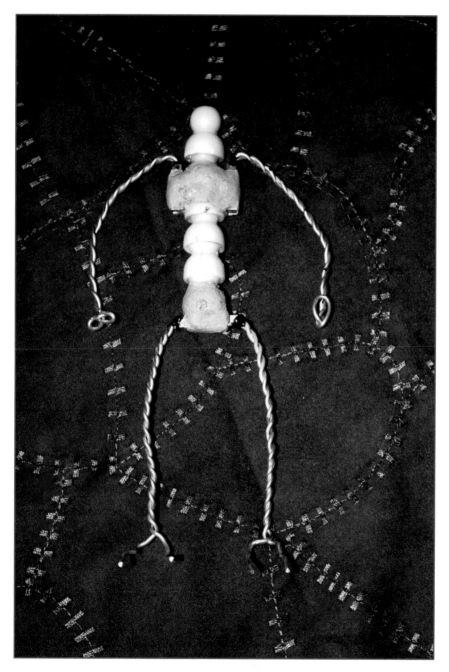

Figure 3.12

Completed armature with plug-in arms and legs.

At this point, you can add a removable head if you wish, using more K&S attachments, or just permanently attach a Styrofoam-ball head to the top bead of the doll armature with hot glue. You can also begin working on building the arms and legs, with corresponding hands and feet (removable or not) as separate pieces. An armature like this can be covered with clay, latex build-up, fabric clothing, or a combination of these materials. With all of these particular materials and more, a wire-and-socket armature is especially handy. A clay puppet, for instance, needs to be resculpted constantly while being animated. The nice thing about being able to take the puppet apart is that it allows for resculpting or replacement of different limbs without the need to put pressure on the entire puppet on set. It is particularly useful if you create a puppet, for example, with clay or latex limbs and short-sleeved clothes made of fabric. Fabric clothing is a relatively forgiving covering in terms of working around it, and if the limbs are skinned with a different material, there is no need to hide any seams where the plug-in sockets are.

Another advanced method for building a plug-in wire armature is presented here thanks to professional stop-motion puppet builder Bronwen Kyffin. This method combines wire limbs with chest and hip plates made of aluminum blocks (Figure 3.13). The blocks have been cut to shape and drilled with holes for the limbs to plug into on the sides. Everything on this puppet can be taken apart, including the arms, legs, chest, waist, and feet (Figure 3.14). In addition to holes for the plug-ins on the sides, the front of the block has additional holes that have been tapped with threads to accept tiny set screws that hold the limbs in place. The end of each aluminum wire limb is covered with a small brass tube and inserted into the plug-in hole behind the threaded holes. Brass is used because the aluminum wire is too soft to have screws embedded into it and would likely snap inside rather quickly. Set screws are put into these threaded holes to fit snugly into notches in the brass to lock the limb into place (Figure 3.15). In the event that the limbs break, the set screws are removed, and a fresh limb can be inserted back in its place.

To help prolong the life of the wire limbs, they are covered partially in electrical shrink-wrap tubing. The tubes are slid over the twisted wire and blown with a hot-air dryer to shrink their form around the wire and make them stronger. The wires used for the torso/waist area are a bit thicker at 1/8 inch, while twisted 1/16-inch wire is used for the arms and the wrists. The fingers are made of threaded 24-gauge floral wire, which is even thinner. The logic behind using different gauges of wire is simply to work out the tension of the puppet from the inside out.

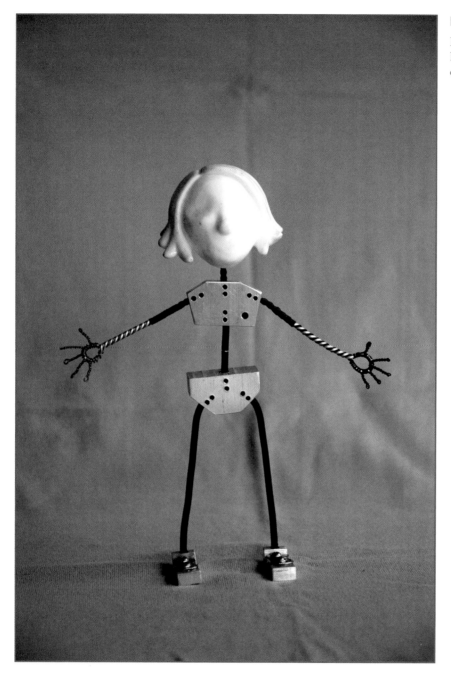

Figure 3.13

Plug-in armature for "Little Bronwen" puppet. (Courtesy of Bronwen Kyffin.)

Figure 3.14

Plug-in armature with all limbs taken apart. (Courtesy of Bronwen Kyffin.)

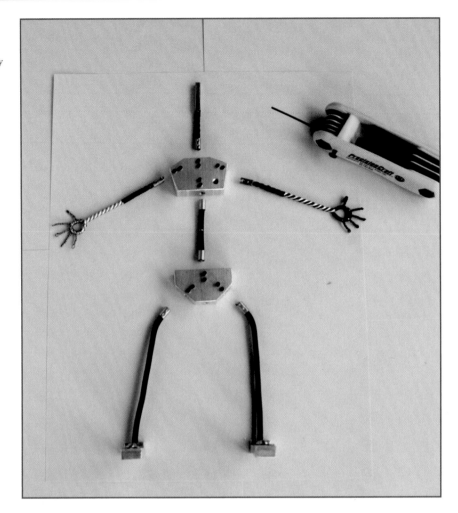

A similar principle is applied to the other puppet, which uses the doll armature for the body and wires for the limbs. When animating either of these puppets, it is likely that most of the pressure from the animator will be placed on the torso. One hand will grip the body tightly, while the other hand moves an arm or a leg, for instance. Ideally, you want to have less tension on the limbs so that they can be moved without putting too much pressure on them. At the same time, the waist should be stronger so that it can take more abuse from the animator and not risk being moved while the limbs are animated. Even with a very strong armature, any of these wire puppets might last only long enough for about one to three minutes of screen time before needing replacement, repair, or retirement. Think and plan ahead for just how much animation needs to be performed and whether those movements are broad or subtle in order to get the most mileage out of the building methods you use.

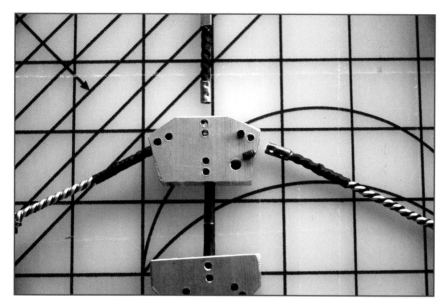

Figure 3.15

Close-up detail of plug-in limbs and threaded holes for set screws to hold them in place. (Courtesy of Bronwen Kyffin.)

For any armature you build, another element that can be added is an extra socket for plugging in a rig. If your puppet has any moments where it needs to jump, fly, dance, or defy gravity in any way, you can suspend it in mid-air for as many frames are necessary by attaching it to a rig (Figure 3.16) or even an anchored piece of strong wire. The rig can remain visible in the shot and can be removed later in post-production. Once again, K&S tubes work well as a possible option for assembling this socket for the rig to plug into. In the example shown here (Figure 3.17), a 3/16" tube has been glued to my arma-

Figure 3.16

Puppet armature on a rig for flying or jumping shots.

Figure 3.17

A simple plug-in attachment for attaching the rig.

ture on his backside, so a 5/32" tube can slide into it and be held in place by a helping hand rig. Dents have also been punched into these tubes to help lock them into place. The helping hand rig, found at most hobby shops, is a great tool for holding puppet parts when building and works great for jumping rigs. The joints on the rig are the made of the same pieces as a ball-and-socket armature, so it can essentially be animated itself. (You can even buy several of them and cannibalize their parts to make your own ball-and-socket puppet armature, if you want.)

Hands and Feet

Once you have your arms and legs built, the next step is to build some hands and feet. If you are covering your wire arms with clay, it is best to avoid an armature for the hands and extending wires into the fingers. In most cases, the wires will constantly poke through the clay, which can usually be posed to hold its shape for tiny fingers without the need for wire inside. If you plan on creating hands in a mold or using the latex build-up process, it will be important to create an armature for the fingers with some form of posable wire.

To create some hands, I used single strands of 1/16" aluminum wire and laid them out in the proper position at the edge of the arm, which had its end loop folded over (Figure 3.18). It's best to cut them a bit longer than necessary because this ensures that they will be long enough (they can always be trimmed down later). A little masking tape helps to keep them in place. Epoxy putty is applied to the arm to create rigid bone shapes in proportion to the rest of the body, and more is applied around the fingers to create the base of the hand. Using needle-nose pliers helps to pinch the epoxy tightly around the fingers, and rolling their shape between them helps to ensure that they will harden with the right shape around the wire (Figure 3.19). If the epoxy is sculpted too loosely over the wire, the fingers can come loose and will need reinforcement with more thin layers of epoxy in the space between the fingers. This shape of the hand should be finessed as much as possible before the epoxy hardens completely.

For the feet, the ends of the legs are cut and twisted to fit snugly around a nut for creating a tie-down (Figure 3.20). A little dab of hot glue may help keep it in place initially and can be trimmed away once it dries. From this shape, epoxy putty can be placed in one slab over the tie-down to cover it and another piece sculpted behind it as a heel piece (Figure 3.21). Leaving some wire between these two epoxy shapes creates a bend in the foot that will help in

Figure 3.18

The beginning of constructing hands for a wire armature.

Figure 3.19

Sculpting the base of the hands with epoxy putty.

Figure 3.20

Placing nuts for tie-downs into the foot pieces.

Figure 3.21

Sculpting epoxy putty around the tie-down to make a basic foot shape.

creating a realistic foot posing in any walking animation. The important thing with these shapes is to keep the bottom of the foot flat the whole time. This is a tricky shape to sculpt using epoxy putty because it must be done quickly before it sets and can get rather messy, but once the battle is won, it works. One thing to watch for amid all the scrambling to get the shape right is making sure the tie-down hole doesn't get filled in with putty (Figure 3.22). Once it hardens, you won't be able to get the bolt into it. This will inevitably happen when applying the epoxy from the top of the nut, so while it's starting to set, I typically push the eraser end of a pencil into the nut to push the epoxy back in and screw the bolt into the tie-down to help ensure that it will screw into it (Figure 3.23). When it's all finished, the epoxy should be flat on the bottom, with the tie-down empty and flush to the sole of the foot (Figure 3.24). As this process unfolds to include both legs and arms, compare the proportions back to the armature to ensure that they are level, not crooked. The last thing you want is to have one leg much longer than the other one. If they are part of a plug-in armature, all of these limbs are still removable and can be worked on independent of the torso (Figure 3.25).

Figure 3.22

Epoxy can get into the tie-down hole, which is not good.

Figure 3.23

The epoxy can be pushed into the hole using the bolt that will go into it.

Figure 3.24

The completed foot with a flat bottom flush to the tie-down.

Figure 3.25

All four limbs finished and laid out.

As an alternative to tie-downs, you can use earth magnets embedded into the feet for the purpose of attaching to a metal platform on an animation set. Magnets are common on TV stop-motion productions, where animation scenes must be churned out quickly and the time-consuming practice of drilling holes into the set and covering them up would be inconvenient. Having a magnet in the foot can restrict the design choices because those strong enough to hold up a puppet are usually a bit large. Television characters in stop-motion (like Bob the Builder or David Pilkey's Dragon) often are designed with large feet as a result. A character with medium-sized to tiny feet cannot likely be held up by a magnet alone, so tie-downs are a better choice in this situation.

To apply latex build-up to the hands, start by dipping the hand in a thin layer of liquid latex (Figure 3.26) and then applying tiny wisps of cotton to the base of the hand and around the fingers. The fingers are covered by applying a wisp of cotton to the bottom, allowing the latex to create some tack to it, and just rolling it around the wire with your finger (Figure 3.27). Applying more latex with a brush, the wrapped cotton will adhere to itself a bit more. To create additional layers and a smooth shape to the fingertips, dipping them into the latex also helps (Figure 3.28), but not so much as to create clumps and fat fingers. Working over the hand and fingers with a small brush and continually building it up with tiny pieces of cotton will eventually create the desired thickness and shape of the hand (Figure 3.29). It is important to continue smoothing it out as much as possible with a brush or fingertip and keep plenty of space between the cracks of the fingers. This area in particular can easily collect clumps of cotton and latex, which can result in a stubby look to the fingers if not kept separated. Eventually, the latex may become too wet to work with without falling apart and getting clumpy. It is best to know when to stop and let the latex dry a bit because it can still be easily tweaked, sculpted, and finessed when it is semiwet but not yet dry (Figure 3.30). With hand designs as well, keep in mind the aesthetic quality of varying the lengths of the fingers. Whether or not you create a realistic hand (four fingers and a thumb) or a stylized hand (three fingers and a thumb), keep in mind that the middle finger is longer than the others, and the pinky is smaller. Creating all fingers the same length tends to make hands look more like rakes or forks.

Figure 3.26

Start the latex build-up process by dipping the wire hand into liquid latex.

Figure 3.27

Wrap cotton around the fingers.

Figure 3.28

More tiny dips into the latex smooths and shapes the fingers a bit.

Figure 3.29

Continue to shape the cotton and latex around the hand with a brush.

Figure 3.30

Completed latex hand before it dries completely.

The same technique of building up small pieces of cotton and latex can be applied to the feet and any other parts of the puppet. Even little details like toes, the ball of the foot, warts, bones, and knuckles can be created with little rolls and wisps of cotton applied carefully to blend in (Figures 3.31 and 3.32). It is best to start with thin layers and build up places where the body needs more bulk, keeping it a bit thinner around the joints, where the puppet should bend. One of the hard things about latex is that it dries very tough and gummy, with a rubber surface that is hard to penetrate. Layers applied too thick can cause the wires to spring back while trying to hold animation poses.

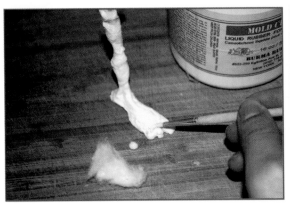

Figure 3.31

Applying latex build-up for a puppet foot.

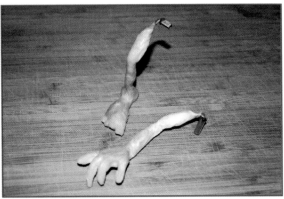

Figure 3.32

Dried latex foot and hand parts.

Therefore, it's important to use latex sparingly and avoid adding too many layers. For any parts of a puppet that require more bulk, try to use more cotton under a thin layer of latex applied with a brush for the outer skin. Wash your brushes often with soap and water; in most cases, the latex will simply peel off the brush. Sometimes, the latex can be difficult to clean off, so it's best to use cheap brushes that are easily disposed of after they are used.

The latex build-up technique is a fun way to create skin for your puppets (Figure 3.33), and it is relatively simple to get used to. The way the skin bulges and stretches over the armature is really fun to play with and offers a quality and texture that can work for many different design styles. Like any method, latex build-up does have its drawbacks. In particular, it generally works better for one-off puppets and can be challenging when trying to create duplicate copies of the same character. Having replaceable limbs does help with this because you can create a bunch of back-up arms and legs to replace when they break. They won't be exact replicas like what you would get by creating molds and casting them, but they can be pretty close if you try hard enough to replicate the proportions as closely as possible.

When painting the latex skin in whatever color your puppet is, you can use regular acrylic paint or any other special acrylic paints you can find that work specifically with latex. A good tip is to mix the paint with a very small amount of Pros-Aide, a special adhesive used by special effects make-up artists. Depending on where you live, you can likely find it at any stores that sell these products or at http://www.pros-aide.com. Pros-Aide helps thin the paint and allows it to stretch over any bends and bulges in the puppet's movement as you animate it. Be sure to use a tiny amount; if you use too much, your puppet

Figure 3.33

The entire puppet armature, half-covered in latex build-up.

will be tacky and sticky to the touch, picking up dirt from your fingers pretty easily. For a smoother matte finish to your puppet and to reduce any tackiness or shiny appearance, you can apply a layer of baby powder or corn starch to the skin by brushing it on or mixing it into the latex as it dries. Overall, play safe and have fun with it—the possibilities are endless. In fact, going back to what I said earlier about clay arms and hands, if you do want to use clay for the skin of your puppet, you can cover your wire armature with latex build-up first, and then apply a thin layer of clay over it once it dries. The latex build-up provides a solid shape over the wire, including over fingers, and can alleviate some of the resculpting needed when using solid clay.

Puppet Anatomy

For this section of the book, I'm pleased to present a look behind the scenes of some puppets created by Bronwen Kyffin and Melanie Vachon for a student film directed by Lucas Wareing at Emily Carr University of Art + Design in Vancouver. Lucas took my stop-motion course at VanArts several years ago and more recently directed his own stop-motion short at Emily Carr called *Ava*, which was about the relationship between a little girl named Ava and her monster friend, Charlie. These characters (Figure 3.34) were designed by Patrick O'Keefe, sculpted by Lucas, and commissioned to Bronwen and Melanie for fabrication, with the assistance of Ian Douglas in machining the armatures. Certain elements of their construction in relation to silicone molding and plastic casting will be detailed further a few pages later, but for now here is a look at how the general fabrication was done. (Except where noted, all photos in this section are courtesy of Bronwen Kyffin and Melanie Vachon.)

Both puppets were built out of metal ball-and-socket armatures (Figure 3.35), which are the strongest type of armatures for stop-motion and provide a great deal of precision and control over the animation. These types of armatures were certainly necessary, considering that Charlie himself was about 16 inches tall (next to the 9-inch-tall Ava), and wire definitely would not have supported his bulk and weight. Charlie's armature (Figure 3.36) was also equipped with chest and waist blocks that were cast in plastic. These blocks were designed to create more leverage with his eventual bulk, cut down on his weight, and give his skin something to hold onto. The blocks were screwed onto the armature with long threaded rods attached to the aluminum chest and waist plates, which had additional holes drilled into them (like Swiss cheese) to cut down further on the puppet's weight.

Figure 3.34

Puppets for *Ava*, a film by Lucas Wareing.

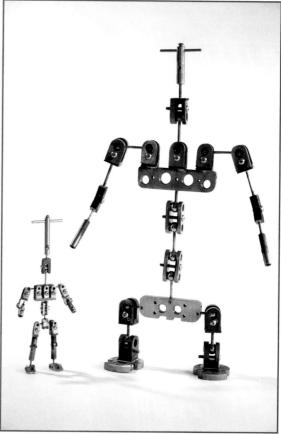

Figure 3.35

Ball-and-socket armatures for Ava and Charlie.

Ball-and-socket armatures consist of many different kinds of joints that can be created. The joints most commonly revolve around a sandwich plate. The plate consists of two long, oval-shaped metal plates with holes drilled into them that wrap snugly around a ball bearing but are loose enough to move in increments. The sandwich plate can also be a U-shaped joint that is about half the size and shape of a full joint. The ball bearing serves as the joint and has a hole drilled into it, into which a metal rod for the limb is inserted and brazed together with a blowtorch. It is possible to buy threaded rods and ball bearings that are already drilled and tapped with threaded holes for this purpose.

Figure 3.36

Armature for Charlie,
the monster.

When designing joints like these, it is important to think ahead to the actual animation and motion that are required, in terms of which joints need to move forward and backward, up and down, or any range of diagonal movement. Ball joints typically provide a great range of circular movement compared to hinge joints, which typically only have lateral movement up and down, like a knee or elbow. In the close-up detail of Charlie's torso (Figure 3.37), there are three U-shaped joints: one for each shoulder and a middle one for the neck. These joints are the anatomical equivalent of the clavicle and the point where the neck joins the spine. The range of movement for these ball joints is mostly left/right or up/down, which allows for tilts of the head and shrugs of the shoulders. The location of the plates in relation to the rod means a small amount of forward/backward motion is possible. However, there is more freedom of movement allowed for in the joints on the other end of the rod, which provides additional mobility for his neck and shoulders. The same principles of motion are applied to the leg joints, based on how they should be able to move (Figure 3.38). When the parameters of movement are specified in terms of the amount of freedom needed in the animation, these parameters can be applied directly to how the armature is constructed. The more you know about real human anatomy and how real joints are capable of moving, the more informed the armature can be in terms of mimicking this motion for animation. If you have any experience in rigging 3D computer models, you may find some similarities to the necessary constraints of movement involved, but the biggest difference is dealing with real physical materials.

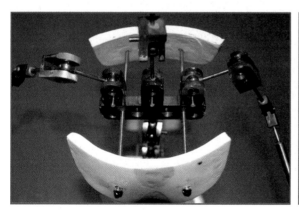

Figure 3.37

Close-up detail of Charlie's chest armature.

Figure 3.38

Close-up detail of Charlie's feet armature.

Both puppets' armatures are covered in foam that is carved into shape to provide the bulk of their bodies. First, two blocks of foam are spray glued to each other around the front and back of the armature (Figures 3.39 and 3.40).

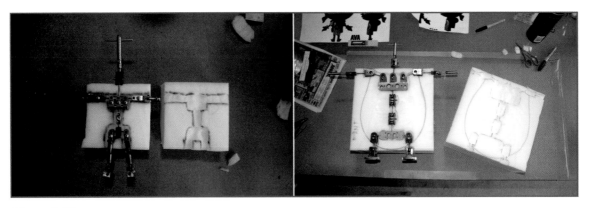

Figure 3.39
Ava and Charlie's armatures laid over blocks of foam.

Figure 3.40
Two foam blocks glued over the armature on the front and back.

The excess foam is simply carved and snipped away until the foam takes on the desired shape. Large pieces are carved out to start, and then smaller pieces are snipped away with scissors (Figure 3.41). For Charlie, the same method is applied to his arms (Figure 3.42). In addition to his foam body, his hands are cast in silicone and his head in plastic. (More detail on these techniques will be explored later in this chapter.) The outer layer of Charlie is then skinned in fabric by cutting out patterns according to his shape and stitching them together (Figure 3.43). For the striped pattern on his skin, masking tape is

Figure 3.41

Ava's carved foam body on the left, and Charlie in progress on the right.

Figure 3.42

Continuing to carve and cut away the foam for Charlie's arms.

Figure 3.43

Charlie being skinned in fabric.

applied to his body in a specifically designed pattern (Figure 3.44), and the exposed parts are airbrushed lightly with white paint. When the tape is removed, the original darker color of the fabric remains in these areas to create stripes (Figure 3.45). With all of these steps completed, Charlie's body is essentially complete. Topping him off are replacement pieces for his eye and lip sync movements, which are made of Sculpey. His eyes are coated with Vaseline on the back to allow them to stick to his plain white eyeballs, and his lips are attached to his head with double-sided tape (Figure 3.46).

Figure 3.44

Creating shapes for Charlie's stripes using masking tape.

Figure 3.45

Peeling the tape away after airbrushing the fabric.

Figure 3.46

Eye pieces and replacement mouths for Charlie.
(Courtesy of Lucas Wareing.)

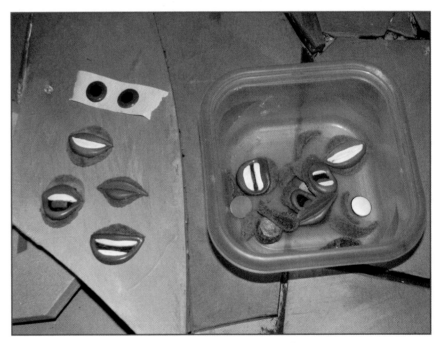

Ava's hands are constructed with aluminum wire to fit to shape under her fabric mittens (Figures 3.47 and 3.48). Her head is coated with primer, and her eyes (as well as Charlie's) are masked apart from the rest of her face and sprayed with Crystal Clear high-gloss acrylic to give them a smooth shine and finish (Figure 3.49). Next, her eyes are masked, and the rest of her face exposed so it can be airbrushed with skin tone (Figures 3.50 and 3.51). Additional paint and doll hair complete the necessary detail on her head (Figure 3.52). The

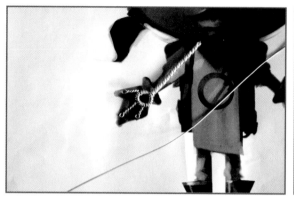

Figure 3.47

Wire hand for Ava laid over the character design diagram.

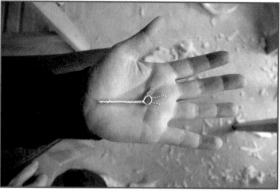

Figure 3.48

Wire hand inside real hand, for comparison of scale.

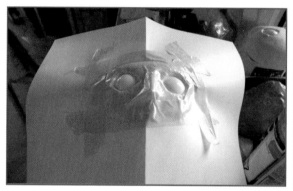

Figure 3.49

Masking the head and exposing the eyes for coating.

Figure 3.50

Beginning to mask the eyes so that the rest of the head can be painted.

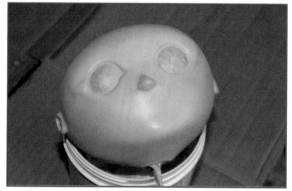

Figure 3.51

The head after being airbrushed.

Figure 3.52

The head with hair and painted details added.

final steps are to sew together tiny clothes in fabric over her body (Figure 3.53) and cast silicone boots to fit over her feet (Figure 3.54). She also has a tiny back-pack made of canvas, with a tiny snap rivet holding in a roll of fun foam (Figure 3.55). Her pupils and replacement mouths, which can be attached, moved around, and removed from the plastic head with Vaseline, complete her facial expressions (Figure 3.56), and she is ready for animation (Figure 3.57)!

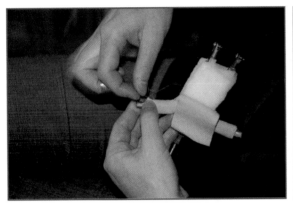

Figure 3.53

Sewing clothes over the armature.

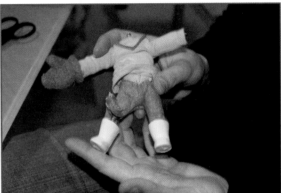

Figure 3.54

Additional clothing and boots are added on.

Figure 3.55

Ava's little backpack.

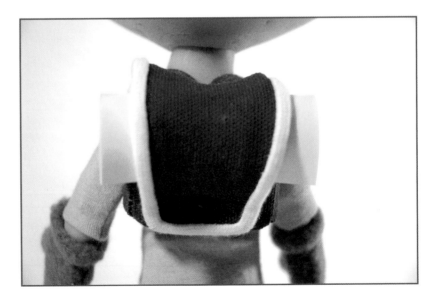

Figure 3.56

Completed Ava puppet, with eye pieces and replacement mouths.
(Courtesy of Lucas Wareing.)

Figure 3.57

Charlie and Ava together in a scene from the film. (Courtesy of Lucas Wareing.)

Silicone

Foam latex has long been a popular material for creating the outer skin or entire body of a stop-motion puppet over its armature. The basic elements that are needed for a foam latex puppet are the *sculpt* (the official term for the original clay sculpture of the puppet) and a plaster mold formed around the sculpt. The foam latex goes inside the mold along with the armature and becomes a cast replica of the sculpt. Foam latex comes as a series of about five different liquid agents that are mixed together to gel into a soft, spongy material. Once it is cured by baking it in a convection oven, it basically behaves like upholstery foam, which springs back into shape even after touching it. Although foam latex is stinky and tricky to mix properly, it is relatively easy to repair and very lightweight, which are both important qualities for a stop-motion puppet.

Another material that has become very popular in recent years for puppet fabricators is silicone. Silicone is easier to mix than foam latex (only two agents are needed, instead of five) and can be used to create both puppets and molds. The appearance of silicone skin for a puppet has a different quality than foam latex; it can potentially be smoother and more translucent. Although foam latex can be cast and painted to appear very smooth, it will often have a certain degree of texture to it. The smoothness and attention to detail from the original sculpt that silicone provides give a great deal of creative freedom for different character designs. The other advantage that silicone has is that *it will only stick to itself*, so it can be worked with alongside a variety of other materials. At the same time, there are some materials that do not react well with silicone, including latex and any sulfur-based modeling clays.

When working with silicone or any other chemicals, it's important to understand what you are dealing with. By law, safety sheets must be provided and sent along with any chemicals you purchase or order, and it's important to read them carefully before cracking the chemicals open. Safety precautions and guidelines will typically tell you to protect your skin, lungs, and eyes from the material, so rubber/latex gloves, masks, and safety glasses are very important to have on hand. The instructions will also tell you how long you can work with the product before it starts changing. The time span for working with silicone before it sets (and is no longer in a pourable liquid form) is referred to as its *pot life*; its *cure time* is how long it takes to cure fully. Pot life is usually only a few minutes, and cure time is typically 24 to 48 hours. Silicone comes in at least two liquid parts that need to be mixed together: the inert silicone base and an additional 10% of an activating agent that causes it to solidify. There are also softening or retarding agents you can buy that can be mixed in to change the silicone's consistency or slow down its pot life, but these are only necessary if you want additional control over it. Once these different agents are one uniform color after mixing (in a cup or bucket, with any kind of stirring tool), you know it's ready to start using before it sets.

Another important thing to understand about silicone is there are some types that are better for *molding* (creating a negative impression of a sculpt) and others better for *casting* (creating the replica of the sculpt that comes out of the mold). Within these two categories, there will be different brands and varieties, each with its own characteristics. Molding silicone is generally much denser and harder, so if you use it for puppet skin over the armature, you won't be able to bend it easily. It also typically comes in specific colors like pink, purple, orange, blue, or green, which are not very convenient base colors for a puppet. Certain brands of molding silicone include Mold Max, RTV, and many others. Most types of silicone that work well for molding are of the tin-cure variety, but others that are platinum-cure can be used as well.

For casting a silicone puppet, the best silicone products are of the special effects variety. These are mostly platinum-cure, much softer, and will easily bend and flex over an armature like real skin. Casting silicone typically becomes transparent or milky translucent when it cures, and you want to make sure the activator that mixes with the base says it's translucent on the bottle. For this reason, if you want a specific color for your puppet, an acrylic tint must be added to the base while mixing. This step has traditionally been important because silicone does not respond well to being painted afterward. In more recent years, however, there have been new developments made in certain silicone products that enable them to be painted. In those cases, tinting may not be necessary. All the same, tinting in the actual mixing process creates one less step later and ensures a smooth surface in the color you want, and you do not need to worry about hiding brush strokes in applying paint. For skin tones, you can alternatively use just a few drops of oil-based foundation from your local drug store's make-up department. Some popular brands of casting silicones include DragonSkin, Plastil, and EcoFlex. There is also a product by Smooth-On called Soma-Foma, a silicone foam that bonds well with other brands and can help to create extremely lightweight puppets. (It also has an extremely fast pot life, about 30 seconds, so it must be worked with very quickly before concealing it into a mold for curing.)

Many different kinds of silicone, both for molding and casting, can be browsed and acquired through Smooth-On (http://www.smooth-on.com), the Compleat Sculptor (http://www.sculpt.com), Sculpture Supply Canada (http://www.sculpturesupply.com), and other special effects/sculpture service companies that sell these kinds of products, depending on your country of residence.

Casting a Silicone Puppet

The general rule for molding and casting, because the mold needs to come apart, is that if your cast is meant to be soft and flexible (like foam latex or silicone), its mold should be created in a hard material (like plaster). If your cast is meant to be a hard material that does not bend (like plastic or resin), its mold should be created in a soft material (like silicone). There are some methods for using silicone in both molding and casting simultaneously, which are mentioned later in this chapter, but for the time being, let's say you need to cast flexible silicone around the armature of your puppet using a plaster mold. A basic overview of this process, using pictures from the creation of Charlie's hands from *Ava*, is provided below. (All photos in these molding/casting sections are courtesy of Bronwen Kyffin and Melanie Vachon.)

The first step is to create the sculpt, which can be of the entire puppet or just part of it (Figure 3.58). When creating a sculpt for eventual casting in silicone,

Figure 3.58

Clay sculpts of hands for Ava and Charlie.

it is important to use a modeling clay that is not sulfur based. Silicone is generally sensitive to sulfur materials, which can cause it not to cure properly. Some brands of clay that can be used include Chavant NSP and Prima Plastalina. Before creating a mold for the sculpt, it should be lacquered with Krylon Crystal Clear spray to create a barrier that keeps it from getting damaged or reacting with any other substances to which you'll be subjecting it.

The sculpt is surrounded completely by a bed of a different kind of clay, commonly a brand called Klean Klay (http://www.kleanklay.com), which is not sulfur based and is ideal for the mold-making process (Figure 3.59). Klean Klay is not recommended for creating the actual sculpt, but it works well for making molds. The clay bed is continually smoothed out and wrapped around the sculpt with a palette sculpting tool so that it is airtight and lines up exactly through the midpoint in a perfectly straight line around its perimeter. The point where the clay bed touches the sculpt is where the seam will be located when both halves of the mold are put together and pulled apart. In many cases, this is at the exact equator of the sculpt, but depending on the design of what you are molding, it is useful to find a point on the sculpt where the seam will not be very visible to the camera. In the clay bed, registration points called keys are created using marbles or any other round or square objects, which will help both halves of the eventual mold to fit together (Figure 3.60). It's best to plan ahead when figuring out how you plan to get the silicone inside the mold. It's possible to just pour it into the open molds, but you might prefer to have a hole for pouring it in while the mold is clamped shut.

Figure 3.59

Klean Klay starting to be built around the sculpt.

Figure 3.60

The clay bed is complete with keys sculpted in.

In this case, it's a good idea to sculpt in a pry point for sticking in a tool to help pull it apart later. You also may want some exit channels built in so you know that the silicone is flowing through the entire cavity all the way to the highest point (like the fingertips for a full body cast). The idea behind the mold itself is to make it as perfectly smooth and functional as possible, think ahead to how you will fill it and get it apart, and think of it as two puzzle pieces that fit together around your sculpt.

Next, the sculpt in its clay bed needs a wall built around it in order to hold the shape of the first half of the plaster mold (Figure 3.61). The wall can be built from almost anything, such as slabs of clay or, in this case, large-sized Duplo or Lego blocks. The smooth, square shape created by the blocks provides a nice surface for the mold to be built against. To avoid leakage and air pockets, the corners of the Lego fortress can be patched with more Klean Klay.

Once the wall is complete, plaster (Ultracal or Hydrocal 30, not art-store plaster of Paris varieties) is mixed and poured in to create the first half of the mold (Figure 3.62). After this hardens, the Lego wall is taken away, the clay bed removed, and all clay remnants washed away with water. The sculpt remains inside the plaster mold, which is coated with Vaseline to aid in eventually prying it apart from the next mold half. The process with the Lego wall can now be repeated as another layer of plaster is poured on top of the first mold half inside. When this is complete, there will be a two-part hard plaster mold for the original sculpt (Figure 3.63), which can now be removed. As an alternative to plaster, you can also create molds for a silicone puppet from a two-part plastic or resin. This would involve mixing and pouring it over the sculpt in a manner similar to this method.

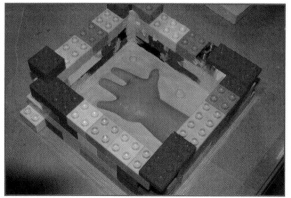

Figure 3.61

A wall made of Lego blocks is built around the clay bed and sculpt.

Figure 3.62

Preparing the plaster to be poured in for the mold.

Now, it's time to get the mold ready to cast some silicone! First, the armature is laid inside the mold, and it needs a way to stay suspended right in the middle because everything around it will be eventually filled in with sticky, gooey liquid silicone. There are a few ways to do this, which may vary, depending on the design of what you are casting. It also depends on how you plan to get the silicone into the mold. For Charlie's hands, the armature was held in place by a lump of Klean Klay placed within the entrance hole where the silicone was poured in. Both halves of the mold should be clamped shut as tightly as possible to avoid leakage and to ensure that the mold will be filled up properly (Figure 3.64). As the mixed silicone batch is poured into the entrance hole, the mold cavity surrounding the armature, which is being suspended upside-down, fills up.

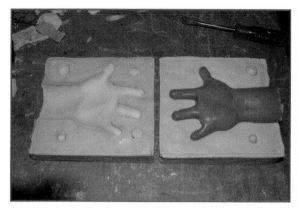

Figure 3.63

Complete two-part mold before the sculpt is removed.

Figure 3.64

Tying the molds together very tightly.

When pouring the silicone into or onto any space, it's important to avoid the creation of air bubbles as it collects and starts to cure. Bubbles can create unwanted warping in the surface of your puppet. To alleviate bubbles, it helps to first tap the container (with the silicone inside it) firmly onto a flat surface after mixing it; this forces the bubbles out. When applying it or pouring it out, you can also drizzle the silicone in a thin, high pour, raising it slowly about one foot above the mold (Figure 3.65). These methods will work well if you're

Figure 3.65

Silicone is drizzled into the space around the clay holding the armature in place.

doing this on your own at home, and if you have the means or space, following this process in a specially built vacuum chamber will help to suck any air bubbles out of the silicone as you work with it.

Another method for getting the silicone into the mold is to leave both halves of the mold open, mix a batch of silicone, and start by pouring a thin layer directly into the mold cavity. This is essentially skinning the impression of the sculpt in the mold and creating the outer layer of the cast, so it's important to get into every nook and cranny of the mold and avoid trapping any air bubbles inside. After skinning the mold, more silicone is poured into the mold to fill it up, and the armature is rested on top of the setting silicone in exactly the right suspended position. Within a few minutes, depending on the pot life of the silicone, the first half will begin to cure. Meanwhile, the second half of the mold is skin coated and filled in with more silicone. Then, the first half of the mold with the armature in it can be flipped over, pressed onto the second mold, clamped shut, and left to cure completely. All of the silicone will bond with itself inside to create the bulk of whatever you are casting.

Once the silicone is cured, the mold is pried open to reveal the cast of the original sculpt, with its armature living inside and totally flexible for animation (Figure 3.66)! The next step is to trim off any extra flash of thin silicone that may have spilled over the mold cavity. This can be done with fine scissors to trim it right up to the edge of the seam. To help conceal the seam a bit more, it may help to cut a groove into the edge and patch it up with a thin layer of

Figure 3.66

Silicone cast hands sitting in their molds.

silicone. During this setting time before it completely cures, continual patching, smoothing, or texture stamping can still be worked into the surface, depending on the design and look you are after.

In another example, for Ava's neck, an additional piece of silicone is cast to form a shape similar to a shirt dickie to go under her clothes. The shape itself is sculpted in clay, and the first part is molded upside-down so that the second half can be molded around it right-side-up. The result is a thin, flexible neck piece that has been shaped to fit around the armature over her shoulders.

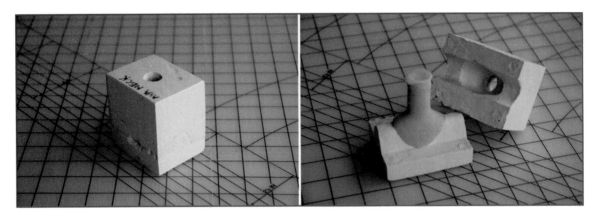

Figure 3.67

Mold created for Ava's neck piece, cast in silicone.

Making a Silicone Mold

As I mentioned before, in most cases, a hard mold is required to create a soft cast, but it is also possible to create a silicone mold (using molding silicone) for a silicone puppet (using casting silicone). If it is a two-part mold similar to the plaster ones I just described, the steps for creating it, like using the Lego wall around the clay bed and pouring over it, are basically the same. The big difference in using this method is that you *must* apply onto your mold and sculpt a universal release agent so that the silicone will not bond to itself and can easily be pulled apart. If you miss a spot, it will bond as one piece because silicone only sticks to itself. If you are casting silicone within silicone, this is very important.

The advantage to a flexible silicone mold is that it is more forgiving than a plaster mold when it comes to *undercuts*. An undercut is any surface on the sculpt (and resulting cast) where the mold can easily get locked in underneath and cause damage to the cast when pulling it apart. Undercuts on the sculpt can be avoided by always creating shapes that are angled the right way toward it, but if they do occur, a flexible silicone mold is a bit easier to twist around it when releasing the cast. Creating a two-part mold that fits together and comes apart like the plaster mold can be done easily in silicone, and then it can be filled with any material that will create a hard cast. Within a soft silicone mold, you can cast duplicate hard copies of props, toys, and any hard parts of a puppet (Figure 3.68), such as accessories or entire heads. Silicone molds can be filled with resins, plastics, and even melted clay for clay puppets.

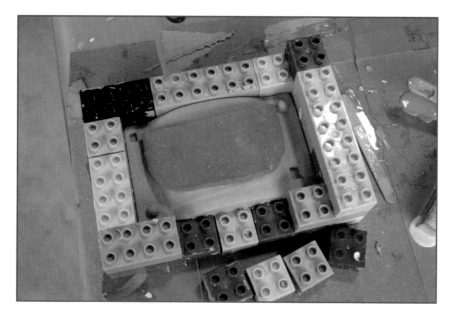

Figure 3.68

Sculpt for one of Charlie's chest plates in a silicone mold.

For *Ava*, the heads for both puppets were cast in plastic in a silicone mold. A different approach was taken in creating these molds, which were created as one piece in a bucket instead of a two-part mold created in two halves. The sculpt for the head is first done in sulfur-free plasticine clay and then attached to a post to hold it in place. For a head or any other object like this, it's a good idea to build the initial sculpt around a ball of foil attached to the post. This will help cut down on the weight and help keep it from slipping off when it's suspended in the mold later.

The next step is to cover the sculpt in a thin skin of molding silicone to create the detailed impression that will be inside the mold. The silicone is drizzled over the top of the sculpt and pushed around with a brush to get inside every nook and cranny, without bubbles. Rather than brushing the silicone on, which creates more bubbles, it's more like pushing it around and into the cracks, without worrying about washing the brush, either. As the silicone drips and collects at the bottom, it can be lifted back onto the top and essentially pushed around to coat it completely. The idea is to skin the entire sculpt in a layer of silicone without bubbles (Figures 3.69 to 3.71).

Figure 3.69

Pushing silicone around the head and into all the sculpted details.

Figure 3.70

Drizzling silicone onto the head slowly to continue covering it.

The next step is to suspend the skinned sculpt upside-down in a bucket (or in a plastic cup for a smaller-sized head). The post to which the head is attached can be attached to a wooden plank that rests over the top of the bucket or suspended in some other way to hold it there. Another solution, to alleviate the possibility of the head falling off the post and into the bucket, is to fill the bottom of the bucket with a layer of silicone and let it cure. This would act as a cushion to rest the head on while it's suspended. Once that is all in place, the rest of the space inside the bucket is filled to the brim with more silicone and left to cure overnight. Bubbles are not as much of an issue in this filler space for the mold itself because they will rise to the surface anyway. The post to which the head or object is attached, suspending it into the surrounding mold, will also serve as an entrance channel for pouring the plastic in during the casting process. As another part of this process, it is important to note on the bucket itself (and later on the resulting mold) the positions of the front, backs and sides of the head inside (Figure 3.72).

Figure 3.71
Completed sculpt covered with a layer of silicone.

Figure 3.72

Bucket filled with cured silicone, marked with reference points to the positions of the front and sides of the sculpt.

Once the silicone is cured, it will be more firm on the surface and much less tacky. The mold can then be pulled out of the bucket or cup, and it will have taken on the same shape of the inside, much like a Popsicle (Figure 3.73). The next step is to get the head out! To accomplish this, an X-Acto blade is used to cut through the silicone as strata-cut layers in a zigzag pattern down a side of the mold (Figure 3.74). The cut is essentially acting as the seam for the mold itself. Therefore, it's important to place this opening near the back of the object being cast, or somewhere the camera won't necessarily notice it, in the event of cutting into the sculpt. The zigzag pattern also serves the purpose of registration keys so that the mold will always go back together in the same place. Cutting a straight seam line will cause it to slide around and could create inconsistencies in the resulting cast. Once the incision is complete, the flexible mold can be pried open to remove the sculpt, leaving a negative impression of the sculpt inside and a spout for pouring in the casting material (Figure 3.75). All remnants of clay that stray inside must be washed away completely with rubbing alcohol and water to avoid any bits of it getting stuck in anything else. Now, it should be ready to fill with plastic for casting!

Figure 3.73

The completed cured mold, now free of the bucket in which it was created.

Figure 3.74

A zigzag-shaped seam is cut into the mold in order to get the sculpt out.

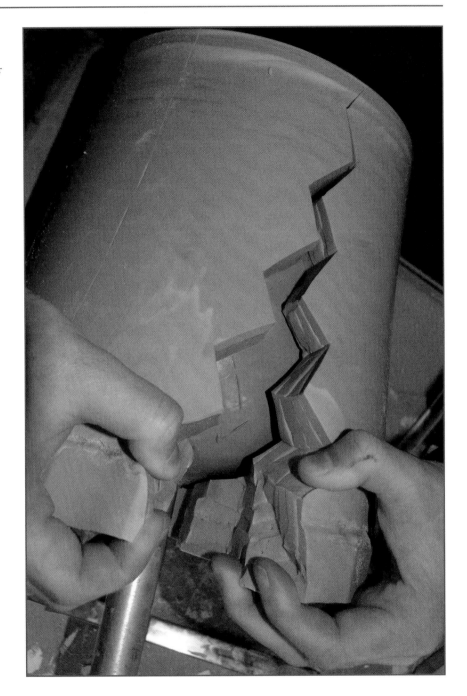

Figure 3.75

A view of the impression of the sculpt from inside the mold.

Plastic Casting

Plastic for casting starts as a two-part liquid that is essentially mixed together and allowed to harden inside the mold. Silicone molds are friendly for plastic casts because of their non-porous nature. Plastic is moisture sensitive, so if it is cast in anything porous, it will not set properly, and it may take longer in humid climates. As always, wear protective clothing like an apron, gloves, and safety glasses when using this stuff.

When you have your plastic ready to mix together, the empty silicone mold should also be standing by and resting back in the same kind of bucket or cup in which it was initially created. The two parts of whatever amount of plastic you use should be mixed together equally (1:1) by volume rather than weight. Each part can simply be poured into a separate cup, with a mark drawn on with a Sharpie to find a common point to pour into. Using patterned Dixie cups helps for finding this common point on two identical cups (Figure 3.76).

After reading all safety instructions and having everything you need ready to go, both bottles of plastic are shaken before opening. The typical pot life for most two-part plastics is about four minutes, with a cure time of about 30 minutes. In each cup, equal amounts of parts A and B are poured separately up to the designated marker (Figure 3.77). Part B is then poured into part A and scooped out with a stirring tool to make sure all of it gets out of the cup.

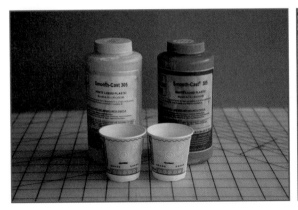

Figure 3.76

Bottles of two-part plastic, with cups marked for the amounts to mix together.

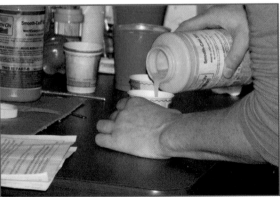

Figure 3.77

Each part of the plastic is poured into a separate cup.

Both parts are then stirred together for whatever length of time is indicated by the instructions (Figure 3.78). The next step is to simply pour the liquid plastic into the mold's entrance hole so that it can fill the empty cavity all the way to the top (Figure 3.79). A little bit of plastic is left inside the cup so that it can be watched while it hardens and act as a barometer for letting you know when the plastic inside the mold is ready to come out.

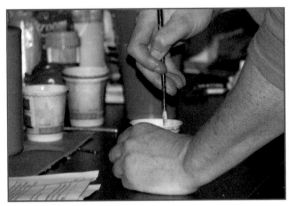

Figure 3.78

The two parts are combined and stirred together.

Figure 3.79

The mixed plastic is poured into the mold.

At this point, at least two different approaches can typically be taken with the plastic inside. If the plastic is simply left to harden while the mold sits still, the plastic will harden as a solid object inside. One thing to keep in mind in this case is that air bubbles in the plastic will off-gas upward as it cures, so it may not be uncommon to find a huge bubble at the top of the cast when releasing it, which would need some patching up with more plastic. The other method, referred to as *slush casting*, involves keeping the mold rotating constantly and slowly while the plastic is curing inside (Figure 3.80). This slushes and guides the plastic to the outer wall of the cast, leaving the inside hollow. A hollow head or other such object will allow for an attachment piece to be placed inside for affixing to a body armature, like a K&S tube, which can be attached inside the head with a bit more plastic to root it in there. A hollow head also cuts down on the weight, which is always important. While slushing the plastic around, it is still a good idea to know where the front and back of the head are inside the mold and to spend more time on the front of the head, where the face is. If any part of the cast needs to be patched, it's better to have this happen in the back, where it might not have as much screen time. It is best to plug the entrance hole with some Klean Klay or a cork and move the mold around over the top of a garbage can in case any plastic leaks out. (The samples shown in Figures 3.79 and 3.80 are for a smaller head that fits inside a large plastic cup, whereas the same process would have been done in a larger bucket for Charlie's head.)

When the cure time has passed and the remaining plastic inside the cup has turned white and hard, the mold can be taken out and pried open, and then you release into the world a plastic cast replica of the sculpt (Figure 3.81)!

Figure 3.80

The mold is rotated slowly over a garbage can to slush the plastic around inside.

Figure 3.81

The sculpt and final plastic cast for Charlie's head.

Face Armatures

A rigid head made of plastic works best for stylized designs with a simpler look, but other puppet designs will call for a bit more mobility in the face. Because human and animal faces are often just as flexible a piece of design as the rest of the body, some puppet faces will be rigged with armature pieces to be animated. Posable paddles, wires, or other mechanisms can be built to simulate movement of the jaw, lips, brow, and eyebrows of the puppet face. In many cases, a movable face armature will be covered with a flexible material like foam latex or silicone. This will cause the surface of the face to bulge and stretch like real skin for the facial features that are manipulated underneath. Pulling and pushing on a jaw or an eyebrow paddle on the surface of the face creates a unique range of possible emotions for the animator. A few examples are illustrated here, ranging from studio productions to independent projects.

For the feature film *$9.99*, director Tatia Rosenthal conceived a system for achieving subtle flexibility in the faces of her puppets. Silicone faces were cast over a hinged chin for jaw movements, with a tiny slot for inserting replacement mouths for dialogue and paddles for eyebrow movements for extra expression. The face mechanisms for the armatures (Figure 3.82) were developed by Philip Beadsmoore. The overall effect given to the puppets is that of being able to combine lip sync that matches each syllable with subtle vertical movements in the jaw. When a character's mouth goes into a long "ah" or "oh" vowel sound, for example, the jaw can drop just as it would on a real human face. This gives a subtle touch of flexibility that couldn't be achieved with a static head made of plastic. For the realistic design of these puppets and the feel of the film, the puppet design serves the aesthetic purpose it sets out to do for this particular independent feature film (Figure 3.83).

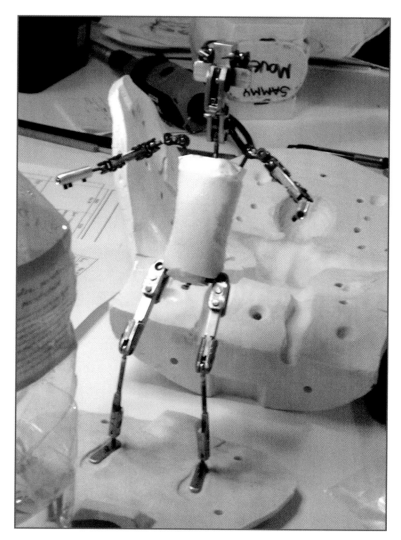

Figure 3.82

An armature with facial controls from the feature film *$9.99*. (Courtesy of Tatia Rosenthal/Here Media/Regent Releasing.)

Figure 3.83

Puppets of Albert and the Angel from *$9.99*. (Courtesy of Here Media/ Regent Releasing.)

Another complex face armature was designed for a puppet of the character Uncle Creepy for a recent stop-motion project for New Comic Company directed by Stephen Chiodo. Based on a sculpt by Chiodo himself, the Uncle Creepy puppet was built primarily on a ball-and-socket armature built by John

Figure 3.84

The armature for Uncle Creepy. (Courtesy of Stephen Chiodo/New Comic Company.)

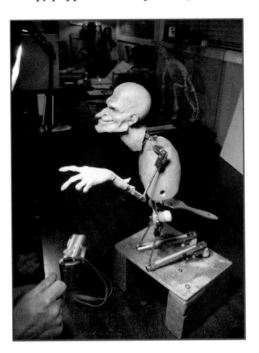

Deall, with silicone-cast skin for the hands and head (Figure 3.84). Underneath the head was an epoxy skull, complete with a jaw piece on a ball joint that could pose open and closed, as well as left to right for a crooked jaw effect. For additional mouth shapes and brow movements, paddles were designed for the upper lip and the eyebrows (Figure 3.85). For the project's animators, Kent Burton and Justin Kohn, the Uncle Creepy puppet allowed a strong sense of control in the face to complement the rest of the body animation. For the lip sync, movement of the jaw is wider or narrower, depending on whether a syllable is accented; it would be opened wider for long vowel sounds and accents in the phrasing (Figure 3.86). To accentuate the fluidity of the actual puppet's animation, certain mouth shapes that required a pucker or tightening of the lips were resculpted photographically using After Effects filters. This gives the puppet a unique sense of lip sync that is completely believable when combined with the aesthetics of the entire project. The amazing *Uncle Creepy Returns* film can be found and studied at http://www.youtube.com/user/creepyuniverse.

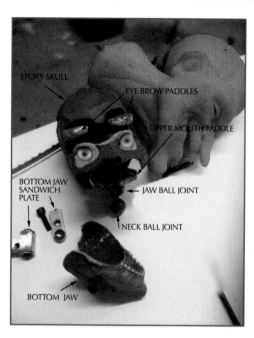

Figure 3.85

The face armature for Uncle Creepy. (Courtesy of Stephen Chiodo/New Comic Company.)

Figure 3.86

Some images of Uncle Creepy showing the flexibility of his jaw. (Courtesy of Stephen Chiodo/New Comic Company.)

Another example of an armature with face controls has been designed by independent animator Dave Hettmer from Michigan, who has worked on stop-motion and miniature effects for films such as *Frostbiter: Wrath of the Wendigo* and *Army of Darkness*. For his personal stop-motion project *Road Rage*, Dave designed frog and snail puppets out of foam latex cast out of plaster molds. The frog (Figure 3.87) is built on an aluminum wire armature (Figure 3.88), and his top and bottom mouth pieces are built out of two 1/8-inch 6061 plates (a typical grade found at hardware stores). Around the mouth plates are lip mechanisms built out of 24-gauge steel florist's wire, which allows for pinching into certain shapes for "oo" or other syllables.

Figure 3.87

Frog puppet by Dave Hettmer, posing his mouth into an "oo" shape for lip sync. (© Dave Hettmer.)

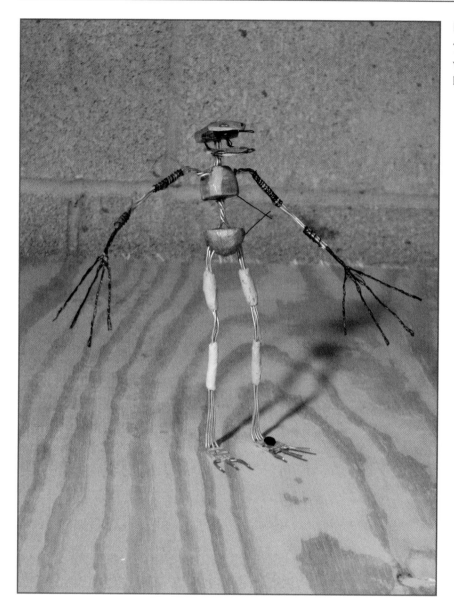

Figure 3.88

The frog's wire armature with aluminum mouth plates. (© Dave Hettmer.)

The snail armature (Figure 3.89) is built on a ball-and-socket neck piece, with a head made of 6061 aluminum blocks filed and ground to shape using a grinding wheel. The snail's dialogue movement is achieved with looped pieces of steel florist's wire, which fits inside the bottom jaw and is bent into various

Figure 3.89

Armature for the snail from *Road Rage* by Dave Hettmer. (© Dave Hettmer.)

mouth shapes (Figures 3.90 to 3.93). The range of movement in the snail's mouth is similar to the open-and-close motion of a hand puppet, but with some additional mouth shapes made possible by the multiple wires. To further accentuate accents in the dialogue, the eyes are attached to bendable wires clamped into the head with set screws. Being able to extend the eye-stalks up and down to the rhythm of the dialogue uses the snail's design to further accentuate the character of his movement (Figure 3.94). The eyes themselves are plastic beads fixed in place, and the pupils are made of thin latex painted with black acrylic paint and Pros-Aide. To make the pupils for both puppets, Dave dipped eye-sized balls in latex for a thin skin that would fit perfectly over the curvature of the ball. Then he cut out several copies of each pupil, which measured only 4 millimeters in diameter. These tiny pupils are stuck to the eyeballs with petroleum jelly on the back for easy sliding around, and the eyelids are added using clay replacement pieces. In addition to the eye and mouth movement, the ball-and-socket joints in the snail's neck allow for smooth animation of the rest of his body to match extreme accents in the dialogue where they are needed. By combining different materials together for the neck, eyes, and controllable mouth shapes, the end results allow for puppets that are designed specifically for great animation and range of expression. Examples of Dave's animation and other work can be found at his website (http://www.hettmerfx.com) and on YouTube (http://www.youtube.com/user/hefflesniggener).

Figure 3.90

The snail's neutral mouth position. (© Dave Hettmer.)

Figure 3.91

The snail's curled lip position. (© Dave Hettmer.)

Figure 3.92

The snail's wide open mouth position. (© Dave Hettmer.)

Figure 3.93

The snail's "F" or "V" mouth position. (© Dave Hettmer.)

Figure 3.94

The snail's up and down eye movements in two superimposed images. (© Dave Hettmer.)

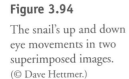

Another example of someone who has used an advanced method for achieving effective face movements is independent animator Ron Cole from New York, who burst onto the stop-motion scene with an innovative, award-winning short film called *In the Fall of Gravity* (Figure 3.95). The puppets for his film move with a unique sense of realism and fluidity that is spell binding in its

Figure 3.95

Ron Cole animating on his short film *In the Fall of Gravity*. (© Ron Cole.)

execution, design, and aesthetic beauty. His work amazed many people in the stop-motion community upon seeing the film's trailer on Ron's blog site and the StopMotionAnimation.com message board. *In the Fall of Gravity* is a philosophical dialogue between the wizard Isomer (Figure 3.96) and his apprentice Trevor Verity. Each puppet's facial expressions and lip sync are achieved through a unique blend of traditional stop-motion puppet animation and a cable control system attached to the puppet's face and connected to an external control box (Figure 3.97). By turning dials on the box, cables attached to the dials run up through the puppet's body into points inside the face (Figures 3.98 and 3.99). The faces are cast in flexible urethane rubber that stretches and bulges into subtle changes created by the cables, and these changes can be manipulated incrementally frame by frame for a certain naturalistic effect.

Figure 3.96

Isomer, the wizard character from *In the Fall of Gravity*, by Ron Cole. (© Ron Cole.)

Figure 3.97

The inner controls for Trevor, a character from *In the Fall of Gravity*, by Ron Cole. (© Ron Cole.)

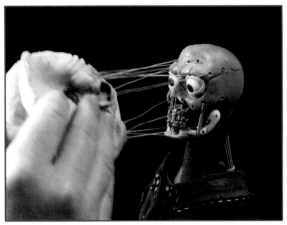

Figure 3.98

Isomer's skin is peeled back to reveal his skull armature underneath. (© Ron Cole.)

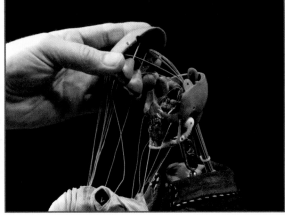

Figure 3.99

Isomer's skull comes apart to reveal the cable system inside. (© Ron Cole.)

I asked Ron to share some thoughts about the evolution of his puppet designs, how they work, and the challenges involved in creating them:

> I had a previous background of 20 years in stop-motion, live-action puppets, and cable controls. Part of my inspiration for getting into cable controls came from a shot Rick Baker did for the 1976 remake of *King Kong*, where Kong drew a breath and blew on the actress after she fell in the waterfall. The cable control technology had been well established further on films like *American Werewolf in London* and *E.T.* This other work for live-action monster effects

had been done with different heads that each did one part of the facial movement. E.T. was one of the only characters made to fully speak, and he would speak in slow motion. My challenge was to miniaturize it and do it frame by frame. With this kind of cable system, there are always tension problems to overcome, and the cables need to be delicate but strong. The skin is paper thin at times, and so many things occur about what nature actually does. For example, not only do lips stretch open, but often there are moments where you need open jaws with the lips closed in order to get many different shapes which happen rather frequently. It's easy to have cables pulling the lips apart, but not pushing, so I needed to have metal pieces inside the lips to push them closed. I also needed to make the world's smallest hinge for a metal piece that had to bend outwards.

A big challenge with this system, which I learned with my first puppet, Trevor, is that the cables would tend to break in the control box end. Because they had tension on them, they would get sucked inside the tube and would not be retrievable, unless I opened up the puppet to get the cable out. So, for Isomer, I built a junction box (Figure 3.100) between the control box and the puppet and split the cables into two halves. Inside the box, the wires were bundled very close together, so I created a map under the lid to indicate which hole and which wire goes where.

On the control box side, there are two types of controls: ones that only pull the cable and others that have a dual function. The dual function controls are only the eyebrows; turning the knob left brings the brow down, and right brings them up. I managed to do that by finding a way to attach two cables to the same controller, which both pull, but in opposite directions. The cables for the face are controlled by 16 dials (Figure 3.101), which achieve the following functions:

1) Outside left eyebrow up and down
2) Inside left eyebrow up and down
3) Inside right eyebrow up and down
4) Outside right eyebrow up and down
5) Left crow's feet up
6) Right crow's feet up
7) Bridge of nose up
8) Top lip up
9) Bottom lip down
10) Lips form "O" toward top teeth
11) Lips form "O" toward bottom teeth
12) Left side smile
13) Right side smile
14) Left side frown
15) Right side frown
16) Jaw open

Figure 3.100

The junction box for Isomer's cable control system. (© Ron Cole.)

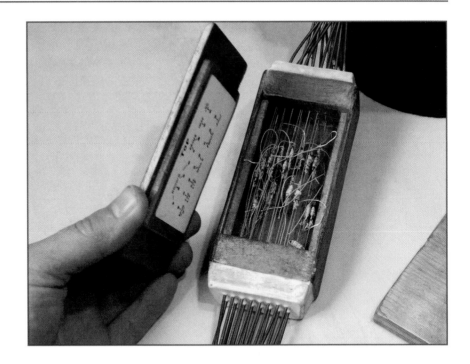

Figure 3.101

Isomer's cable control box, labeled with functions of the different dials. (© Ron Cole)

When animating realistic dialog, the face moves as a whole in order to portray both the words and expressions that give them further meaning (Figures 3.102 to 3.107, showing various expressions for Isomer). That's also true even when the character isn't speaking at all. The human face is obviously the most expressive part of our bodies and is virtually always in motion, expressing moods, thoughts, ideas, comfort, and concerns. A personal rule of mine about animating is the idea that "stillness equals death." Even if only in the tiniest increments possible, I made my best effort to keep every part of a puppet moving at all times.

Outside of the facial controls, the animation for everything else on the body, eyes, and eyelids is done by touching the puppet. I also have a clay tongue that slips into the mouth when I need it, as there is no point in mechanizing that. Isomer has replacement plastic eyelids, and Trevor's eyelids are just clay. My cable technique will continue to be refined, and my dream is to eventually fit the control box inside the puppet.

A detailed tutorial for the inner workings of Ron's cable control system can be found on his blog (http://wobblytripod.blogspot.com), as well as other behind-the-scenes looks at his work and how to order a copy of *In the Fall of Gravity*.

Figure 3.102

(© Ron Cole.)

Figure 3.103

(© Ron Cole.)

Figure 3.104

(© Ron Cole.)

Figure 3.105

(© Ron Cole.)

Figure 3.106

(© Ron Cole.)

Figure 3.107

(© Ron Cole.)

Replacement Faces and Rapid Prototyping

Another emerging technology being implemented into various aspects of stop-motion puppet and set construction is rapid prototyping, or 3D printing. The basic concept behind this technique is to create a 3D computer model and have it printed out as a physical replica. The technology behind rapid prototyping has many other uses and implications in itself, but the film *Coraline* helped put it on the map for use as an animation technique. The area of the film where it was used the most was the facial animation on certain main characters. The faces on characters like Wybie, Coraline's Mother, Other Mother, and Coraline herself consisted of thin replacement masks that were removed and replaced for each frame of the animation.

Replacement animation for facial expressions is a technique that has been around since the very beginning of the stop-motion medium. It likely grew out of the logic behind hand-drawn animation, where every frame consisted of a separate drawing that was different than the one before it, and each drawing was replaced under the rostrum camera for shooting. Adapting this idea to stop-motion meant that every frame would consist of a separate face that was replaced for each frame. The earliest known use of replacement faces appears to be from the MoToy Comedies by American filmmaker Howard S. Moss in 1917. Most of these films are lost, but the few that exist feature a dopey character with exaggerated facial expressions (Figure 3.108). A small number of in-between faces would help to transition from one key expression to another for a caricatured effect. Later evidence of replacement faces is found in the Kinex Studio short films from 1928 to 1930, in the characters of Snap the Gingerbread Man and a recurring witch character (Figure 3.109). It is not entirely clear what materials were used to create the faces for the characters in these early films, but they appear to be sculpted in clay and then either baked or molded. To keep the consistency between faces, it is likely that a clay sculpt was made and cast out in a mold, and then a tiny transitional change was made in the sculpt for each sequential cast. These puppets usually had only one or two in-between faces between each expression. *The New Gulliver* in 1935 also used the technique, with a decidedly more crude clay appearance.

Figure 3.108

A series of replacement faces from the MoToy Comedy *Cracked Ice* by Howard S. Moss (1917).

Figure 3.109

A series of replacement faces from Kinex Studio (1928).

George Pal took the idea of replacement animation to another level by carving entire puppets out of wood and replacing the whole puppet for each frame. Later feature films produced by Pal would revisit the replacement face technique with varying complexity and design ideas, including Wah Chang's work on *Tom Thumb* and *The Wonderful World of the Brothers Grimm*. Commercials for the Pillsbury Doughboy and Speedy Alka-Seltzer brought replacements to TV production, and in more recent years the technique resurfaced in some of the puppets for *The Nightmare Before Christmas* and *James and the Giant Peach*. In these cases, faces were sometimes rigged with magnets on the back to help them snap onto the head and keep them registered in place. Obviously, it was very important to have a numbering and labeling system for the different faces because many of them would have only a subtle difference in appearance. The advantage to replacement faces has always been the ability to achieve a fluidity and range of expression that is not possible with just one static head. The challenge behind them is the incredible amount of work involved in sculpting each individual piece and in keeping them properly registered onscreen. The materials used, whether clay or plastic, would often warp over much time and re-use on set, which would cause major problems in keeping their look consistent.

The advancement in technology using replacement faces for *Coraline* bridged the gap between modern computer animation and bringing the precision it offered into a physical stop-motion universe. Animator and sculptor Martin Meunier, who had worked with director Henry Selick on previous stop-motion films, served as the facial animation designer and coordinated an entire rapid prototyping department for *Coraline*. The process started with traditional means before going digital. Facial expression changes and lip sync were designed and animated in 2D, and then key poses were sculpted as clay maquettes and scanned into the computer. The computer animated in-between positions, and entire animated face sequences were animated in CG. Each individual frame of the computer animation was exported as an STL (stereolithography) file and printed out on an Objet 3D printer (any one of three printers installed for the production). A 3D printer is basically like a photocopy machine that prints liquid resin on a flatbed in layers. Starting from the bottom of the model it is printing, an ultraviolet light cures each layer of resin as it prints until a hard replica of the model is completed.

Once printed, each modeled piece needs to have any extra support material removed, washed, scrubbed, sanded, and then sent to the fabrication department for painting. Each character could have as many as 15,000 faces and up to 250,000 facial expressions available, all in perfect registration to each other. The variety in expressions was created by dividing the face into upper and lower halves (Figure 3.110), so that mouth movements and lip sync could be combined with eyebrow movements in many different combinations.

Figure 3.110

Photo of the Coraline puppet, showing the face divided into halves.
(© Focus Features.)

The seam between the two halves of the face was removed in post-production by digital effects artists. In addition to the outer appearance of each face piece, inside were details like teeth, tongues, and uvulas, as well as a complex registration system to help the pieces fit together like a puzzle. The amount of sculpting and modeling work that went into the film was estimated to be the equivalent of nearly 30 years of traditional sculpting; rapid prototyping allowed this amount to be completed in about 18 months. It allowed them to experiment with using CGI against itself by printing it out into the real world and getting artists involved in the CG process. Overall, amid all the new technical precision and subtlety offered through this technology on *Coraline*, the end goal was for the audience to have an emotional connection with the characters.

The Objets used on *Coraline* are designed to operate like a printer or photocopier, with a head that moves back and forth to print out each layer of the model. There are similar machines under different brands that employ a similar process and print a plaster-like material that also have the ability to print in color. Other machines such as EnvisionTEC printers are operated by a 250-watt bulb inside the hub of the printer (Figure 3.111), which projects the computer data from each layer onto a metal plate on the outside. The metal plate rests in a bed of liquid resin, cures each projected layer, and raises up incrementally for each layer until the model is complete and suspended upside-down (Figure 3.112). Any negative space within the model can be supported by a mesh-like support material, which is generated within the actual computer modeling software. The plate and model are removed from the printer, and support material must be cut away from the model with a hot knife (Figure 3.113) and placed in a bath for cleaning.

The future implications for this technology to continue stop-motion productions have yet to be seen, but there could be a great deal of potential for bridging the gap between stop-motion and the capabilities of CGI. For artists who specialize in modeling or sculpting in CG using tools like Maya, ZBrush or Mudbox, printing their work in 3D can be a valuable way to transition into stop-motion if they want the experience of seeing their art in actual space. The process also has implications for easing the duplication of objects that would otherwise be cast out of molds, likewise eliminating the issue of undercuts and inconsistencies that can occur. In addition to creative applications for animation, architectural models can be realized with a great amount of detail for

Figure 3.111

Interior bulb for 3D printer at Protodemon Creative Studio in North Vancouver, Canada. (Photo by Ken Priebe. Courtesy of Protodemon.)

possible aid in creating elaborate stop-motion sets (Figure 3.114). A world of ideas and options is opened up by CG modeling's ability to create intricate details that would be very difficult to sculpt by hand or to physically cast in a mold. In addition, these details can be duplicated in different scales. The effect of any 3D object growing, shrinking, or morphing is possible simply by scaling or modifying the CG model and saving each change as a separate object to be printed. Entire replacement puppets can also be animated in the computer and printed out for each frame.

Figure 3.112

A finished model suspended from the resin bed.
(Photo by Ken Priebe. Courtesy of Protodemon.)

Figure 3.113

Cutting away meshed support material from the model.
(Photo by Ken Priebe. Courtesy of Protodemon.)

Figure 3.114

Different scaled building
models printed by a 3D
printer. (Photo by Ken Priebe.
Courtesy of Protodemon.)

There is much that can still be explored, although for the average independent filmmaker, there is not only the issue of using it creatively, but also the issue of cost. The printers themselves have various ranges in cost and quality and require a certain amount of space and material to support the maintenance behind them. The most convenient method for utilizing rapid prototyping technology is to enlist the services of a company that specializes in servicing prototypes based on your own 3D models. Companies like Shapeways (http://www.shapeways.com), Protodemon (http://www.protodemon.com), and others can provide this service if you upload your files to their websites and place orders for 3D printing production. They all typically have their own guidelines for submitting files and parameters for what they are able to produce. If you feel inclined to explore this technology and bring it further into the realm of stop-motion production, it can certainly achieve some effects that would be much more difficult to get otherwise. When used creatively and combined with a good dose of hand-crafted elements, there is a good realm of opportunity for bridging media and enhancing the art of stop-motion storytelling.

Replacement Animation Puppets

Scaling back to puppets of the simpler variety, the idea of replacement animation can also be achieved with materials much less costly than a 3D printer. I recently created a series of replacement figures for an animated logo sequence done in stop-motion. My friend and colleague Steve Stanchfield created a hand-drawn animation logo for his company, Thunderbean Animation (Figure 3.115), which provides animation services and produces DVDs of rare lost films from animation history. The logo starts with a lightning flash and the word "Thunder," and then a happy animated bean comes in and places the word "Bean" into the title. Steve and I had been collaborating on a DVD full of rare stop-motion films called *Stop-Motion Marvels*, so I thought it would be cool if the logo was also done in stop-motion. Steve's animation style is very rubbery,

Figure 3.115

Logo for Thunderbean Animation by Steve Stanchfield. (© Thunderbean Animation.)

with lots of squash and stretch to the drawings, so I knew that replicating the same look in stop-motion would involve replacement puppets, much like the George Pal Puppetoons of the 1940s.

To create an understructure for the beans, I simply used tiny Styrofoam ball pieces for the top and bottom, glued them together with aluminum wire (Figure 3.116), and covered them in clay. Using the Styrofoam balls helped me keep the shapes relatively consistent from one puppet to the next and cut down on the weight. Studying Steve's original animation told me I needed a pose where the bean's eyes and mouth were closed, a slightly squashed version of the same expression (Figure 3.117), and at least one in-between position. I also needed a severely squashed pose for the anticipation (Figure 3.118) before he stretches up to place the words into the title (Figure 3.119), which also required separate puppets. Coming from the stretch was another in-between pose and a final pose to end him on as he stops to look upward and smile. I was able to streamline the original animation and simply re-use these basic shapes to get the effect I needed, without necessarily adhering to the need for that many replacement figures (Figure 3.120). For the arms and legs, I used small pieces of aluminum wire wrapped in black masking tape, and his hands and feet were made of sticky tack and white plasticine clay. I knew I would need a rig in the shot holding him up the whole time because the spindly legs would not be strong enough to hold him up on his own, and there would be several frames where he was in mid-air. A helping hand rig worked just fine for this, with the pincher on the end either holding a wire to stick into the puppet or sticking into the puppet itself. The rig was visible in every frame and later erased digitally in post-production.

Figure 3.116

Styrofoam armature structures for the clay replacement beans.

Figure 3.117

Basic shape for the bean as he enters the frame.

Figure 3.118

Squashed anticipation pose.

Figure 3.119

Big stretched pose.

Figure 3.120

The final resting puppet, along with some of the other replacement puppets.

For the animation of these puppets, I set up a white poster board curved into a cove to create a plain white limbo space for the action to take place. This was lit with some ambient lighting to help soften the overall effect but still create a shadow under the puppets, emphasizing the fact this would be a 3D stop-motion version of the logo. I imported an image of the logo into my frame-grabbing software and used it as an onion-skinned image to line up the framing of the shot and size of the puppet in the frame (Figure 3.121).

Figure 3.121

Author Ken Priebe framing his Thunderbean Animation shot. (Photo by Shawn Tilling.)

The logo would be composited into the shot later, and I wanted to match the exact framing as closely as I could. Once I got the framing right, I traced the edges of the logo with a dry-erase marker on the monitor to give me a reference point for when the puppet would actually make contact with the logo and where he should step and land. Using all of this as a framework, I started animating (Figure 3.122).

Because of the different positions caused by the extreme squash-stretch movement and the fragility of the various puppets, in most cases I took the entire puppet apart between each frame. If the arms or legs needed to dramatically change position, I would take the wires out, bend them into shape, and stick them back in their new pose. The onion-skin feature was very useful for registering the extreme movements after removing the puppet from the set, and toggling the frames gave me an idea of how the arcs and movement were working. The whole sequence took me about four hours to shoot once it was all set up, and the end results were a happy stop-motion jumping bean!

Check out the accompanying CD for the final animation, as well as the *Stop-Motion Marvels* DVD, available from http://www.thunderbeananimation.com.

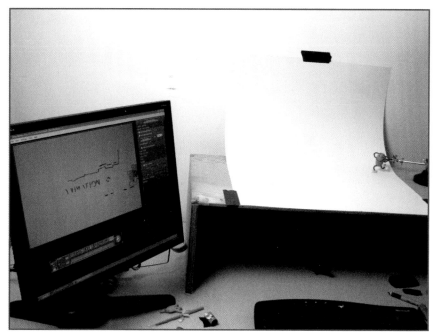

Figure 3.122

The Thunderbean animation in progress, with reference markers on the monitor and onion skin for positioning.

As some final notes for this chapter, let me point out just a few other excellent resources for a few specific things related to advanced puppet-building:

Online tutorials for making your own ball-and-socket armatures:

- Lionel I. Orozco:

  www.stopmotionworks.com/ohspics.htm

  www.stopmotionworks.com/drlballs.htm

  www.stopmotionworks.com/ballbrz.htm

  (Above tutorials also available with more written details in Marc Spess's book, *Secrets of Clay Animation Revealed*.)

- Sven Bonnichsen:

  www.scarletstarstudios.com/blog/archives/2006/06/how_to_make_a_b.html

- John Hankins (Castlegardener):

  http://castlegardener.wordpress.com/2008/06/29/beginners-guide-to-ball-and-socket-armatures

■ For additional tutorials and tips on creating silicone molds and casts, check out some of the issues and videos provided at http://www.stopmotionmagazine.com and http://www.marklagana.com/siliconemould.html, and consult the message board at http://www.stopmotionanimation.com.

■ Armature kits and other services/supplies:

Stop-Mo-Tec: http://www.stop-mo-tec.de

Animation Supplies: http://www.animationsupplies.net

The Clay & Stop Motion Animated Store: http://www.animateclay.com/shop

4

Digital Cinematography

Stop-motion photography is not just one image, but rather a series of images that create motion when strung together. Shooting stop-motion relies on having the following things: a story to tell, puppets to tell that story with, and a camera to be the eyepiece for that story. If you have the first two nailed down, reading this chapter will help you focus (no pun intended) on what you should know about your camera, some details on how to shoot with it, and some practical effects you can try.

When stop-motion was shot on film, each frame would exist as its own separate image, strung together on a strip of 8mm, 16mm, or 35mm film (Figure 4.1). The film would be registered with a series of sprockets that pushed the strip of film through a gate in front of a square window blocked by a shutter. Exposing one frame of film with the touch of a button would open the shutter and expose light through the lens onto the film. Then, the sprockets inside would advance the film-strip to the next unexposed space for the next image to be captured. Each image was essentially a separate photograph with its own established focus, exposure, color, and lighting. These elements would essentially be a continuous tone, and the features on a film camera could be set manually, although fluctuations could happen because of uneven shutter speed, changes in temperature, or the film moving around in the gate. There was no way to make sure each frame was consistent with the next one. The result of the whole process was basically a series of still images on the strip of film that would exist only in negative form until it was sent to a lab to create the positive print. Looking at the strip of film itself, all of the separate images are visible, so an editor can see exactly where scenes begin and end, and the images can be rearranged and spliced together.

Figure 4.1

A series of 35mm frames from *Meet the Raisins.* (© Will Vinton Studios.)

As film use declined over the years and was replaced by video, the most popular method for stop-motion became using a MiniDV camcorder with an IEEE-1394 Firewire connection (Figure 4.2) that provided a live feed to a computer with frame-grabbing software. The video camera basically acts as an "eye" and feeds a constant live image into the software, so if one moves a hand into the frame, this should all appear in real time on the computer monitor as well. The software then grabs separate still images from the live feed each time the animator hits the capture button. The flexibility of this method provides instant access to the images for preview purposes and playback. However, even with an HD camera and frame averaging provided to improve the quality of each frame, the image being fed into the computer is essentially a compressed image, and there may be limits to how much resolution can be attained for high-quality broadcast. Watching the animation play back on a computer monitor might look fine, but if it is meant to be blown up on a huge screen at a film festival, the image quality might not be as strong as it should be. Of course, some software does have frame averaging and HD capabilities to help with this.

Despite these challenges to work around, using a live Firewire feed is still a perfectly valid way to shoot stop-motion. However, even though Firewire cards and converters are still on the market for installing into computers, most video cameras no longer come with the Firewire output or cable included. Video camcorders at average consumer prices (or higher) now typically shoot movies onto a hard drive, and a USB connection is used to transfer the video off the camera. Flip Video cameras operate on the same principle, allowing you to shoot video easily in the palm of your hand and upload movies as AVI files directly to your computer. From there, you can burn your videos to DVD or upload them straight to YouTube. More and more standard hard-drive camcorders also shoot in HD, which is quickly becoming standard for all broadcast media. This is all fine if you are shooting home videos of your friends, your kids, or your cat playing the piano for YouTube. However, for stop-motion it presents a problem because a USB connection from these cameras (Figure 4.3) will not provide you with a live feed for your frame grabber. Without a live feed, you cannot use the onion skin or frame-toggling features that frame-grabbing software allows you to take advantage of to help keep your animation registered.

Figure 4.2

A MiniDV camera with Firewire cable output. (Photo by Jeff Bell.)

Figure 4.3

An HD camcorder and Flip Video camera with USB outputs. (Photo by Jeff Bell.)

Meanwhile, as Firewire outputs on computers and camcorders have become harder to find, there has been an explosion of popularity of digital SLR still cameras in the past few years. Gone are the days of taking pictures with a film camera, dropping off the tube of film at the drug store, and waiting an hour for your photos and negatives to be ready. Tiny digital cameras that allow you to point, shoot, and get your pictures instantly for uploading to your computer, printing, or posting online have taken the world by storm. (I don't even remember the last time I took a picture using film.) Then came the digital SLR camera (Figure 4.4), which had the appearance and image quality of the more professional film cameras but allowed for manual controls and creative freedom in a digital universe. Now it seems like everyone has a digital SLR camera because they have quickly become more affordable for the average consumer.

Along with this trend has been the realization that one can shoot stop-motion with a digital SLR camera. Part of the appeal of shooting stop-motion this way is that it essentially takes the process back to its roots of shooting a string of still images on film. After taking a series of high-quality still images, the next step is to download them straight to the timeline of an editing software program and play them in sequence. The manual controls for image quality make the stop-motion frames look as sharp and clear as a film print, or potentially even better.

However, this has presented another problem: By itself, a digital still camera will not provide a live feed for your frame grabber. The solution in this case is to mount a camcorder next to the SLR or attach a tiny spycam or webcam to the viewfinder and use that image for the live video feed. The animator can then use the live feed image to utilize the frame-grabber's functions of onion-skinning and toggling, while at the same time capturing their actual frames in high-resolution with the SLR camera. As long as you remember to take a picture with each camera, this gives you the best of both worlds. This method is still a common way to shoot stop-motion, but even better is the fact that digital SLR cameras now are available with an HDMI or USB live video feed (Figure 4.5). They are more expensive than the lower consumer brands without live preview, but as they rise in popularity, the price continues to come down and become more affordable. Before too long, digital SLR still cameras with a live video preview function could likely become the standard for personal video use (including filming your cat for YouTube). The more affordable these options become, the better it will be for everybody. The other convenient factor to the digital SLR camera's popularity has been the development of several stop-motion software programs to communicate directly with the functions of certain Canon or Nikon SLR cameras. At this time, the latest versions of Stop Motion Pro and the newly popular software Dragon Stop Motion have this functionality, and many more could easily come onto the market before too long. Software programs now have the capability to work with the manual controls of the camera from within the computer, capture the HD images directly into the timeline, and provide a multitude of other convenient functions for digital workflow.

Figure 4.4

A Canon EOS Digital Rebel XT digital SLR camera.
(Photo by Jeff Bell.)

Figure 4.5

A Canon EOS 5D Mark II digital SLR camera.
(Photo by Jeff Bell.)

This book is not intended to focus on any particular software program (although a few specific ones are mentioned throughout) because this information will always change as new versions come out. Whichever software you use is up to your own preference, operating system, budget, and reasons for shooting stop-motion in the first place. Indie stop-motion filmmakers all have different financial situations, living conditions, and responsibilities outside our puppet-pushing; not everyone may be able to afford a fancy digital SLR camera with live video. They also may not necessarily need a super-high-quality image if they are simply doing stop-motion tests or learning basic student-level animation. A webcam can still provide a live feed for a simple image through a USB, but most of them won't allow for manual control or a suitable image for a semiprofessional production. A MiniDV camcorder with a live Firewire output had always been a good compromise, but being without this option puts stop-motion filmmakers on a budget in a difficult transitional stage. Hopefully this will pass, and another simple method will come onto the market that allows all filmmakers to make their films look the best they can at any budget. The software you are able to use may also be determined by your camera. If your version of the software does not support the live-feed option for your digital SLR camera, you are limited to using a webcam or an SLR with a spycam, or trying to find a used DV camera with Firewire (perhaps on eBay). Another option may be to use a special video adapter or a video capture converter like a Canopus, which coverts an analog video signal to digital for a live feed. With a bit more simple technology and a little creativity, you can find other solutions that work to achieve your purposes, according to your budget constraints or shooting needs.

Independent animator Ron Cole describes his method for connecting his stop-motion set-up as follows:

> I have a Lumix SLR camera, which has manual controls and a good image. My camera is not compatible with the Dragon software I'm using, but for the end product I use the following method: I have a live feed coming from the camera to an analog-to-digital converter into my software. The live feed is a bit grainy, but hi-res images are coming in through my camera's Eye-Fi card, which is a memory card that can upload images wirelessly to my computer. Dragon has a feature called "folder watch," which takes an image from the Eye-Fi card and replaces the live feed image in the timeline. This gives me the ability to back up after taking my picture to check the hi-res image. This is very useful when I'm shooting stop-motion to match up with a live-action shot and need the puppet's foot to be in the right place, for example, after taking the exposure. Since the grainy image coming from the viewfinder is harder to see, it helps to be able to double check the alignment of my puppet after capturing my hi-res images into the timeline.

As a stop-motion filmmaker, you can also decide for yourself whether a live feed is necessary at all, especially if you have a bit more experience with animation. If you are shooting frames with an SLR or any other type of still camera, you can simply load the still images into a timeline on your computer as you shoot. The only computer function that may be available to you is the ability to advance through your frames to check the registration of your animation, but only after you capture each frame. As far as the positioning of your puppet is concerned, you are shooting blind, as you would be if you were shooting on film. Without the ability to toggle between your last stored frame and your live frame in your computer, the exact reliability of your puppet being properly registered is essentially done by observing the puppet on set and seeing the movement in your head. The difference is that *after* you capture your frame, you can look at your timeline and advance your frames to see whether the animation is doing what you want. If there is a problem with the registration, lighting fluctuation, or otherwise, you simply delete the frame you just took, fix the problem, and reshoot. This is a different method of frame toggling with an extra step, but it still does the job. The only other convenience not offered without the live feed is the onion skin, but you can work around this by using the old-school method of drawing on the computer monitor with a dry-erase marker. Overall, it's up to you and how spoiled you have become by the luxury of the live feed. If you are experienced enough in stop-motion to know instinctively where your puppet should be without using these tools, you can likely get by without them. With your camera, simply shoot blind, take your pictures, load them up, and watch the magic happen. (While you're at it, you might as well break out those rusty surface gauges, too!)

Whatever method you decide to use, it does look like the digital SLR still camera is continuing its popularity, so this chapter will mainly focus on shooting in this method for creating an advanced, high-quality stop-motion film.

Digital Camera Basics

With a digital SLR camera, the images are not captured onto a strip of film, but rather onto an image sensor. The sensor is made up of millions of pixels, which are like tiny buckets that gather light. The light is essentially converted from analog into electric photons in digital format, and this will typically give increased quality through a full-frame sensor. The resolution of the captured image is measured in megapixels; the resolution increases based on the megapixel number. Most digital cameras range from 8 to 21 megapixels. When a picture is taken, a mirror (which reflects the image seen through the viewfinder) flips up, and light enters through the lens and hits the sensor, creating an exposure that is sent through a processing engine to create a digital file on the camera's memory card.

When taking these individual images, you have the option of saving them either as JPEGs or in RAW format. JPEGs are a relatively standard format, even for compact digital cameras, and can be captured in high quality, although they are compressed images. They are only 8-bit, but perfectly suitable for loading into a video timeline for editing and giving you this flexibility. RAW files are unprocessed and essentially serve as a digital negative, going up to 14-bit and giving you an expanded range for editing in post-production. RAW files imported as a sequence into your editing timeline or Adobe Photoshop will give you more flexibility for changing brightness, correcting color, or adding digital effects. The main thing to realize is that it also means each individual frame will have a significantly larger file size and will require more hard-drive space to back them up. Shooting in RAW format is probably best for a professional film that is commissioned or intended for HD screening or a film festival. Depending on your intentions for shooting, you can either shoot in both formats (RAW for high-quality edit, JPEG for back-up and simple playback) or just stick with whatever suits your needs.

The lens you use can vary greatly, but its quality will have a great impact on the quality of your image. Shooting at a small scale for stop-motion does not require a telephoto lens, because you are typically much closer to your subject. Most stop-motion filmmakers typically use any lens in the range of 24mm to 85mm (or higher) and follow the recommended practice of interchanging lens brands with camera brands. One of the biggest challenges in shooting stop-motion with still cameras is the flicker caused by fluctuations between exposures. Often this will be caused by outside elements, such as uneven wattage or gradual dimming of the lighting set-up, but it can also be caused by fact that most digital SLR camera lenses have an iris that defaults to being open and only moves into the setting you want when you take a picture. Using a truly manual lens from an older camera is one way to help keep all your images at the same exposure.

The settings for the basic exposure elements of your camera should all be set to manual controls when shooting stop-motion to alleviate the fluctuations between separate frames that can result from using automatic settings. The essential elements to keep on manual settings include focus, aperture, shutter speed, white balance, and ISO.

ISO

The *ISO* determines how sensitive your image sensor is to light. On film, the ISO would be predetermined by the type of film stock being used, but digital ISO can be adjusted for each frame and shooting situation. If you are shooting a dark scene for your stop-motion project, increasing the ISO will increase the sensitivity to light and allow for a slower shutter speed. However, it will also create more digital noise, which is one of the shortfalls of digital photography. Heightened sensitivity on the sensor causes heat build-up and will create chunky blotches in low-light areas and shadows, unlike film grain, which is smoother and moodier. This was one of the challenges faced on Tim Burton's *Corpse Bride*, which had many scenes with low light, so dark sets were often over-lit and adjusted in post-production. A lower ISO setting combined with a shorter shutter speed will typically create less digital noise, but ultimately the relationship between noise and your manual settings depends on your camera. In most cases it's best to keep the ISO setting lower; most stop-motion filmmakers keep it around 100 to 200.

Aperture and Shutter Speed

Controlling the *aperture* affects the amount of light coming into the camera through an iris-shaped mechanism inside the lens. Capturing light through exposures in photography is measured by *f-stops* (Figure 4.6), which are either half or double the amount of light in the previous stop. To increase aperture by one f-stop, for instance, means doubling the amount of light hitting the sensor.

The shutter speed consists of how long the shutter is open and exposes the sensor to light. Therefore:

> Wide aperture (lower f-stop number) = more light = faster shutter speed.
>
> Small aperture (higher f-stop number) = less light = slower shutter speed.

Placing a digital light meter directly in front of your central focus (like your stop-motion puppet) and pressing its meter button will help you determine which f-stop and shutter speed to use for getting the right exposure for the lighting situation you are using. This is pretty straightforward if you just have one puppet in a long or medium shot on stage for a simple scene. For a composition that requires a bit more depth to the puppet's surroundings, there are a few other things to consider. Whatever is closest to your light source may have a lower stop than anything that is farther away in the background, so you may want to take a reading for both your foreground and background and stop your camera at a point in between.

Figure 4.6

Chart for some of the f-stops provided by a camera lens. (Image provided by James Emler.)

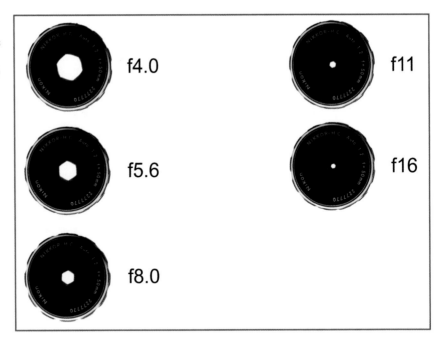

Depth of Field

These camera settings will also be affected by the *depth of field* you want for your shot. Depth of field refers to how much of the distance of your composition is in focus. For stop-motion, as opposed to live action, everything is scaled down to miniature size, including the distance between your camera and your subjects. In most cases you don't want the audience to feel like they are watching a miniature set, but rather a world they will recognize as having a natural sense of distance. This natural feeling of distance will be accomplished mostly by having a wider depth of field where more elements are in focus. A shallow depth of field will mean that if you focus on the central part of your composition, the background and surrounding elements will be blurry. Shallow depth of field is typically caused by a lower f-stop and faster shutter speed and a wider depth of field by a higher f-stop and slower shutter speed. For a happy medium in a basic animation scene, most stop-motion filmmakers set their camera in the area of f11 with a shutter speed of 1/2 to 1 second. Stopping at f16 or f22 will create a more extreme depth of field, and stopping at f8 or lower will soften the background. It all depends on the mood you are going for when telling your story.

The illustrated examples shown here show how different moods and effects are created through camera settings and also through composition of the shot itself. For a happy, light, or comedic scene (Figures 4.7 and 4.8), the composition is usually flat, with the camera centered and perpendicular to the set. Figure 4.7 is shot with a shallower depth of field, which blurs the character in the background. Figure 4.8 is shot with a wider depth of field, so the whole scene is in focus, and the faces of both characters are much clearer. This clarity is important for a playful scene like this and communicates the relationship between the two characters.

Figure 4.7

Shallow depth of field, shot at f2.8 and a 1/8-second shutter speed.

Figure 4.8

Wider depth of field, shot at f11 and a 2-second shutter speed.

For a creepy, dark, or dramatic scene (Figures 4.9 and 4.10), the composition is usually shot at more of an angle to give a more unsettling effect. Figure 4.9 is shot with a shallower depth of field, blurring the background character and heightening the mysterious mood. Figure 4.10 is shot with a wider depth of field, bringing both characters into focus.

Depending on what your story calls for, there will be times when you may want a shallower depth of field and times when you won't. It helps to know how to use your camera as a story-telling tool to get the effect you want.

Figure 4.9

Shallow depth of field, shot at f2.8 and a 1/8-second shutter speed.

Figure 4.10

Wider depth of field, shot at f20 and a 6-second shutter speed.

White Balance

White balance is a function that removes certain kinds of color casts created by different light temperature situations. Color temperature of light is measured by the Kelvin scale, which is based on the color that would be cast by an object as it is heated. Higher temperatures will appear cooler; this seems backward, but it's based on the fact that although we think of objects as being red or orange when they get hot, they actually will go blue to white the hotter they get. Therefore, warm-feeling lighting situations, such as candlelight, have the lowest light temperature (1,000 to 2,000 K), and cool-feeling lighting, such as an overcast day, have the highest light temperature (9,000 to 10,000 K). In any lighting situation, our eyes can always recognize whether an object is white, but digital cameras do not have this interpretation, so improper white balance setting will create unwanted blue or orange casts to an image. Simply put, you need to tell your camera what is white so it has a reference point for it. For any photographic situation, including stop-motion photography, custom white balance is typically set by placing a white card in front of your entire frame and allowing the camera to set the white balance to the color temperature of your lighting situation. Most cameras will also have preset white balance settings for certain lighting scenarios, such as tungsten, daylight, overcast, and fluorescent.

In terms of how this relates to stop-motion, in most situations you would not be shooting outdoors, so higher color temperatures would rarely be taken into account. In most cases you are shooting indoors on a miniature set using artificial light. Most lights used for stop-motion have a quartz or tungsten filament, which has a color temperature of up to 3,500 K. To achieve a particular mood for your scene, you can play with the white balance to make your shots appear warmer or cooler, if you feel this adds some atmosphere to your film. A standard set shot in tungsten can be made to look warmer by setting the white balance to daylight (about 5,000 K) and giving it a more orange cast (Figure 4.11). For a sad or creepy mood, letting in more light and balancing to a lower tungsten setting can add a darker blue mood to your scene (Figure 4.12). In many cases this may seem like extraneous tweaking to your imagery, but mostly it helps to know how to set the balance properly so that you also know how to control the way your film should *not* look. Adjusting the white balance should ideally be done on set if you are shooting JPEGs only, but if you are shooting in RAW format, you also have the option of changing the white balance in post-production.

Figure 4.11

White balance set for a warm feeling.

Figure 4.12

White balance set for a cooler feeling.

All things considered, there are endless combinations of settings and scenarios for making your stop-motion films look a certain way, and they will always change, depending on an equally endless range of factors. Within whatever means you have, set things up until they look good enough to serve your story.

(Photos for this section shot by James Emler. Monster puppet by Emi Gonzalez, and hamster puppet by Frida Ramirez.)

Camera Effects

Once you have set up your sets, puppets, lights, and camera, the shooting process is relatively straightforward. You take a frame, move the puppet or object, take another frame, and move the puppet or object again. That is essentially what it's all about, but at the same time there are plenty of options for embellishing your shots for a richer cinematic experience. Certain effects can be achieved by your camera right on your stop-motion set, with little to no additional work done in post-production. *Post-production* refers to the process of adding certain elements to your scenes after they have been shot and is typically referred to in the business as simply *post*. When a filmmaker talks about doing something "in post," including "fixing in post," it means that effect or fix will be done later. Fixes in post can include attempts to line up frames where the camera was accidentally bumped, for instance, or where there were fluctuations in the lighting. Today's digital tools give us more options for fixing and adding effects in post, but all the same, it's a good idea to avoid using this as a crutch too much. Ideally, you want to shoot your stop-motion properly enough that very little post-production work is needed to fix mistakes. Effects are another story; there is a great deal of artistic and technical freedom allowed today that not only enhances the film itself, but also creates ease in production. (More detail on post-production effects is provided in Chapter 9, "Visual Effects.") The decision of whether to create an effect in post or in camera during production will often depend on several factors—anything from artistic reasons to technical or budgetary restrictions. Most importantly, how you shoot your film and what kinds of effects you create are all determined by your story. Changes in focus, lighting, composition, or movement by the camera should happen because the story dictates them, not because of the technical "wow" factor behind it. The filmmaking, in essence, should become transparent so that your audience becomes involved in the story and the characters.

Rack Focus

A particular composition often seen in live-action films or still photography is when there is a foreground subject close to the camera and another subject in the background or middle ground of a shot. This composition is often used for over-the-shoulder shots between two characters having a conversation, for example. If there is a considerable distance between these foreground and background subjects, and the camera is focused on the subject in the background, the subject in the foreground will be out of focus. Alternatively, if the foreground subject is close enough to the camera lens to be focused on, if the focus is on that subject, the background will be out of focus. If the focus between these two subjects shifts visibly in the middle of a shot, this is referred to as a *rack focus* shot. Aesthetically, a rack focus is used purposely to draw the audience's attention from one subject to another within the same shot. In a live-action film, the rack focus is typically done by a camera assistant called a focus puller, who physically moves the focus dial on the lens while the cinematographer looks through the viewfinder. Since the focus puller cannot see what the final shot looks like, the start and end points of the rack focus must be determined in advance so that he can simply move it based on the numbers on the focus dial.

In stop-motion, a rack focus must obviously be done frame by frame, so often it will be the animators themselves who do this, along with animating their subjects. The same principle applies of knowing where the start and end points are on the focus dial and moving them incrementally between frames. For stop-motion, of course, it is important to avoid touching the camera itself because this can create unwanted bumps and jitters in the shot when played back at speed. On big-budget stop-motion productions, shifts in focus are often programmed by a motion-control system, where a computer programs the start-end points of the focus and moves them infinitesimally between each frame, along with all other camera moves. Before motion control was an option, or even today for those who cannot afford a motion-control system, a rack focus can only be achieved by touching the lens. This is still possible without touching the camera, but it must be done very carefully. According to stop-motion director of photography Pete Kozachik (full interview in Chapter 5, "Interview with Pete Kozachik, ASC"):

> [A] solution that many people employ is to attach a stick (such as a chop stick) to the lens with hot glue. This provides a more accurate lever arm with more control and doubles as a pointer to line up with calibrated marks on cardboard or tape around the lens. Another thing that helps is to include a slight preload from a rubber band so the lens can't flop around, and it helps to move in one direction only.

This functionality of hand-animating a rack focus has been taken a step further by Brett Foxwell, a mechanical engineer, machinist, and stop-motion animator originally from Chicago. Brett devised a special focus-pulling mechanism (Figures 4.13 and 4.14) that he describes here:

> For the rack focus, I attach a stiff metal strip sticking radially out from the camera's focus ring. Then a lead screw or a micrometer is mounted in a position such that its travel pushes the metal strip and turns the focus ring. The lead screw has a ball attached to the tip, and a spring pulls the strip onto the ball.

The lead screw typically has an inch of travel for the typical rack focus shot. The rig is attached to the camera base, so a firm mounting and a very light touch on the lead screw helps. The focus ring is still a problematic aspect and is likely to be bumped during the animation, so I have had to restart some shots or just live with a slight shift midway through the shot. Higher-quality lenses have sturdier focus rings, and the tension spring helps with this problem.

Figure 4.13

Focus puller designed by Brett Foxwell. (© Brett Foxwell.)

Figure 4.14

Focus puller on set with a different arrangement for the short film *Fabricated*. (© Brett Foxwell.)

Figure 4.15 shows a series of frames that display the stages of a rack focus shot from Brett's independent stop-motion short film *Fabricated*, a creation myth of the life-forms present on Earth after the age of man. His film is still in progress and has been in production for about six years.

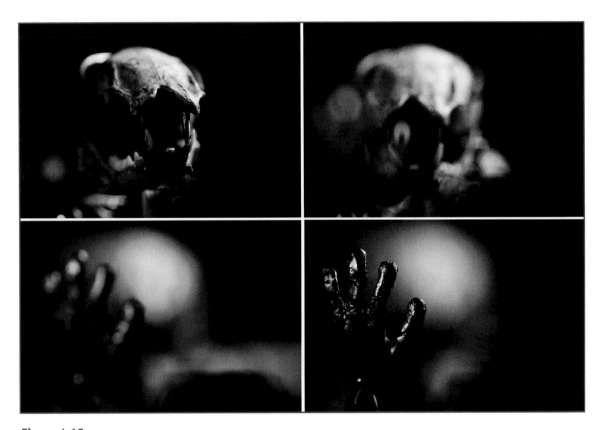

Figure 4.15

A rack focus shot from *Fabricated*. (© Brett Foxwell. Website: http://sites.google.com/site/bfophoto)

Blurring Effects

If a subject you are shooting with a stationary camera moves while the shutter opens to take the picture, the result will be a blurred image of that subject. You may have seen this happen when taking pictures at a party or any other situation. For instance, your friend was talking when you took the picture or spun around quickly without realizing you were snapping the frame, and the result is that his head is all blurry. This is one example of unwanted motion blur in a picture, but in other cases there are aesthetic choices for deliberately using the technique. You may have seen images of cars zooming down a highway at night and becoming long streaks of light caused by the headlights moving across the frame. This is caused by the light moving in a consistent direction while the shutter is open for a longer shutter speed, typically a full second or more. A long shutter speed is typically the key to making this happen, and it's important to remember to combine this with a low f-stop, since light is entering the lens for a longer period of time. The effect is to artistically achieve a feeling of motion within one static image.

For *Fabricated*, Brett Foxwell employed an artistic application of motion blur for a certain scene. For the effect of a surreal flame that is encountered by his puppet character, a pleated copper sheet was mounted on a motor shaft spinning along its vertical axis. The motor would be turned on to spin in front of the camera shooting a 1-second exposure, which made the sheet appear blurry, while the puppet was static and stayed in focus (Figure 4.16). Between frames, Brett progressively cut the sheet apart and tacked on curved pieces of brass foil, continually bending and twisting them to create additional movement (Figure 4.17).

Figure 4.16
A motion-blur effects shot from *Fabricated*. (© Brett Foxwell.)

Figure 4.17

Another motion-blur effects shot from *Fabricated*. (© Brett Foxwell.)

Motion blur can also be added to a puppet character or object that is meant to be moving very quickly across the screen or as a method of making the animation appear smoother. If the individual frames from the animation are blurred, the shot has the potential for a closer resemblance to live-action photography, which will typically have blurred action if any motion being filmed is faster than the camera's shutter. One simple method for achieving a blur effect on set is to place a sheet of glass onto the camera lens or directly in front of it and then use Vaseline to smudge the place where the puppet is. K-Y can also be used since it is water based and easier to wipe off the glass. The smudging would need to be removed and re-applied for each frame as it follows the motion of the object. Using this method means your puppet or object still needs to be static, but the illusion of an unfocused blur is created by the glass effect. The alternative is to find a way to actually move the puppet while each frame is being taken. People have achieved this in various ways. Attaching invisible strings to the puppet and yanking on them while capturing is one method. Finding a way to vibrate the set is another. Whichever method is used, the trick to effective motion blur is finding a way for the blurring action itself to follow the path of action in which the puppet or object is moving. If an object is moving diagonally from left to right, for instance, the direction of the blur should appear to be trailing behind in that particular direction. Applying motion blur to a puppet can also be done through various post-production methods, which are covered in Chapter 9, "Visual Effects."

Camera Moves

Depending on the film project you are creating and the kinds of shots required, you may want to create shots with camera moves like trucking/tracking shots, pans, tilts, and any other variety of motion. For subtle camera moves across one shot, digital pans or zooms can also be created in post-production through After Effects or other programs. Pans done in post will change the framing of your shot, but the perspective of the shot will not change. You are simply shooting a wider composition of your shot and moving the dimensions of your screen around within that composition. With a zoom, you are doing the same thing. For this effect, be aware that there may be a change in resolution quality when you zoom into your frame. When planning ahead for camera moves in post, this might give you reason to shoot your images in RAW format so that you reduce the amount of image quality loss.

In a shot where the actual camera is moved around the set, the perspective will change throughout the shot, which gives a different cinematic effect. To accomplish this effect, your camera needs to be mounted on some kind of rig that can also be moved frame by frame, along with whatever you are animating. Usually the camera itself will be mounted on a base that can be moved forward and backward or left to right. If you want the option of tilting the camera up or down, the base itself can be a geared tripod head with incremental-motion dials on it. As usual, you generally don't want to touch the camera itself but rather only move the track it's attached to. It also helps to have a ruler or some kind of marking system for registering each tiny move you make to the track. Even a long strip of tape with marks drawn on it will work just fine; there should be a point on the base where the camera is attached to line up with each mark. Your camera move can be planned beforehand, especially if you are using an exposure sheet and know exactly how many frames long your shot is. You can plan where the camera move starts and when it ends and also plan out a slow-out and slow-in. Some software programs now have a special calculator that will help you plan out how much to move your camera over any number of frames.

Camera rigs can be very simple or more complex, depending on your skill level, building tools available, and what kind of shots you ultimately want to create. You want to think about the camera moves that are needed to tell your story or achieve a certain effect, not just move the camera for the sake of moving it. One instance where you might want the option for a camera move would be a scene where a puppet character is walking through a tunnel or hallway, and you want the camera to follow him. This action was called for in the script for Brett Foxwell's *Fabricated*, so he set up his camera rig to do this, with the camera suspended from above (Figure 4.18). Having the camera rigged from above allowed for it to move through instances where the floor is visible through most of the scene. The rig can also be interchangeably assembled to have the camera supported from below.

Figure 4.18

Camera motion rig designed by Brett Foxwell. (© Brett Foxwell.)

Brett describes the construction of his rig here:

> The camera support bracket is constructed out of 1-inch by 0.5-inch aluminum bar stock. I machined several different lengths and drilled many through holes and threaded holes at 0.5-inch intervals. The camera sits on a 0.25-inch aluminum plate Swiss-cheesed with holes. The result is a somewhat modular system that can accommodate many different arrangements and setups. The camera rig is in turn attached to the overall set structure, which is a commercially available aluminum extrusion system called 80/20. This extrusion system is the backbone of the whole setup. The visible set and the camera setup are both attached to the extrusion framework, so everything is integral and quite resistant to jostling. Another important factor with all of the mechanical movements (the focus puller setup, the geared heads, and the dolly track) is to have all of the components biased in the direction they will be moving before you start animating them. When you are returning to the start point, go well past the start point, and then go forward in the intended direction, stopping at the start point.

On a larger set, your camera track can be built to move through the set itself to create a trucking shot that is level with the ground. (Although in terms of scale this would be equivalent to a camera on a tripod trucking through a real set.) This was the approach taken by a former student of mine named Lucas Wareing on his student film *AVA*, made at Emily Carr University of Art + Design in Vancouver. For one particular long trucking shot in the film, the script called for an establishing shot moving through a large set, with a puppet sleeping at the far end and the sun moving across the sky (Figure 4.19).

Figure 4.19

A set from Lucas Wareing's film *AVA*. (Courtesy of Lucas Wareing.)

The camera track itself was relatively simple, just consisting of long, flat pieces of wood (Figure 4.20). Two long, rectangular pieces are glued to a flat base, and the tripod head is affixed to a smaller piece of wood that fits snugly inside and can be slid back and forth. The track was designed with additional pieces that slot together like a puzzle so that as the camera moves forward and reaches the end of the track, more pieces can be added so that the move can continue (Figure 4.21). This also helps conceal the track at the beginning of the shot and is created in steps outside the camera frame. This solution was also used because the shot included the camera tilting upward, which may have been easier to achieve with the camera mounted from below rather than above. The camera was moved forward by hand on the sliding track, and about midway through the shot the camera also began to tilt downward while still moving forward.

Figure 4.20

A wooden camera track. (Courtesy of Lucas Wareing.)

Figure 4.21

Taking the camera track apart. (Courtesy of Lucas Wareing.)

To figure out exactly when the camera tilt should start and get the desired effect, a virtual camera move was programmed beforehand using Final Cut Pro, as explained by director of photography Chayse Irvin:

> Final Cut Pro 7 has the ability to create logarithmic curves over a timeline. Basically what I did was create a sequence that was the same time as the shot. Since we were working on one's and not two's, a 23.98 timeline is perfect. I took a video-generated filter called "color," and I could manipulate the motion settings of that, using the scale function to animate the dolly and rotation function to animate the tilt. I found the beginning and end marks by physically moving and setting the camera where I wanted it to begin and end. That would give me a measurement in distance, as well as a degree in tilt. I made those values my beginning and end in FCP over the 23.98 timeline and duration of the whole shot, then guessed where I wanted it to accelerate or decelerate and applied those "curves" in the FCP motion tab. During animation I would just press the forward key, moving to the next frame. Then I would click on each text slug, and it would give me FCP's calculation of what the next frame's movement was. Then I applied that to what we were working with physically. The movement in the shot was 15 seconds, which equaled 360 frames of animation.

For another animated element in the shot, in the background there was a large plank of wood with a light attached to the end, which was meant to represent the sun moving across the sky (Figure 4.22). A large chart was drawn on a sheet of wood to which the plank was attached and could be moved frame by frame according to the timing marks drawn on the chart. The light itself, although visible to the camera, was not intended to be the actual sun in the

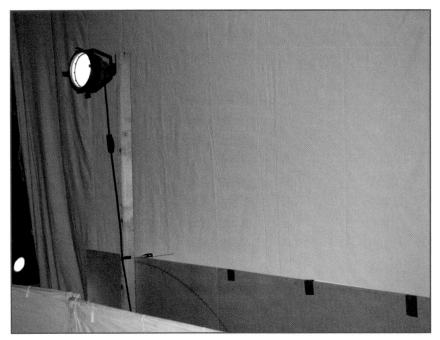

Figure 4.22

Adjustable rig for a moving sun light. (Courtesy of Lucas Wareing.)

film. An illustrated sun would be composited over it in post, so the animation of the sun light was only there as a guide for tracking it. On the set, between the background and the camera, a circular disk on a wire was positioned to line up with the sun in each frame, thereby covering it. The end goal of animating the sun light throughout the shot was simply to give the proper light and shadows moving across the set.

Animator Anthony Scott, animation supervisor for *Corpse Bride* and *Coraline*, designed and built a camera rig of his own (Figure 4.23) for a recent stop-motion music video he worked on, a collaborative project with artist K Ishibashi of the band Jupiter One. Anthony named his rig "the LumberFlex" (which started as a joke, but the name stuck) and designed it for shots that need to get close to the set and move through it. The wooden camera base moves along a track made of two pipes on a long wooden platform, which is hinged in the middle and essentially works like a teeter-totter. It's weighted on the opposite end with about 20 pounds of weights to counter-balance the heavy geared head for the camera as it slides forward, and a bungee cord keeps things from going flying if the camera is removed. Another device, a Model Mover (Figure 4.24), which incrementally pushes the platform upward by turning a wheel at the bottom, was added to the front for boom shots. For some tilt shots, Anthony would move the geared head and also attach a stick and a sheet of foam core to the back of the camera, marking the increments for the tilt motion on the foam core (Figure 4.25). All of the mobility for the LumberFlex, like any camera rig for stop-motion, is designed to be moved in increments frame by frame. The animation of both the camera moves and the objects on set was primarily shot on twos (two frames per movement) for this project, which is surprising because the general rule for camera moves has traditionally been to shoot them on ones (one frame per movement) to avoid a strobing effect. However, on Anthony's previous animation work for the titles to *United States of Tara* (which won the stop-motion team an Emmy), they found that camera moves on twos actually looked better. More information on Anthony and K's new animated music video project is included on the companion CD in Appendix B, "The Stop-Motion Community."

Figure 4.23

The LumberFlex camera rig. (Courtesy of Anthony Scott.)

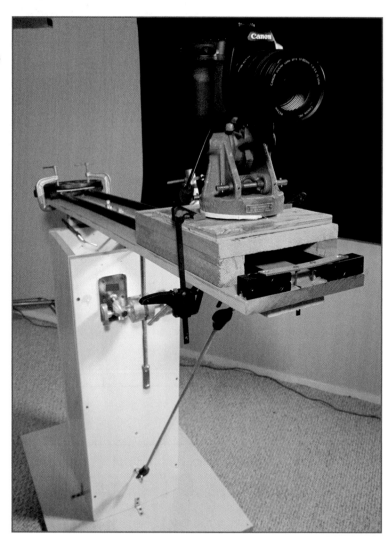

Figure 4.24

Model Mover device for
the LumberFlex. (Courtesy of
Anthony Scott.)

Finally, going from these rather advanced methods and large-scale rigs back to
the very simple, filmmaker Patrick Boivin creates many of his tracking camera
moves simply by attaching his camera to a miniature train track and pushing
it along (Figure 4.26). His short stop-motion films, which have become a big
sensation on YouTube (http://www.youtube.com/user/PatrickBoivin), such as
Bboy Joker and *Iron Man vs. Bruce Lee*, also use a lot of dynamic camera moves that
mimic a handheld quality. Patrick explains how he does this in stop-motion:

> I do a lot on set with a classic photo camera tripod. There is a crank on the side
> that allows me to raise the head gradually. I also work with a digital camera with
> a much higher resolution than what I need at the final, so I can easily crop and
> move inside the image in post-production.

Figure 4.25

Tilt-measuring device for the LumberFlex. (Courtesy of Anthony Scott.)

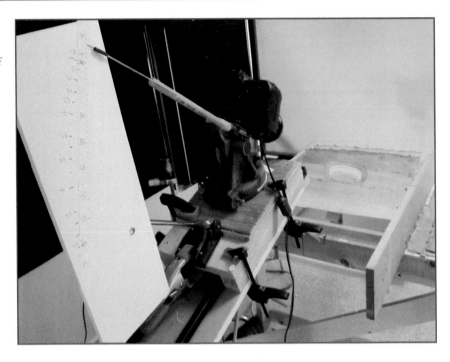

As these various examples show, no matter what tools or resources you have, a little creativity can go a long way when it comes to achieving the effects you want.

Figure 4.26

Patrick Boivin's moving camera rig using a miniature train track. (Courtesy of Patrick Boivin.)

Stereoscopic Photography

One of the biggest emerging technologies in filmmaking today is stereoscopic photography and projection. The term "stereoscopic" is a more technical term for what most people simply know as "3D." The idea of *projecting* movies in 3D is nothing new. It had been experimented with since the beginning of film, but it first became popular in the 1950s. The way it worked was by rigging up two projectors, each running a duplicate print of the same film, synchronized exactly to the same frame. The projectors' images were shown through a polarized filter and lined up in such a way that both images were spaced slightly apart on the screen, creating a small overlap between them. When viewers put on the special 3D glasses (Figure 4.27), they repolarize the overlapping images to create the illusion of depth and actions popping out from the flat screen. The overlapping images were an attempt to mimic the fact that when we are looking at an image, our right and left eyes see the image from a slightly different perspective. (If you stop reading for a moment and look at any object close to you, first close your left eye, and then close your right eye. You will notice that the object shifts a little bit. These are the two views seen by each of your eyes, and your brain puts these images together to recognize the depth of what you see.)

Figure 4.27

3D glasses. (Courtesy of Justin and Shel Rasch.)

3D movies in the 1950s came about mostly as a gimmick to increase declining movie attendance. Once television came along, people moved towards getting their entertainment and news from the comfort of home, rather than going to the movies. Seeing movies in 3D made the theater experience more of an event, something you couldn't get from television. Most of the 3D movies were horror films like *House of Wax* and *Creature from the Black Lagoon*, with cheap thrills and chills to heighten the horrific effect. Because of limited projection technology and audiences complaining of headaches, the trend didn't last very long, so movies went back to being projected normally. 3D movies emerged again for a while in the 1980s, when the availability of cable television and video rentals kept audiences at home rather than in the theaters. Once again, the trend died off until large-screen home theaters (and the practice of downloading movies onto computers and phones) became another threat to the movie-going experience. Today, many films (animated films in particular) are marketed and projected in 3D and 3D IMAX to bring people back to cinemas for a unique experience. Whether this is just another passing gimmick has yet to be seen, but the phenomenal success of James Cameron's *Avatar* and the development of 3D televisions could mean that 3D is here to stay.

For the latest crop of animated films, their theatrical projection may be presented in 3D, but the films themselves are not typically made that way originally. Like the films before them, they are made with one camera and simply reformatted for 3D projection. In 2006, Walt Disney Pictures re-issued *The Nightmare Before Christmas* to theaters in 3D by creating a digital copy of each frame for the overlapping image. The 3D formatting was done by a team of artists and technicians at Industrial Light & Magic, some of whom had worked on the original film. The original puppets were scanned into the computer and the sets re-created in a virtual 3D environment of featureless geometries for each scene of the film. Then each frame of the original film was digitally projected onto the geometry, the camera moved over slightly, and the frame re-photographed. This image would be shown as the right-eye image, while the left-eye image was the original version of the film. Viewing *Nightmare* in 3D in a properly equipped theater allowed for the detail of the hand-crafted sets and puppets to come forward in a way that brought more attention to their actual third dimensions.

Around this same time, production was going forward on *Coraline*, which would take the third dimension to another level of artistry and technology. The main difference was that *Coraline* was actually *shot* in stereoscopic 3D, in addition to being projected in 3D for certain screenings. Shooting in stereoscopic 3D means that instead of having one camera view that takes a flat picture of a three-dimensional scene, there are two images taken from different views of the same scene to mimic the different perspectives of our left and right eyes (Figure 4.28).

Figure 4.28
A view of left-eye and right-eye images taken for the short film *Line*. (Courtesy of Justin and Shel Rasch.)

The distance between our eyes is referred to as *IO* (interocular distance). This same sense of distance is mimicked by stereo photography—the greater the distance is, the greater the sense of three dimensions and depth that will be created. However, having the IO too far apart will also create a ghosting effect, where the double image shows up even with the glasses on, and the focus distracts the eye towards the edges, rather than the illusion of one solid object on screen. Also, if the IO is too great, the effect would be much too intense when projected in 3D, which would cause major headaches for the audience. However, once the comfortable parameters for the IO have been set, since the IO creates the depth to your shot, animating that distance (having the IO incrementally change throughout the shot) will cause your scene to visibly stretch away from the audience.

Putting this principle into context of stop-motion, in terms of how the viewer receives the image that is projected, the distance between our eyes is very slight, not much more than a half-inch or so. The eyes of a typical miniature stop-motion puppet are even closer together, only a few centimeters apart. Therefore, when shooting at miniature scale for stop-motion, taking the two separate images at this very small distance apart from each other is necessary to achieve a stereo effect that our brains can actually handle. On a miniature scale like a stop-motion set, two camera lenses cannot easily get as close together as mere millimeters or centimeters, so the solution is to use one camera on a slider that moves the camera back and forth (Figure 4.29). The animator positions the puppet, the camera takes a left-eye view of it, and the camera slides over slightly to take a right-eye view of the same puppet. The camera then slides back to the left-eye view in preparation for the next image, the animator moves the puppet, and the process repeats, with the camera taking two separate images for each frame of the animation. Stereoscopic films shot on a larger scale may possibly combine two lenses in one camera, but with stop-motion being on a miniature scale, if you want to shoot in stereo, it is better with the slider option.

Figure 4.29

Camera-sliding tripod attachment for stereoscopic photography. (Courtesy of Justin and Shel Rasch.)

Once you set your IO, the other step in figuring out how deep your scene will go in or pop out of the screen has to do with *alignment* of your shot. If you treat the screen as the middle ground of your shot, the trick is to have your left- and right-eye images line up with each other wherever you want the middle ground (also called a *zero plane* or *zero parallax*). In many cases, you may want to focus this middle ground on your puppet character or another object on screen. This way the background will appear to be deep behind the character, and if it stretches out its arm or throws something forward, for instance, this will seem to pop out at the audience.

One way to focus on the photo subject is to shoot your scene with *convergence* on the point where you want the middle ground. This simply means that in addition to the camera sliding back and forth, the camera is angled slightly inward in each side. It would be like two eyes crossing towards each other slightly to focus on one point. The mechanics involved to shoot with convergence are more costly because the slider not only needs to move the camera back and forth, but also turn the camera inward towards the subject. In addition to the technical end of figuring this out, the end results are pretty much configured there on set, with little room for adjusting in post. The other option, favored by most for stop-motion production (including on *Coraline*), is to shoot *parallel*, meaning the camera is simply pointing straight ahead at the set while capturing the left- and right-eye images. Shooting parallel allows you to play around with the alignment in post, creating more freedom of choices for how much stereo you want to create. As far as your camera settings, you can do things however you would on any other set, although keeping a wide depth of field, with everything in focus, will tend to enhance the stereo effect.

When you have left- and right-eye images shot and want to view them in 3D on your computer to test the 3D effect, the simplest method is to create an *anaglyph* image that can be viewed with a pair of red-blue 3D glasses. The two images can be layered over each other in Photoshop, each on its own separate layer. Hide the left-eye layer; then for the right-eye image layer, double-click on the layer in the Layers window to bring up the "Layer Style" window. Under Advanced Blending are three checkboxes for the red, green, and blue channels of your image. Check off the Red box, and you will notice a color shift in the image to a bluish tone (Figures 4.30 and 4.31). Click OK, and when both layers are still visible, you will see a double image and can move

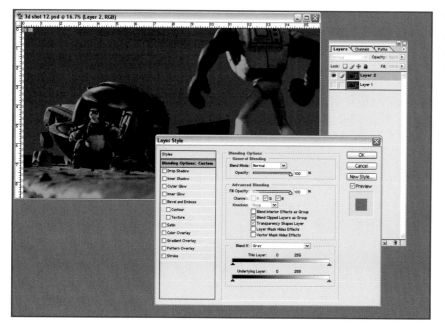

Figure 4.30

Checking off the red channel for preparing an anaglyph image. (Courtesy of Justin and Shel Rasch.)

Figure 4.31

A view of the left- and right-eye images in anaglyph format. (Courtesy of Justin and Shel Rasch.)

the right-eye layer around to find the alignment you want. Viewing this anaglyph image with your red-blue 3D glasses will show it in eye-popping 3D (Figure 4.32)! The same principle of creating an anaglyph image by turning off the red channel can be applied to an entire image sequence in After Effects, along with other options for adjusting the channels for the desired effect.

Figure 4.32

Anaglyph 3D image, which can be viewed through a pair of red-blue 3D glasses. (Courtesy of Justin and Shel Rasch.)

When shooting in stereo, this obviously complicates the workflow of your digital images, since you will have two different versions of each frame of animation you capture. For this reason, it's a good idea to have some kind of a system for storing these images in two separate folders, ideally while you are shooting. It's possible to shoot all your images in a row and sort through them later, selecting every other frame and copying them en masse to separate folders. However, if your software allows for automatically separating the left- and right-eye images, that might make things easier.

Independent stop-motion filmmakers Justin and Shel Rasch (Figures 4.33 and 4.34) have recently been working on a stereoscopic short film called *Line* in a studio they have set up in their garage, with the help of some consultants in the stereoscopic field. Here they reiterate the principles of stereoscopic production by describing their shooting process in detail:

> Basically we have a tripod with a little motion-control device, with incremental numbers we can type in for how far to move the camera left or right. Then there is a little button where we press positive or press negative, for the right eye or the left eye. In the Dragon software we're using, we take a shot and then the software has an Exposure 2 layer for a second set of exposures into a different directory. We hit the button for the right eye, and the camera moves over, takes a shot, and moves back to the left. We have to remember we've done this for every frame.

> It's all a distance thing, based on how far your character is from the camera, and how 3D you want it to look off the screen is the distance of how far you put your camera movement, either left or right. We've been experimenting with it in After Effects to see what it looks like. You can also choose where you want the middle ground to be, so basically you decide which part of your scene you want to be screen depth, and everything in front of that will come off the screen. Also, in terms of what you want to be behind the background and what you want in the middle, you can choose that for each shot.

> When you have the two images and you put them on top of each other in After Effects, you can find the point in your animation (where, for example, the character is coming forward) where everything lines up perfectly with your character so there's no double image. That's called the zero plane, and you'll see a double image in the background and foreground, which are the parts popping off the screen. You can choose how close to the camera you want that zero plane to be, and all the 3D is based off that.

(For more about Justin and Shel's lives and work, see the full interview with them in Chapter 13, "An Interview with Justin and Shel Rasch." Also check out the files Justin Rasch_3D.mov and Justin Rasch_3D_2.mov on the accompanying CD with a pair of red-blue 3D glasses on!)

Figure 4.33

Justin Rasch animating on set. (Courtesy of Justin and Shel Rasch.)

Figure 4.34

Shel Rasch views their work in 3D. (Courtesy of Justin and Shel Rasch.)

Whether shooting in stereo or not, I hope this chapter has helped you understand some basic things about how to set up for shooting stop-motion effectively. All things considered, once you know the basic fundamentals for your camera functions, you are free to be creative and play. When applying this creativity to a short film, though, make sure the effects and settings you experiment with serve your story first and foremost. Knowing how to use the technology to enhance the art and become part of the storytelling process should be your ultimate goal so that you can bring your audience through the story along with you.

5

An Interview with
Pete Kozachik, ASC

Figure 5.1

Pete Kozachik poses on the Land of the Dead set from *Corpse Bride*. (Photo by Simon Jacobs/ © Warner Brothers Pictures.)

Pete Kozachik (Figure 5.1) has worked in the film industry for over 30 years as an animator, visual effects artist, and cinematographer. He was the director of photography and visual effects supervisor on *The Nightmare Before Christmas, James and the Giant Peach, Corpse Bride,* and *Coraline.* On the latter two films, he was instrumental in adapting the technology behind the first uses of digital SLR cameras and stereoscopic photography for stop-motion. He also grew up in Michigan, like me, so for this reason and so much more, I'm glad to have his contribution to this book.

KEN: *Can you tell me about your background and how you got started in stop-motion?*

PETE: As a kid I had seen both *King Kong* and *Seventh Voyage of Sinbad* within a few weeks of each other, and they got completely seared into my cerebrum (or wherever those things get seared). It wasn't clear to me at the time what I was looking at, but it affected me so much. I remember sitting with my mom in the theater at age 7, watching *Sinbad*, and out of concern that it might have been too scary for me, she leaned over and suggested the creatures on screen might have been giant robots. So for the next few years I had it in my mind that the U.S. government had a secret fleet of giant robots with rubber suits on and let Hollywood use them.

Then at some point I saw a photograph of Ray Harryhausen posing next to his Cyclops and Dragon puppets, and it all became clear. I realized those figures weren't as big as I thought they were, so it was something I felt I could do. There wasn't any information out there about how Ray's films were made, but I managed to experiment enough to start making my own stop-motion films. By the time I was in high school, we had moved to Tucson, Arizona, and I showed some of my films around town. This got me some jobs working at various TV stations, mostly shooting and working with some industrial filmmakers. After graduation from University of Arizona, I put my name out as an animator, picked up a few years of work on commercials and industrial films, made a reel, and then headed to Hollywood in the late '70s.

I got lucky enough to start working for Gene Warren and later with Phil Kellison, both having backgrounds in stop-motion. Phil was a director at Coast Special Effects and became one of my early mentors in the craft. I ended up working there for several years, and it was such a valuable learning experience. I had it in mind to watch the animators work, but stop-motion animators are actually not that interesting to watch, because they move very slowly, and it's all just going on in their heads. But I remember one of my first nights there, cleaning up after someone's shoot, and opening up a drawer with a row of Pillsbury Dough Boy heads. I was so totally transfixed by that, because these heads seemed too precious to even look at, and I've never really lost that fascination.

KEN: *What kinds of projects did you work on there?*

PETE: Coast Effects made most of their money on commercials, but they would also bring in low-budget features to keep Phil Kellison happy, since he liked to work on those. We would use stop-motion whenever we could, even if it was just a spaceship, or whatever. It was a small part of a larger company, consisting of only a dozen or so of us, so we all did a little bit of everything. If a star animator like Laine Liska was too busy, sometimes I would animate something, and they would just tell the client that Laine did it. At one point I had brought a motorized spaceship prop I built to the set, and the cinematographer suggested that since I had built it, I should shoot it. This led to me transitioning from animation to more work in camera, motion control, and photography. After a few years at Coast, I answered an ad for a cameraman at Industrial Light & Magic (ILM) and moved up to the Bay Area to work on feature films.

KEN: *How did you end up getting involved with* The Nightmare Before Christmas?

PETE: I had worked with Phil Tippett on *Willow* while at ILM and ended up working for him exclusively at his own studio for the last two *Robocop* films. I essentially brought motion control to Tippett Studio and spent some serious time there, at a point when they were starting to gain more momentum. Phil Tippet's studio worked organically, a lot like Coast. That's not too surprising, as he was an earlier alum from Coast. Henry Selick had been renting space there for his short film *Slow Bob in the Lower Dimensions*, which we shot as a pilot for MTV. Around that time, Tim Burton asked Henry to direct *Nightmare* and, based on the strength of *Slow Bob*, approved the idea of bringing me on as director of photography.

At exactly the same time across the studio, Phil Tippett was gearing up to shoot stop-mo dinosaurs on *Jurassic Park*. He made a tempting case for me to work on JP, doing this really cool stuff with dinosaurs, and I said "yeah I know, but Henry's got this thing going where it's not just effects, it's a whole movie." So we went back and forth on it, but I ended up going with *Nightmare* because I felt it was a great opportunity to tell an entire story with stop-motion, which I had never done before. It is a major commitment to jump onto a show like that, because you are basically throwing about 3% of your life into it, so it had better be good. It becomes a much bigger part of your life than making shots for a single sequence.

KEN: *On a stop-motion film, how is the decision typically made whether to do effects practically on set or in camera, versus doing it later in post-production?*

PETE: I'd like to say it comes down to personal taste. When Henry Selick and I work together, the personal taste would usually be to do as many effects in camera as possible, but there are practicalities to consider, too. Back when we were shooting on film, there was no such thing as digital compositing; you got better quality if you did everything in camera, but that doesn't really hold water anymore. Composites used to be hugely expensive, and now they're not. It used to be worth risking a reshoot as opposed to having a grainy film composite, or an "optical," as it was called then. On a film like Stanley Kubrick's *2001: A Space Odyssey*, shots would be done in camera and spending months of laying images onto the same negative.

These days there is a lot more green-screen shooting going on, which I think is good, because then the animators can focus exclusively on their performance, rather than all the steps of multiple passes through the camera. Directors have a lot more freedom now, too, so rather than being told that elements have to be shot with all sorts of restrictions, they can call for more ambitious shot designs, and darn near anything can be lined up digitally into a seamless composite.

On *Nightmare*, we did our best to get a lot of effects in camera, so we used a lot of front and rear projection directly on set, in order to add real flames to the torches and things like that. My personal take is that stop-motion should have some degree of real-world physics in it. Elements like water splashes, smoke, and fire are from the same world that the puppets are, and I feel it can be a richer experience for the audience using elements that are shot in real life. I also still respect films that go with the cute approach of using cotton or stylized cartoon animation for smoke, and we've done a few things like that in our films, too. I remember enjoying that kind of approach as a kid, watching things like *Gumby*.

KEN: *Is there any particular shot you've worked on that stands out, in terms of capturing the magic of stop-motion with brilliant effects work?*

PETE: There is a sequence with the *Corpse Bride,* starting with her coming out of the ground, all the way to when she and Victor are on the bridge surrounded by a flock of crows. There are a lot of shots in that sequence with complex composites (comps) in them, and some of the most painstaking animation ever done, in particular on her clothing. There were a couple of shots where we had to throw in the towel and use computer animation on her veil. It was still supposed to look like stop-motion, and luckily the animators pulled it off (Figure 5.2). Some of the shots don't even look like they needed post work to begin with, but in some instances we had to add extra background just because we couldn't practically fit it into the stage. Overall I love everything about that sequence, and when I signed on to the movie, that scene was the one I was thinking about. I was envisioning an image that might have been in old horror comics, part spooky, part sexy, pretty much everything that parents didn't want us to spend our allowance on.

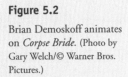

Figure 5.2

Brian Demoskoff animates on *Corpse Bride*. (Photo by Gary Welch/© Warner Bros. Pictures.)

KEN: *What were the challenges you faced using digital SLR cameras for the first time on* Corpse Bride?

PETE: I think the biggest challenge was taking this new technology that wasn't really designed for that purpose and very quickly adapting it to professional work. We had challenges with everything, even including stringing the images together and looking at them.

There are all kinds of agreed-on standards to the century-old film technology, including how sensitive it is, in terms of its ISO rating. We got into a pickle early on in *Corpse Bride*, shooting test images with these cameras. When we viewed the images on stage in Photoshop, it would show us a better image than what we were capturing. So unbeknownst to us, for several shots in the movie, we were drastically underexposing them and had to ask the visual effects crew to tweak them into usable shots. To establish a safe standard, we had to pretend we were shooting on relatively slow film and not plan on enhancing it in post. This made it feel like we were going backwards, but ultimately it made life a whole lot sweeter in the color grade, since the shots did cut together without much tweaking.

Another problem was dust falling on the unprotected image sensor, which wouldn't be there when we started, but each time the mirror flipped, chances were that some dust mote would get in there to drift down on the sensor.

So there were minor issues like that, but on the other hand, the SLRs allowed for things that were unheard of back when we used those 30-pound Mitchell cameras. With those, you really had to consider how much the camera weighed, how you were going to support it, and how the animator would get his head around it. Suddenly, when the cameras were tiny, we were more on par with what live-action could do (Figure 5.3). If live-action film had to mimic how stop-motion used to be shot, the camera would be the size of a Volkswagen.

KEN: *So what kinds of things should a stop-motion filmmaker shooting with his own SLR camera keep in mind or watch out for?*

PETE: There are a few things which now seem rather obvious. First of all, turn off everything that is automatic: iris, exposure, focus, ISO, white balance, everything, and dumb the camera down to the point where you are manually in control. But much more important than the technical stuff, is that people seem to be losing time waiting for the ultimate perfect camera to show up, and it hasn't happened yet. The closest thing right now is probably the Canon 5D, which will be valuable for a few years until something better comes along. There is a lot of hot air wasted on the minutia of how much better photography can get, or how much more resolution you need. As filmmakers, we should help the audience focus on the story, the drama, and the characters. That's what they buy tickets for. If you're only sitting there admiring the image sharpness, then somebody didn't do their job. So my most heartfelt advice is simply to get off the Internet and start shooting with what you've got.

Figure 5.3

Pete Kozachik goes over a motion-control shot with Caroline Wilson on *Corpse Bride*. (Photo by Graham Pettit/ © Warner Bros. Pictures.)

KEN: *What would you say are the differences and similarities between shooting for live-action and shooting for stop-motion?*

PETE: The thing we have been trying to do, with all of the crews I have worked with, is to emulate the same film language and techniques as are used in live-action. Most of the time it can be done, in terms of lighting, composition, lens choices, color, contrast, camera movement, and things like that.

On *Nightmare* we were first experimenting with camera techniques that were fairly well accepted in the live-action world. As we experimented, we often wondered if it was going to end up being a bad fit. As an example, the character of Sally (with no disrespect to the puppet builders) is essentially a crude representation of a woman. There are visible signs like seams, brushstrokes, or other imperfections that make it obvious to the audience she is only a few inches tall. So the question became, can we take this puppet and give it the 1930s/40s glamour treatment with the lighting and camera, or will it just look ridiculous and ghoulish? Well, to our surprise, it worked! Through using diffusion filters and other techniques, there were many shots in the film where we treated Sally the same way we would have treated the romantic leads in Hollywood's golden age.

The differences between live-action and stop-motion lie in the disciplines you have to apply to setting up a shot. In live-action it can be OK to rig setups somewhat precariously, with the understanding that they only need to last as long as the take, so there is a certain amount of serendipity involved. In stop-motion, you need to consider the long haul when setting up a shot. The demands are greater these days, and nobody finishes a shot in one day anymore. A shot may take several days or even weeks, so there can't be any opportunity for things to slowly change over the passage of time, like a light bulb slowly getting dimmer, a set warping from the humidity, or a camera slowly losing its position. It's the same with light leaks. Back when we shot on film, even if we had a good camera (and usually we didn't), it was wise to bag the whole camera so that some little unseen crack didn't slowly leak in light and fog each frame.

The other thing to think about is access for the animator. They will be walking back and forth several hundred times during a shot, so you don't want to have too many c-stands or cables getting in their way. Chances are, if there's an obstacle, they will step on it or bump it, and it's really hard to get things back to where they were. A lot of visual effects work in stop-motion has to deal with getting elements into a shot that couldn't be there while the animator was at work. When possible, devices like trap doors or walls that can be pulled apart and back together between frames can be designed into the set instead.

Another unique element of stop-motion is that in order to get shots out in a timely manner, we need multiple crews. On *Coraline* I had about 30 people who were broken down into about eight or nine different units. They were primarily cameramen, electricians, and assistants, plus some tech support people, so there is a lot of parallel processing going on. We had about 40 sets all going at the same time, simply because we had to. You couldn't live long enough to finish that show with just one crew.

So it's also really important that every single crew person goes to dailies, not just the lead crew members. Everyone needs to see what others are doing, so the shots cut together properly. Part of my job as DP was to make sure communication was indeed happening between sets, because it takes effort to walk 200 feet through a maze of sets to check out a set on the other side of the building. There were some electronic aids there, used for sending still frames to other people's computers, but direct communication is still vital.

KEN: *What are your thoughts on the future potential for this new stereoscopic technology that was used on* Coraline, *and 3D movies in general?*

PETE: I'd like to see 3D used in the same way that music, color, and sound have always been used in film. It needs to get to the point (and I think we are getting close now) where it is no longer the main reason for going to the show. I can remember back to the point where almost half of the movies I went to as a kid were black-and-white, and we would sometimes choose which movie to see based on whether or not it was in color. That's ridiculous, of course, and I would say the same for 3D. But there is room for everybody, and hopefully we will also start to see films where everyone agrees that 3D won't add much to it. Then we can spend our resources on more time on set, better filmmaking, and things like that. 3D is a great technique, and I'm glad that *Coraline* was made that way, as it makes it more fun to watch. But I've talked to people who didn't see it in 3D, and they liked it, too.

KEN: *What are your thoughts on the future potential of stop-motion as an art form?*

PETE: Stop-motion has done a lot in the near century it's been in use, mostly on the fringe. It started as a visual effect technique, and then it got blown away in 1993 with *Jurassic Park*. All the same, I would still love to see or work on a classic Harryhausen-style monster movie in stop-motion, so we'll see what happens. Stop-motion's best future is most likely in the niche it's forming into now, which is stylized imagery that has something different going on than CG animation. Luckily, most people know what they're looking at now, thanks to MTV and the glut of media and information we now have. Because of that, stop motion can be appreciated for itself.

6

An Interview with
Trey Thomas

Figure 6.1

Trey Thomas animates on *Corpse Bride*. (Photo by Brian Demoskoff/Characters © Warner Bros. Pictures.)

Trey Thomas (Figure 6.1) is one of the current generation of professional animators who got their start during the animation boom of the late 1980s and early 1990s. Since then, he has been a stop-motion animator on *The Nightmare Before Christmas, James and the Giant Peach, Monkeybone,* and *Corpse Bride*; the lead animator on *Coraline*; and a CG supervising animator on Walt Disney Feature Animation's *Dinosaur* and DreamWorks SKG' *Shrek 2* and *Madagascar*. I'm very glad to have Trey's thoughts on the process of feature animation as part of this book.

195

KEN: *Can you tell us about your background and how you got started in stop-motion animation?*

TREY: It was always an interest of mine, sort of the classic story of being a Ray Harryhausen fan when I was a kid. I always liked animation and special effects in general, but when I was a youngster, I wanted to get into gore effects and make-up, like Tom Savini–type stuff. When I was in high school, I was focused on making zombie movies. I grew up in Washington, D.C./northern Virginia and went to art school in Richmond, Virginia, for a couple years. I took film courses, which introduced me to animation. I applied to film schools in California and ended up attending the film program at Brooks Institute of Photography. Unfortunately, it didn't have any animation instruction, so I just did my live-action assignments in stop-motion. I didn't really know how stop-motion was done, so what I ended up producing was pretty crummy looking. But after I graduated, it was enough to get me a job on *The New Adventures of Gumby*, and that's where I learned the basics of animation. So I never really took an animation class in my life, but I picked it up by not taking "no" for an answer, begging for jobs, and stuff like that.

KEN: *Then how did your early work on* Gumby *lead into working in features?*

TREY: There was a period of about three or four years in-between there where I worked on several seasons of Pillsbury Doughboy commercials. I also worked on a couple of pilots for series by Dave Bleiman and Ken Pontac, who were producer/directors on *Gumby* and had some other projects they were trying to start. There were a few bits and pieces of work I was picking up from Colossal Pictures in San Francisco, where I eked out a living until Henry Selick brought me onto his film *Slow Bob in the Lower Dimensions*. Shortly after that, Henry got the green light for *The Nightmare Before Christmas*, and all my dreams came true right there. It was such an honor and privilege to work on *Nightmare* since I loved Tim Burton's work and really enjoyed working with Henry. When I started in stop-motion, there was no such thing as a stop-motion feature, so I never thought I'd be able to make a living at it. I thought it would just be more of a hobby in my garage or something. But to be on a film like *Nightmare* was just mind blowing. It was being in the right place at the right time.

KEN: *I can imagine that working on* Nightmare *would have been a major high point.*

TREY: It was an absolute high point because it was the first feature I had worked on and because it was what it was—a dark Tim Burton movie with Danny Elfman music and directed by Henry. It was more than I could have asked for. I haven't felt that kind of pride in my work (again) until *Coraline*. After *Nightmare* and *James*, stop-motion just kind of dried up, so I went to Disney to learn the computer and ended up being in CG for the next eight years. When I heard Tim was doing *Corpse Bride*, I started making plans to try and get on it. As soon as my contract with DreamWorks ended, the very next day I was on a plane to London to work on the last six months of production. After that, I hung out in London until I was ready to head out to Portland for *Coraline*.

KEN: *Was that your first time in London?*

TREY: I had been to Manchester once before, to visit Paul Berry, shortly before he passed away.

KEN: *I know there are many people, including myself, who admire the work of Paul Berry* (The Sandman, Nightmare, James and the Giant Peach). *What can you tell me about him?*

TREY: He first came onto the *Nightmare* crew about halfway through production. Before that, it was mainly the small group of us who had started on *Gumby* and gone through the commercial jobs at Colossal, etc. It seemed like we had reached a bit of a plateau in the quality of the animation, and then Paul Berry showed up with *The Sandman* and an Academy Award nomination. I think we, as a group, loved *The Sandman* and found Paul's passion and expertise maybe a little intimidating. He came in and raised the bar, and I think the crew responded. I think everyone took the challenge and ended up doing the best animation of our careers. He was very unique, with his weird, bright red hairdo and his pillbox cap that he wore every day. He was a brilliant, crazy, and truly inspired animator. We were good friends, and I really miss him.

KEN: *Since most animators typically have a personal style of approaching their work, how are scenes assigned to specific animators throughout the production?*

TREY: Animator casting is really important in stop-motion feature animation. You get the most out of your crew if you play to their strengths. You find where people excel, and you keep them there. But the reality of production doesn't always allow for casting to take priority. I mean, *Coraline* was pretty crazy, with 50 stages and 30-something animators, but *Nightmare* was about half that, more like 20 stages and 15 animators. So it was quite easy to give everybody a chunk of the movie, and that has a much better flow. Of course, it depends on the sequence, too. If you have a montage sequence, there can be a montage of animators. But when it's two characters interacting, it's nice to keep those people in that one moment so they can keep the speed, rhythm, and emotional place of the sequence. As soon as you switch sequences, it switches the pace, mood, and rhythm. So, in my opinion, smaller productions are generally more successful stylistically. But then again, *Coraline* came out pretty great, so what the hell do I know?

Figure 6.2

Concept art for Sally from *The Nightmare Before Christmas.* (Courtesy of the Animazing Gallery/Touchstone Pictures.)

Figure 6.3

Concept art for *The Nightmare Before Christmas.* (Courtesy of the Animazing Gallery/Touchstone Pictures.)

KEN: *What kinds of scenes do you like to animate or typically get assigned to animate on a production?*

TREY: In the past, I've typically landed scenes with female lead characters. I kind of fell into it; it wasn't by design at all. On *Nightmare*, I had been given a bunch of Sally shots and did well at it, so they said, "OK, he's a Sally guy." So I got locked into lots of the Sally animation and loved it (Figure 6.2). I had a few of the girls on the stage doing video reference for me, and it was great. On *James*, I focused on animating the centipede, who was more of a tough New Yorker type, but then got back into the female lead characters on *Dinosaur* and then the Other Mother scenes on *Coraline*. I did some *Corpse Bride* shots, including a lot of Bonejangles, but I came in late on *Corpse Bride*, so I don't claim ownership of any of those characters. I was there to just help them wrap up the production.

KEN: *Another scene in* Nightmare *(Figure 6.3) I was told that you had animated is one of my favorites—when the Harlequin Demon sings "Won't they be impressed? I am a genius!" and makes a hat out of a dead rat.*

TREY: That was my very last shot on the film, and it was a nice 30-second epic to go out on. My cameraman Brian Van't Hul (who was also visual effects supervisor on *Coraline* and worked at WETA for many years—very brilliant guy) cracked open a bottle of champagne at eight in the morning after it was completed. It was such a beautiful way to end such an amazing experience which I felt had gotten me into peak form. I lucked out on that shot because I was totally flying on adrenalin at that point.

KEN: *It's amazing hearing you say that, when you consider what's happening in the shot itself acting-wise. It seems you really put a lot of yourself and how you felt about the show into that shot.*

TREY: Absolutely! Plus I was really flying blind at that point. I mean, after a year and a half of production, you're pretty much running on vapors, but my confidence level was high. It was an incredibly cool shot, and they gave it to me because they believed I could pull it off. When I finished it, I was really proud of it, although I look back at it now and all I see are the flaws. But several people have singled out that shot as being particularly good. It's weird—it seems like five lifetimes ago.

KEN: *From the angle of an actor breathing a performance into a puppet, how do you prepare yourself for a shot, in terms of the posing, timing, and overall acting decisions?*

TREY: Well, first I listen to what the director is looking for and to the quality of the voice recording. Second, I make a plan. Although sometimes you just have to wing it, that's not ideal. It's always best to know what you're going to do and how/when you're going to do it. You can act out the shot, or you can use a stopwatch to refine your timings. Some animators like to videotape themselves or others acting out the shot, and often some unexpected stuff happens that can enhance the believability of the performance. In feature production, we have the luxury of being able to rehearse shots, and generally that allows you to anticipate problems, gives you the opportunity to work out the performance, and gives the director a clear idea of what you plan to do. Then, do it with confidence, since you only get one shot at it—be bold and sell it.

KEN: *Were there any major differences in production among the various films you've worked on, particularly with* Corpse Bride *being done in the U.K.?*

TREY: The puppet style for *Corpse Bride* was different because MacKinnon & Saunders went out on a limb to make those really impressive mechanical heads, so it had a very different look compared to the others. In the U.K., there is a long tradition of stop-motion that we don't have here in the U.S., where it's a little bit harder to sell. But there were no significant differences in production style—it was an American production in London. Several of the same key people who were on *Nightmare* and *James* were on *Corpse*. I love London, and I love Tim Burton's aesthetic. I do tend do gravitate towards the dark stuff since I grew up loving horror movies. Each film I've worked on was cut from a different cloth, particularly when you consider the CG films at Disney and DreamWorks compared to Tim's and Henry's more left-field art films. I first got into CG when the producer on *Nightmare* had offered many of us the chance to go down to Disney and work on *Dinosaur*. It was a weird thing, becoming a supervising animator in CG without ever having touched a computer in my life. I was given six months of training, which doesn't happen these days, but I hated the process. The levels of directors, the politics, the constant polishing, and on *Dinosaur* in particular, watching the spirit of the film being destroyed over three years...I found it demoralizing, but the money was great. So it's hard to compare the two since the peak point of my career financially was the low point of my career artistically. Stop-motion is more of an art form, and CG is more of a technical thing. In stop-motion, you only get one chance—you animate from beginning to end, and if it's not good enough, you do it again. If not, we're moving on. I like that simplicity.

KEN: *Any advice for aspiring stop-motion animators or thoughts on the current stop-motion scene?*

TREY: Just grab a puppet, some clay, or whatever you can, start experimenting with it, and build up a body of work that you can start showing to people. I didn't learn animation in school; I just started doing it. *Gumby* was the key to the kingdom for me. It was an incredibly naive-style show, and it allowed you to experiment and make mistakes and hone your craft, which is a great way to do it. When you're forced to bang out two or three shots a day, you learn so much so fast. So I would say get a couple of bits together, show it to a preschool television show, and get in there. It's a boot camp, and you want to do as much work as possible and learn as quickly as possible.

There is definitely a resurgence of stop-motion at the moment, which is probably a backlash against the saturation of CG. Of course, if it keeps up like it is now, it will just become another thing that people will get sick of. Everything goes in cycles, and we happen to be hitting a peak, much like we did in the early/mid-'90s before it dipped again. There could be as many as five stop-motion features getting produced next year. I feel lucky to be around at this time of the industry. But as it will come, so it will go, and in a few years we could hit a lull again. I hope not, though; as long as there are entertaining stories to tell, stop-motion is the coolest way to tell them.

7

Character Animation

Animation is an amazing thing. This can be hard to remember when you are immersed in it day in and day out—talking with other animators, watching animated films, teaching it to students, creating it, or even writing about it. But every now and then, that initial spark just hits you, and you realize what a mind-boggling concept is behind the whole idea. In stop-motion, whenever you see a puppet on a set, suspended in absolute stillness between frames, there is a notion of the stillness that is only visible on that set. In our dimension of time, under those hot lights and in that stuffy air, the puppet is merely a figure that sits there until an animator touches it. Once touched, and when the playback button is pressed, a whole new life is created in that other dimension of time on the monitor. All of a sudden, this tiny being of earthbound materials appears to have its own thoughts, fears, and speech . . . a complete life of its own, living in its own world.

It would seem as if that life comes only from the mind of the animator. However, anyone who has sat back and watched his puppet come to life after sweating over it for hours will know that there is something cosmic about these worlds we create. The puppets do seem to take on lives of their own, as if they are discovering it along with us. It's like the scene in Walt Disney's *Pinocchio* where the wooden puppet, crafted by Geppetto and given life by the Blue Fairy, finds out, "I can move! I can talk!" and then goes out to explore his new world. The adventure of Pinocchio is a loving metaphor for the art of animation itself, created by animators who lived and breathed in our own world. Other animators have explored the relationship between puppets and their creators using stop-motion, such as Peter Lord's *Adam* and Nick Hilligoss's *L'Animateur* (*The Animator;* Figure 7.1). I love films, like these, that play with the notion of a puppet's creator within the very medium in which they are made, as if to remind the audience of the sheer magic behind what they are actually watching. I could go on exploring these philosophical implications, but I will digress for the time being and leave you to ponder that on your own. All things considered, the privilege and challenge of an animator is to bring things to life, and that is serious business, all the while being serious play. This chapter will give you some things to think about as you seriously get down to breathing life into your puppets.

Figure 7.1

A scene from *L'Animateur* by Nick Hilligoss.
(© Nick Hilligoss.)

Animation Technique

You need a certain discipline to create believable animation. Much like learning a musical instrument—if you want to play improvisational jazz, you first have to learn your notes and scales, and then apply those foundations to everything else you do. All animation is based on certain principles and foundations based on how things move and how this movement is broken up into frames. Disney went so far as to break many of these principles down into specifics, which are explained in detail in the famous animation textbook *Disney Animation: The Illusion of Life,* by Frank Thomas and Ollie Johnston. These principles include squash and stretch, anticipation, overlapping action, follow through, secondary action, basic elements of timing, holds, and many others. Different authors and animators often have different ways of defining these principles and have developed them in further detail for various mediums of animation. In my first book, I introduced many of these principles in Chapter 5, "Basic Animation," in a way that they could be applied specifically to straight-ahead stop-motion. In this more advanced volume, I will elaborate on a few other ways to apply solid animation principles in your own work.

Timing

When regular folks hear about how stop-motion is done, a questions that often comes up is, "How do you know how far to move the puppet or object?" This is a very good question, but it doesn't always have a simple answer! The simplest answer lies in the essential principle of slowing in and slowing out and the fact that *movements closer together will slow down the action, and movements farther apart will speed up the action.* So, how does one know what's too fast or too slow?

The concept of timing is one of the hardest things to grasp as an animator. Even once you learn it, it is easy to forget. At 24 frames per second (12 movements per second if shooting entirely *on twos*, with each movement captured for two frames), each movement is a tiny part of a much bigger picture. At times, I still catch myself falling into the trap of getting excited about how effective just four drawings on a light-table or four poses on the frame grabber look when flipping through them. That spark of getting excited about the concept of animation comes back in that moment, as I constantly flip through the images that I worked on so hard to get right. It gets to be very obsessive in those moments when everything clicks because they can be rare. (Plus, it's fun!) But when the whole completed animation sequence plays back, those four great images go by way too fast. It's frustrating because you wish the audience could share that same revelry you felt when you created those four perfect drawings or poses and watched them move. In the blink of an eye, they are gone, and it's kind of depressing.

Of course, provided you continue to do your job well, those four poses are followed by four more poses, then another four, and so on, all coming together into a full performance in motion. Like the individual notes in a piece of music, the individual drawings or positions of a puppet are not that significant by themselves but are immensely significant in context of entire work. What matters is where those notes are and how they are played. Timing for animation is no different; the discipline is in knowing how each frame is placed to bring it all together. For example, master animator and director Richard Williams (*The Animator's Survival Kit*) has worked with Warner Bros. animator Ken Harris and has often observed in interviews that Harris' unique talent was that he knew exactly where to place each drawing in every frame for the timing that was needed. In the same manner for stop-motion, one should strive to know exactly where to place each position of the puppet in every frame.

Of course, in hand-drawn animation (and similarly in CG animation), there is the advantage of creating key poses first to create the right timing and then filling in the in-betweens later to smooth it out. Stop-motion does not have this luxury because it is all done straight ahead, with no chance to go back and finesse the timing once it has been shot. Some contend that the terms *keys* and *in-betweens* are useless for stop-motion animators for this reason—because it is straight ahead, and every pose simply leads to the next one. Although this is true, I think it's still useful to sometimes think in terms of keys and in-betweens when approaching stop-motion, especially if one crosses over into other mediums on occasion. At the end of the day, it's all animation, and the basic principles still need to be relevant no matter how it's done. Hand-drawn animation can also be executed completely straight ahead, and it is often necessary to get the right motion (such as the follow-through motions of a tail on a character).

A general rule when it comes to timing straight ahead is to decide which poses the audience really needs to see. The keys do not refer only to the main parts of an action; they can also refer to the main parts of the story being communicated to the audience. Which parts of any particular action or performance are the important parts that the audience should not miss? When you are moving straight ahead with the various poses of your puppet, and you find yourself getting to these important parts, slow down the positioning into a few tiny increments that "favor" those key poses. Those are the poses you want to hang out with for a while so the eye has a chance to see it. Better yet, you may need to cushion your positions into a hold so the pose is really noticeable. My general rule, which I picked up learning animation and often reiterate to my students, is that at 24 frames per second, it takes *six frames to feel something, eight frames to see it, and 12 frames for it to really soak into the brain.* If you are shooting on twos, this principle translates into *three, four, and six moves,* respectively.

Animating straight ahead in stop-motion contains a deadly trap—how easily an animator can get locked into a repetitive, trance-like act of move puppet, take picture, move puppet, take picture, move puppet, and so on. True, this is basically what happens, but it becomes very easy to get sucked into this so much that the timing of the animation becomes too even, floaty, and aimless. There should be some planning and rhythm to these movements—some close together, some far apart, and, when appropriate, grinding to a halt, not moving at all, and settling into a hold. It is perfectly fine to have your puppet stop moving; I find myself reminding my students of this at times. I will admit this concept is hard to grasp because if the puppet is not moving, it's not animated! What matters is that when it's not moving, it still feels alive. This can be controlled by knowing how long to hold an expression or pose to make it real, and when it begins holding too long.

If a character moves into a hold, it can probably only do so for a maximum of 2 or 3 seconds before it loses its breath of life. At the very least, a hold this long or longer should be broken up by a blink or subtle secondary movement to keep it alive. For instance, if a character turns its head to look at something and holds before reacting to what it sees, holding for six or eight frames would be a very quick glance, and holding for 16 to 24 frames would be a more intent look. A longer hold would indicate a slower reaction and denser character, whereas a shorter hold would indicate an immediate reaction from a character who is more alert. Breaking up a puppet's actions with an eight-frame hold here and a 12-frame hold there, and so on, is vital to good timing and ultimately a good performance. It is more natural and lets the audience soak in the moments that are most important to the scene as a whole.

It is also important to remember that starting any animation exercise with a minimum eight-frame hold at the beginning is vital to let the audience's eye acknowledge the character before he starts moving. If the character starts moving on frame 2 or 3 of a scene, you are starting the action much too early for your audience, and their brains may explode trying to catch up. Start moving your character on frame 9, 13, or even 24. Holds are a good thing, so do not be afraid to hit the capture button a few extra times. The nice thing about shooting a long hold is that you can always cut frames if it does end up being too long for the timing you want. Putting frames back in is a bit harder. Holds are also your friend when you are animating a long sequence that has a lot of complicated movements, and you can gladly welcome any moment when your puppet can slow down and pause for a few seconds.

The other general rule to remember regarding holds is that they should always be a minimum of six frames. A six-frame hold is still very short and is often used only for very quick glances or pauses in a character's thought process on screen. At two frames, there is only enough time for an image to appear on screen before being replaced by another image, where the brain does not register the images as being separate. At four frames, the eye just starts to notice the separation between sequential images, so a four-frame hold in the middle of an action will always look more like a camera mistake and cause a jerk in the flow of the animation. An entire character should never hold for only four frames, and the same principle applies to any individual part of a character as it overlaps with the rest of the figure. For example, if a character is being animated and several parts of him are moving perpetually at the same time (head, arms, eyes, etc.), if any individual part stays in the same spot for four frames, it will cause a little "stick" in the animation and will look choppy. It is important to keep track of all these different parts of a character and make sure that every little gesture, as they overlap with each other, takes at least six or eight frames to happen on screen.

If any part of your puppet is moved accidentally for only two to four frames, it is best to try covering it up by just adding three or four more moves in the direction the part is moving (unless you go back, delete the frames, and re-do them). For example, let's say you are focusing on animating the head and left arm of your character without paying attention to the right arm. A few frames into the animation, you realize that the right arm has shifted to the left for four frames, and your intention was that it should not move at all. From this point, it is better to cushion it farther to the left for at least four more frames and write it off as a subtle secondary action. Any tiny move or hold on a puppet that lasts only four frames will not look right, but if it lasts at least six to eight frames, it will at least appear more natural.

Overall, timing is a discipline that you can continue to experiment with until you get a sense of how long it takes to achieve a certain action. In many cases, it will be through timing things too fast, slow, or even that you will learn your own sense of timing. Try to apply what you've learned to each subsequent piece of animation you do.

Arcs

Nearly all patterns of movement occur along a curved path of action called an *arc,* rather than a straight line. Arcs are an important principle to pay attention to, and they are especially effective when applied to stop-motion animation. One of the biggest challenges in stop-motion is keeping each frame properly registered to the next one so that the movement is smooth. Because you are manipulating a puppet in three-dimensional space, it is very difficult to gauge exactly where the path of action is for any motion on the actual set. Making reference to what is on the monitor helps, and being able to place markers and use onion-skin features in frame-grabbing software makes a huge difference. But a frame grabber doesn't understand how to animate, and neither does a computer—only an animator can understand this!

When planning out any movement, look for every opportunity to register your puppet so that the path of action it follows is an arc. You can draw this arc on your monitor or use markers in the software to establish where the points along the arc should be. Then, find a common point on your puppet that you can line up with this arc and keep it moving along that path as you animate. If the path of action does not travel along a steady arc and is not registered properly, the end result will be jittery. Even if one frame moves outside the path of action, it will be noticeable to the audience and create a small jerk in the animation. Having a path of action of any sort in mind during the animation process, whether you actually mark it on your screen or just picture it in your head, is vital to alleviating that "jerky" quality that often occurs in stop-motion. Basically, think hard about the direction things are moving. If a hand or head is moving to the right, keep it moving to the right until it's supposed to change direction, perhaps up or down along an arc. A few frames (say six or more) later, it may even start moving to the left, depending on what's actually being animated. Simply put, if you forget which direction your puppet is supposed to be moving, it will be all over the place, and you will inevitably get that jittery effect of a puppet on way too much caffeine.

Arcs can be applied to nearly any movement to give it more life and a natural flow. Moving a puppet's head along an arc is effective when snapping into an anticipation pose, in any direction, and using the eye as a guide to move it along this path can be a useful point of reference (Figure 7.2). The same principle can be applied to a hand moving in space, using the finger or any part of the hand as a point to guide along its arched path (Figure 7.3).

Figure 7.2

The head moves down and up on an arc, using the eye as a point of reference.

Figure 7.3

A hand with pointed finger moving along an arc up to the head.

For a character jumping, running, or walking forward, moving the entire puppet along an arc is very important to make the action smooth. An extreme motion like a jump will be even more noticeable if the frames are not registered along a steady path (Figure 7.4).

Figure 7.4

The Thunderbean, jumping along an arc path of action.

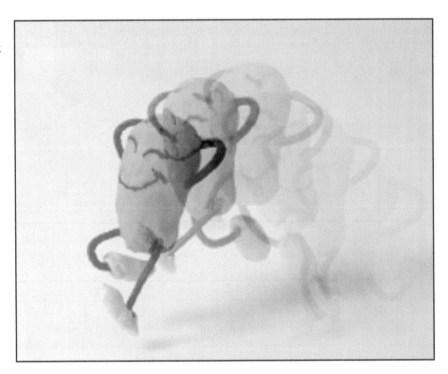

In a walk, there are even more elements to pay attention to in keeping the arcs consistent. The head and torso should be continually moving forward in each frame as well as up and down on an arc (Figure 7.5), and the arms should be swaying back and forth along an arc of their own.

Figure 7.5

The head and torso moving forward in an arc for a walk sequence.

Overlapping Action

Another very important principle that brings an animated character to life in a very big way is overlapping action, which means that not every part of a character will start or stop on the same frame. Movements should be staggered by a few frames so that all elements of the character overlap with each other for a much more natural appearance. To demonstrate some examples of the difference overlapping action can make in stop-motion animation, let me introduce you to my character, Goth Mime (Figure 7.6). On the accompanying CD, there is a series of short animation movies where Goth Mime goes through various movements both with and without overlap to the action. I have deliberately animated some of these exercises in a very basic, rushed manner for the purpose of comparing them to other variations that are animated with more attention to detail. The versions that are not animated well do not have nearly as much life and natural movement as those that are animated with the principles applied.

Figure 7.6

Goth Mime puppet by
Ken Priebe.

The first example is through a simple head turn, from left to right, as if Goth
Mime hears something off screen that causes him to turn around. Looking at
the movie called Head Turn 1.mov on the CD, you will notice that it feels
very stiff. The eyes don't move at all, and it's simply the head being turned
from left to right, without much of an arc and only a certain degree of easing
in and out (Figure 7.7). This was simply done by turning the head frame by
frame without putting much thought into it. The end results are functional
in achieving the simple motion of a head turning, but there is not much life
in it.

Figure 7.7

Frames from a head turn with no overlapping action. (Head Turn 1.mov on the CD.)

Compare this movie to the next one, Head Turn 2.mov, and you will notice that some overlapping action has been added. In this version, the eyes move first, a few frames before the head is moved (Figure 7.8). The results are much more natural and have a better sense of realism. The eyes essentially lead the head into its movement, preparing the audience for the action that takes place. There is also a stronger arc that the eyes and nose move along, which was actually planned out on the monitor to help provide a smooth path of action and ensure a better result to the animation (Figure 7.9).

Figure 7.8
Frames from a head turn with overlapping action in the eyes. (Head Turn 2.mov on the CD.)

Figure 7.9
The arc for the head to follow drawn on the monitor.

In another version, Head Turn 3.mov, an added element of overlapping action is employed by animating a blink before the basic eye movement and then leading into the head movement (Figure 7.10). Blinks often add more life to the movement of a character, especially on a head turn. When the head moves, it is very common for the brain to send a signal for the eyes to blink as it happens to help control the sensory overload that can occur when shifting the eyes' whole perspective.

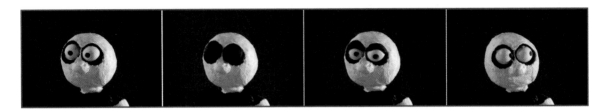

Figure 7.10
Frames from a head turn with a blink and overlapping action. (Head Turn 3.mov on the CD.)

The same principles of overlapping action are demonstrated in some other exercises, which extend the simple motion of a head movement into the entire body of the puppet. Take a look first at Body Turn 1.mov, where the whole body turns from left to right without any overlapping action (Figure 7.11). Everything moves at the same rate, from the eyes to the head and through the arms and hips, starting and stopping on the same frame. The end results are not very believable and feel very stiff and robotic.

Figure 7.11
Frames from a full body turn with no overlapping action. (Body Turn 1.mov on the CD.)

Now, compare this first body turn to the next one, Body Turn 2.mov, and you will notice what a difference the overlapping action makes. In this example, the eyes move first, followed by the head; the arms and hips follow afterward (Figure 7.12). The arms themselves overlap in their timing and spacing, with the right arm settling into a hold a few frames after the left arm. There is a scientific and anatomical logic to overlapping action that occurs in the whole body as it turns from left to right. The idea to turn in the first place is simply a signal triggered by the brain that shoots very quickly down the spinal cord, sending that signal to the rest of the body. The eyes are the closest thing to the brain, so they are the first parts of the body to receive that message from the brain that says, "Turn!" The next part to receive it is the neck, followed by the shoulders, arms, and hips. In the blink of an eye, the simple act of turning around is like a memo being sent from management to all the floors below it. Animation needs to break this up, slow it down, and overlap the body parts getting this signal frame after frame.

Figure 7.12

Frames from a full body turn with overlapping action. (Body Turn 2.mov on the CD.)

Anticipation

Another set of movie files on the CD shows the difference anticipation can make to an action, combined with proper timing for the eye to read the various poses in the animation. These animated exercises show Goth Mime performing the simple act of picking up a ball from a table. The first example, Pick Up Ball 1.mov, is deliberately animated much too fast, with very little thought put into animation principles (Figure 7.13). The hand does grip the ball for at least six frames before picking it up, which is important to read as him actually gripping it. Otherwise, there is very little life or proper staging in the way it is posed and timed. The biggest problem is that there is no anticipation for him grabbing the ball, and it goes by much too quickly for the audience to fully appreciate and be prepared for it.

Figure 7.13

Frames from an action of picking up a ball with no anticipation. (Pick Up Ball 1.mov on the CD.)

The next version, Pick Up Ball 2.mov (Figure 7.14), is an improvement in that there is easing in and out, overlapping action in both arms, and most importantly, the left arm comes up for a short anticipation before coming down to grip the ball. There are drag and overlap in the elbows and wrists of the puppet, making it feel much more flexible and believable.

Figure 7.14

Frames of an action of picking up a ball with anticipation. (Pick Up Ball 2.mov on the CD.)

Performance

All the technical animation principles should be thought about, planned for, and injected into any animation sequence for it to move properly and read well for the audience. But even more important are the performance and acting choices made for the character. These choices should have a direct impact on how the animation principles are used, because the way a character moves depends very much on who that character is. Its inner thoughts, attitude, and mood will affect how long you shoot your holds, how much easing in and out is needed, and the overall tempo of the animation. If the character is nervous, stressed, happy, or alert, its movements should be faster and farther apart, which will require fewer frames to move the character around. If the character is sleepy, depressed, or dimwitted, its movements should be slower and closer together, which will require more frames. Whatever goes on *inside* your character will affect how it moves and performs on the *outside*.

All animators have different methods for planning out their scenes and making their acting choices. Often, they will use a combination of different ways to plan. Stop-motion animators who also like to draw (or at least have some drawing skill) may prefer to make tiny thumbnail sketches of a sequence. Drawing out the key poses and nuances of a scene helps an animator visualize what each frame should look like and explore many different options for approaching the posing. The poses explored through drawing can be applied to the puppet to make sure the armature is able to mimic those same ideas. Other animators may use live-action reference by recording themselves with a webcam or video camera so that they can make a QuickTime movie to analyze frame by frame. This also helps to visualize difficult movements, like the rotation of a wrist, arc of a limb movement, or overlap in the timing of different body parts. Whatever is learned from this analysis can be applied to the animation, but with an extra dose of exaggeration to the timing. Animation is stylized motion based on real-live movement, not necessarily a replica of it.

To practice acting for animation, it is a good idea to think of some scenarios to place your puppet into that allow for it to go through some kind of thought process. They could be opening a gift, talking on the phone, waiting for a bus, looking for something, or any other situation you can think of. Act out the scenario based on who your character is and how it reacts to things. Ask yourself things like:

- Who is the character?

- What kind of mood is he in?

- What is he doing in this scene, and why is he doing it?

- What happened right before this scene takes place?

- How does the character feel about what is going on?

You don't need to have a fully detailed answer for all these questions, but it helps to have a sense of the basic "who, what, when, where, why, and how" of the scene so that your audience will understand what you are trying to communicate. The most basic question to ask yourself throughout the whole process should be how you would behave if you were that character in that particular situation.

You can learn a lot by studying other animation as well, in terms of analyzing frame by frame the techniques used in animated films across all media. Study stop-motion films, but also look closely at the acting choices made in hand-drawn and computer animation films. When you notice a good performance in animation, figure out what makes it good by studying it. Think about the beats, timing, posing, and overall feeling you get by watching it. The only major trap to watch out for is an exclusive reliance on other animation to inform your own work and personal style of acting. One of the most useful resources to study to become a better animator in terms of performance is real actors. The best animators will often use live-action films as their inspiration more than other animated films to avoid the possibility of recycling posing and acting choices that are commonly used or overused. Watch all kinds of movies and take note of the acting styles inherent in them. If you start a library of movie clips for different scenarios and analyze them frame by frame, you will see all the animation principles there as well. A real-life actor's performance will have overlap, anticipation, and even go into holds. If he is holding still, his performance will mostly come through his eyes and very subtle movements. If he is performing broad actions, there will be strong posing and staging with arcs in the movement, cushions into poses, and dynamic facial expressions. It is all there and fascinating to watch. In the courses I teach, I always use live-action clips alongside animation examples to show this connection. All acting and movement comes from the same source. The only difference is that you are creating it all from scratch in animation and have control over every single frame. So make it count!

Two-Character Dialogue

The only thing more challenging than animating one character alone on a set is to animate two characters engaging with each other at the same time. The basic principles are the same, but there is the additional need to keep track of two puppets. On most hand-drawn feature productions, a dialogue scene involving two characters will typically be done by two different key animators who guide each character's individual performance. Communication between these animators is vital because their drawings need to line up, mesh, and interact seamlessly within the same sequence. On a stop-motion film (and similarly in CG), the animated performance of both characters is typically done by a single animator, who needs to keep track of what both characters are doing at the same time. This is a very advanced test of an animator's ability as an actor and a very important skill to learn. If you aspire to work in studio production, you will likely be expected to pull off scenes with several puppets at once and do it well.

The most important factor when animating two characters at once is to keep both characters alive. In most cases, dialogue between two characters means that while one speaks, the other listens and then responds. When one character is listening to the other, it may be still, but not so much that it seems dead. It still needs to have subtle movements that are a reaction to what the other character is saying. The trick is to guide the eyes of your audience back and forth between the two characters, overlapping actions between them and making it feel natural. Depending on the context of the scene, their lines may interrupt each other or overlap at times, and the performance element will vary, depending on who these characters are. Are they having a civil conversation or a heated argument? Are they really listening to each other, or is one distracted? Do these characters like each other, or are they enemies? It is usually most effective to have some contrast between the two characters—age, voice, appearance, scale, personality, or attitude. One may be skinny and the other fat, or one may be uptight and the other easygoing. If you think about many of the great on-screen duos from film and television, such as the comedians Laurel and Hardy or *Sesame Street*'s Bert and Ernie, there is usually some contrast like this between them that creates much opportunity for drama, conflict, and comedy.

For this section of the book, I did a short piece of animation to demonstrate a few different things: animated performance with two characters, lip sync, and some basic compositing that is covered later in Chapter 9, "Visual Effects." I also made it to amuse my young daughter, Ariel, who provided one of the voices. I made a recording of her one day when she was getting a kick out of playing with a little toy dragon that shoots a plastic fireball out of its mouth. I edited together some of the things she said, including her laughing, and put it in context for an animation scene. The monster puppet breathes a fireball (because that's what monsters do) while her hamster friend is reading, and the two characters share a little moment of dialogue together. The complete animation is on the accompanying CD for study (Two Character Dialogue.mov), and some of the steps and techniques involved are referenced in this section. Both puppets were designed and built by former students from my VanArts stop-motion course—the monster by Emi Gonzalez, and the hamster by Frida Ramirez (Figure 7.15). I still had these puppets in my "puppet vault" at the school and thought they looked great when I put them together. (Maybe it has something to do with the fact they were both built by students from Mexico who I had in two different courses, which is only a mere coincidence.)

Figure 7.15

The monster and hamster puppets for a two-character dialogue scene.

In Chapter 9, "Puppet Animation," of my first book, *The Art of Stop-Motion Animation,* I briefly covered how to break down a dialogue track and prepare it for animating to. Once I had my soundtrack edited for this new dialogue scene, the track was broken down in the same basic manner onto an exposure sheet (or dope sheet). The opening line was simply a very emphatic "Wow!" followed by a laugh, which is a rather unique sound to break down and actually a lot of fun to animate to. Because the whole point of breaking down a dialogue track is to break it up phonetically rather than using the actual spelling of the words, if the sound is not necessarily words, it can be broken up the same way, as it is (Figure 7.16). Listening closely to the sounds that make up the laugh, there are several little exhales, inhales, and a series of tiny "Heh" sounds. Some of the "Heh" sounds are shorter and some accented more than others. It's just a matter of listening to the pattern and finding the exact frame that each sound lands on. When recording a laugh onto the dope sheet, I find it best to mark the sounds down to look like the actual sound waves and make notes next to them about what kind of sounds they are. The blank frames between them break up the various sounds and can be referred to in the actual animation. The rest of the scene was relatively straight-forward dialogue, where the hamster (which has my voice) asks, "What are you doing?" and the monster replies, "I'm shooting fire!" Then, the hamster replies, "You're crazy" (Figure 7.17). I will explain some of the particulars of the actual lip sync in a moment, but first I'll go over some of the other steps applied to the animation as a whole.

I set up the composition of the shot based on the fact that I knew I wanted a fireball composited into the top-right part of the frame, coming out of the monster's mouth over the hamster's head. It is always important to think about the movements that may occur and to make sure there is enough negative space around the characters to make this happen. It's also useful to position the two puppets in such a way that it is easy to reach around them and touch them for the animation. You want to avoid bumping one character while animating the other. I also wanted them to be in a position where they were angled to each other enough to be able to turn and look at each other. Any shot should be composed in such a manner that the characters can interact based on what the scene requires. In moments where they actually make eye contact, they might not actually be doing so on the actual set. They may actually be looking slightly past each other, but the idea is to match their eye lines so that on screen, they appear to be making eye contact. If the character's head moves, the eyes will often need to be adjusted in the actual animation between frames to keep that eye contact consistent. For example, if a character's head moves to the left, away from the other character on the right, but the characters are supposed to

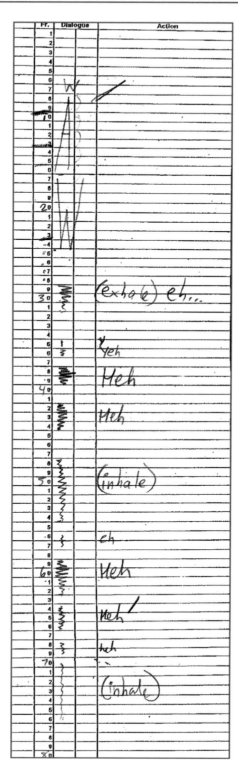

Figure 7.16

Broken-down dope sheet for a laugh.

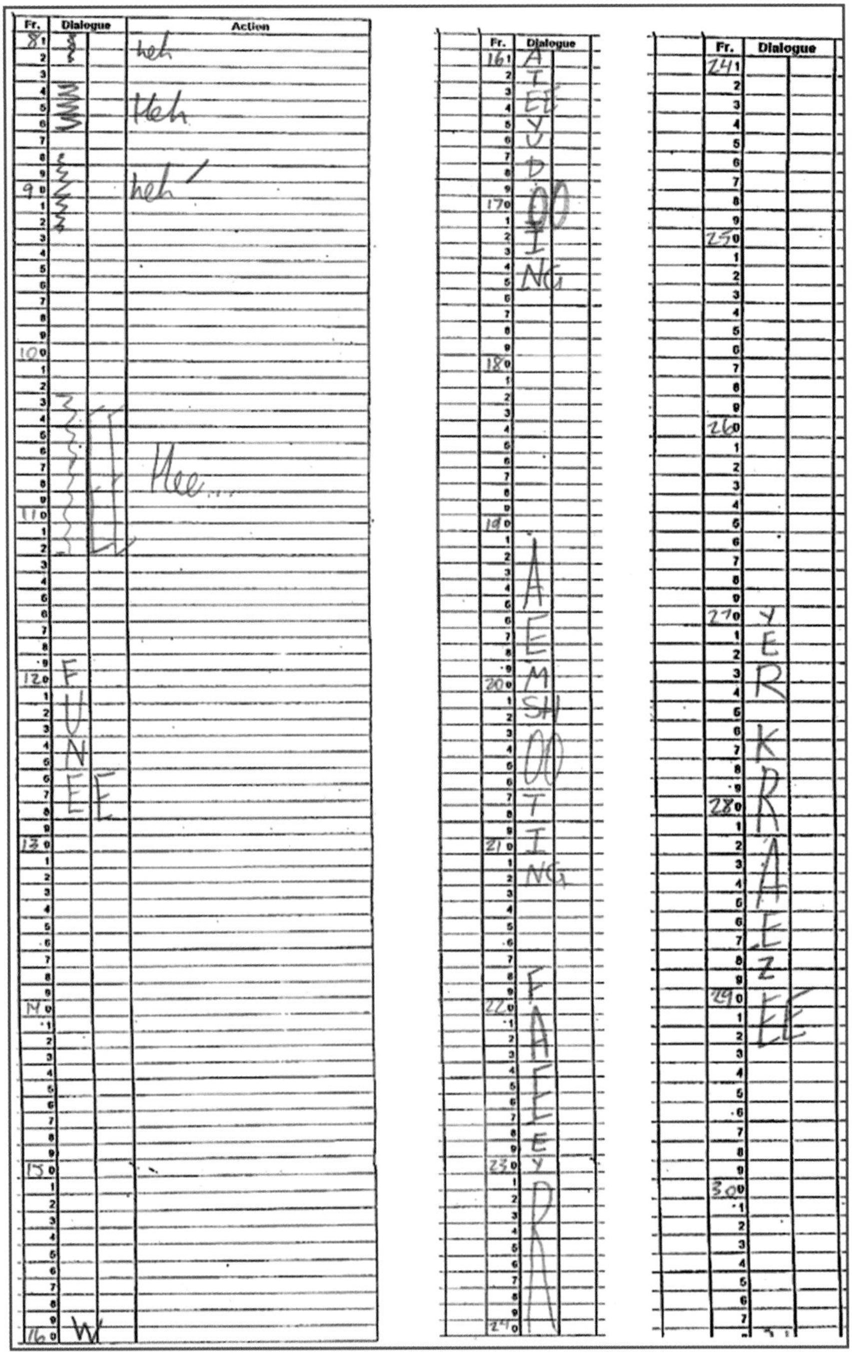

Figure 7.17

The rest of the dialogue track broken down on a dope sheet.

maintain eye contact, the first character's eyes must be moved to the right incrementally as the head moves to the left. Otherwise, the character's eyes will simply stay rooted to the head and will not appear to be making eye contact with the other character anymore.

The personality, design, and construction of these two characters had a direct impact on how they moved. The monster is built on a plastic doll armature, with very long arms and lots of mobility in the neck joint. The head is sculpted in clay over a Styrofoam skull, and the hands are sculpted entirely in clay. This flexibility in the puppet design allowed for some very broad, flamboyant movements. The dialogue itself also gave me clues about how the characters should move. The monster needed a really big accented movement when shouting, "Wow!" and some sweeping gestural poses on the line, "I'm shooting fire!" These kinds of movements perfectly suited the personality I wanted to give the monster—a wild, theatrical personality (very much inspired by my daughter). The hamster, by contrast, does not really have an armature, other than two Styrofoam balls for his round body, a removable round head covered in clay, and solid clay arms and feet. He is much more subdued and mellow than the monster, so he didn't need to move much, other than his head and facial expressions. All he says is, "What are you doing?" and "You're crazy" in a relatively monotone voice, so he didn't need to move as erratically as his co-star.

Using the dope sheet as a guide for where the phrases and accents were in the dialogue, I first did a pose test of the animation, which can also be viewed on the CD (Two Character Pose Test.mov). The purpose of a pose test, also referred to as a pop-through, is to block out the poses and acting decisions for the two characters. The results of a pose test are always going to be a choppy version of a smoother animation sequence because there are no in-betweens. All you are seeing are the key poses, in accordance with the approximate frames they should land on, in sync with the accents in the dialogue. The lip sync itself is really the icing on the cake in a dialogue scene because the actual animation of the body language and movement is what really sells the acting. The idea is to block out a practice run of what the animation might look like in the final version. Shooting a pose test is also very useful for planning the overlapping action between the two characters. They should not change position on the same frame, but rather have some delay between them. If one character snaps into an emphatic pose, the other character can react to the pose, but it should happen a few frames afterward, not on the same frame.

This pose test allowed me to explore the initial approach I wanted for the performance and figure out what did and didn't work. I found that a few too many poses were blocked out for the laugh, for example, making the animation a bit jittery, so that prompted a mental note to soften this action a bit in the final version. There were essentially three different laugh phrases, so I found a different key position to move the monster around in for each of them. When doing the final animation, I would often refer back to my pose test as a reminder of what I wanted the key poses to look like, so I had a reference point for what kind of pose the puppet should be progressing toward. If I didn't like a particular key pose, I could make a mental note of how I wanted to change it or simply take another stab at it. Since there are not many frames or changes to the puppet positions in a pose test, it is much less risky to make changes to the timing or posing until it's working right. Once I had gone through this test and studied it a few times, I was ready to line up my puppets into their zero poses for the final hero shot.

In animating the actual frames straight ahead, including the extra preamble sequence of the monster looking around before she blows the fireball, I paid attention to the overlap between characters and when they should move. To feel natural, the starting and stopping points of these movements should overlap between the two characters, and they should not both stop moving on the same frame. When one character spoke, the other character would be stuck in a hold for the most part, so I could just let them sit there in many instances while I focused on the other puppet who was speaking. Then, when I felt it was needed, the holding character would occasionally blink or move his head in a very subtle six- to eight-frame motion, as if he were following the actions of the other character. This kept each character alive while they were waiting for their "cue" to speak. It is important to avoid overdoing this, which can be an easy trap to fall into. Because the actual animation takes so long, it may take one hour to animate just one or two seconds of screen time. You may find yourself saying, "This character hasn't moved in a while; I'd better move him." But if you forget that you are in another time dimension, it really hasn't been that long for the puppet, only for you. Think in terms of the timing inside that *other* time zone, because that's where the puppets live and what your audience will be watching.

Lip Sync

The lip sync itself for both characters was done with a set of replacement mouths for the main syllables in the dialogue. Being made out of plasticine clay that is still malleable, a good level of control is possible to manipulate the mouths for some fluid animation. The trick to making the sync look right is to choose mouths that take on the character and appearance of how the syllables sound. The largest mouth, which is a wide open shape for long "ah" syllables, can be placed onto the face on the accent and then squished together slightly for the frames that come after it until the need comes to replace it with a different mouth. This effect was used on the word "wow," which is broken up on the dope sheet over about 19 frames, half of which are the "wah" and then going into "w." For the "ah" frames, the wide open mouth is animated on twos, then replaced with a transitional "eh" shape, and finally kept on a transitional "w" mouth that suits the character of how the word is said (Figure 7.18).

Figure 7.18
Frames from the monster saying, "Wow!" in full lip sync. (Two Character Dialogue.mov on the CD.)

Another important aspect of the lip sync, when breaking it down, is to break down phrases based on how they are said phonetically. In many cases, not every single syllable needs to be accentuated verbatim, especially if any lines are mumbled or spoken very quickly so the words kind of blend together. For example, when the hamster says the line, "What are you doing?" the way it sounds is more like, "What-ee-yuh-doo-ing?" The word "are" is not really accentuated as such, so it's not broken down that way. The mouths used to match the dope sheet reflect the quick, slurred way the line is said, so it appears natural.

The other lip sync technique applied to this line is ending it on a mouth shape that reflects the character of what is being said and holding it there for a few extra frames. The very end of the line stops on a mouth shape that is indicative of the "ing" of the word "doing," hanging slightly open with the teeth showing. This mouth position holds for about 24 frames after the line finishes (Figure 7.19) before transitioning to a neutral mouth after the monster starts speaking. In many cases, this technique of holding on the final mouth position of a frame is best suited for when the character asks a question or says a line where he is thinking of something or its not entirely confident.

When a character says a line with more finality and confidence, it looks better to just snap right into a closed neutral mouth right at the end of the phrase. This is the case with the monster at the end of her line, "I'm shooting fire!" After the "r" mouth on the last word, the animation segues right into her closed mouth because she is proud of her little trick. That particular mouth reflects the character of what she is saying and how she says it (Figure 7.20).

Figure 7.19

Mouth shape on which the hamster ends for his line, "What are you doing?" (Two Character Dialogue.mov on the CD.)

Figure 7.20

Mouth shape on which the monster ends for her line, "I'm shooting fire!" (Two Character Dialogue.mov on the CD.)

The closed neutral mouth shape is also typically used for the syllables of "b," "m," and "p," which are sounds made by the lips being pressed together. This shape needs a minimum of two frames in order to register on screen. Even if a line is said very quickly and that syllable is only audible on one frame, it should be cheated to be photographed for two frames, or it won't be seen and might look sloppy in the overall sync. Another trick that can be applied with this mouth shape, if it is recorded on the dope sheet for more than two frames, is to nudge it up slightly before replacing it with the next mouth. The next mouth is usually going to be a vowel shape, like in the word "my" (broken up as "mm-ah-ee" on a dope sheet). Simply put, if an "m" is there for four frames, shoot it in its initial position on the face for two frames, push it up a tiny bit for the other two, and then replace it with the "ah" mouth. The effect will add a nice punchy anticipation to the lip sync (Figure 7.21).

Figure 7.21

Frames of the hamster demonstrating lip sync.

Animation is difficult and very hard work, but it's also fun and fascinating. This is particularly true with stop-motion. Because it deals with tiny figures that are touched between frames, I've always felt it has a strange connection to childhood fantasies about toys or robots coming to life. But it's not only the imagined movement of them that fascinates me; it's also the stillness. When I was a kid, I would play with puppets and make stuffed animals move around like they were living, but I was also obsessed with arranging them next to each other in the toy chest and just looking at them. I had the same obsession with the animatronic robot characters at pizza restaurants that existed in those days, like Chuck E. Cheese's, ShowBiz Pizza Place, and another place in Michigan called Major Magic's (Figure 7.22). When the lights went down, my friends and I would put down our pizza and rush over to the stage. The curtains would open, and these clunky cartoon animals would come to life and sing the Beatles or some popular '80s song. Then, the curtains would close until the next show. Between shows, my friends and I would often sneak up and peek behind the curtain, and these amazing creatures were frightening and fascinating as they sat there in the darkness. In that stillness of the dark stage and the toy chest, these puppets were still living and breathing in their own world, as if they were in a meditative state, waiting for their next cue. As I was focusing intently on the animated dialogue sequence for this book for about 10 hours, I sometimes would be struck by particular poses of the puppets that brought some ethereal feeling of these memories back. It was in the life behind that stillness of the puppets on set (Figure 7.23) that I found myself taken back to this same sense of fascination that I can't really explain.

Figure 7.22

The animatronic rock band from Major Magic's All Star Pizza Revue, Detroit, MI, circa 1982.

Figure 7.23

Stop-motion puppets on set, waiting to be brought to life.

8

An Interview with Bronwen Kyffin

Figure 8.1

Bronwen Kyffin.

Bronwen Kyffin (Figure 8.1) is a stop-motion animator and director originally from Quebec, whose career has literally taken her across Canada. She has worked on several shows for Cuppa Coffee Animation, including *Henry's World, JoJo's Circus,* and *A Miser Brothers' Christmas,* and many other award-winning productions, such as the Leo Award–winning CG series *Jibber Jabber* (as a co-director.) She now lives and works in Vancouver, BC, and we first met at the Vancouver SIGGRAPH Spark Animation Festival in 2008. I'm glad to present her experience, sense of humor, and passion for the art of stop-motion as a contribution to this book.

Website: http://bronwenkyffin.com

KEN: *So how did you get started with stop-motion animation?*

BRONWEN: Well, it was actually totally by accident. I went to Dalhousie University in Halifax to study costume design and theatre, and while there I started getting really interested in live-action puppetry. Near the end of university I made my first short film, which was a combination of live puppets and actors. After graduating I stayed in Halifax and started working in the film industry doing wardrobe, props, set dressing, and directing the odd music video. One winter through the film co-op there, a fantastic woman named Helen Hill offered an experimental animation program. Helen was someone who loved animation and was passionate about sharing her enthusiasm for it. Through that program, we each got 100 feet of film to create any style of animation we wanted. I figured that stop-motion had to be just like live-action puppets, right? I would just move the puppets really, *really* slowly (laughs). I had no idea what I was getting myself into. That was my first venture into stop-motion, a short film called *Cecil's Insomnia*, about a sock puppet who gets separated from his mate and can't sleep anymore (Figure 8.2). It was really fun, but I still wanted to be a puppeteer and make children's films, so I moved to Toronto and started looking for work. Then in that funny way that things just happen sometimes, after about a year of being in Toronto I got offered a job at Cuppa Coffee Animation Studios, working on their series *Henry's World*. I applied to be an animator, but got offered a job building puppets, due to my previous experience. This was great in itself, and then about half way through production I got the chance to join the animation team and ended up staying at Cuppa Coffee for four years. I was hooked. This stop-motion thing was quite frankly the best thing since sliced bread.

Figure 8.2

Still from *Cecil's Insomnia*.
(Courtesy of Bronwen Kyffin.)

KEN: *Did you have a favorite project or series at Cuppa Coffee?*

BRONWEN: It's hard to say, since each one was so different and had its own little charm, and I got to work with some really great people throughout my time there, which is more important that anything. But if I really had to choose, I'd say *Henry's World* was really fantastic because it was the first stop-motion series I worked on, so it will always have special place in my heart. The crew was a very tiny, close-knit group of people, and everything was so new to me; I was learning like a sponge every single day (Figure 8.3).

Figure 8.3

Cuppa Coffee director Dave Thomas (left), electrician Dennis Murphy, and animator Bronwen Kyffin hanging out on the *Henry's World* set. (Courtesy of Bronwen Kyffin.)

KEN: *What were some of the challenges that you would face working in a studio?*

BRONWEN: The hardest thing about working at a studio animating for television, I think, is the volume of footage and the pace at which it needs to get animated. Like live-action TV, you're always on a very tight schedule, and with every show you're trying to do so much more than you did last time. Then add in the fact that the whole thing is being done in such a painstaking medium as stop-motion animation. The fast pace is hard on animators. You have to be able to deliver high-quality straight-ahead animation day in and day out. And you have to learn to sometimes say "that's good enough," which is hard for any animator. Sometimes the animation may only be 85% of what you wanted to accomplish, but you can't sacrifice four hours of work to go back and do it again to fix one little hand movement you didn't like. You have to do your best and just make a note to do it better the next time. But that's also the fun of it. You're always animating a little bit by the seat of your pants and you have to embrace that. When a puppet breaks in the middle of a shot and you have to keep going, some really creative ideas can come out of that situation.

KEN: *How did your transition from being an animator to an animation director come about?*

BRONWEN: Well, I had *Henry's World* under my belt, and I was animating on *Jojo's Circus*. I knew *The Wrong Coast* was coming up, and that they still needed an animation director. It was certainly always my goal to direct, and being animation director would be a great opportunity to move towards that. But I also knew that I wasn't one of the senior animators who would more naturally be in line for that position. It was one of those times where I had to let someone know I had the experience to do it. I went to the producer of the show and asked her if I could book five minutes of her time. I prepared a whole little pitch outlining how my previous experience as an independent filmmaker, live action film tech, and music video director actually made me the perfect candidate. Unbelievably enough, it worked. So that brought me out of animating for a couple years, but I loved animation directing! You get to spend a lot of time working directly with the series director, discussing what they see for the episode and the shots and animation they need to make that happen, and then you get to say, "OK, I'm going to get that for you!" There are guidelines for what the director wants, but you still have lots of creativity within those guidelines. It's not easy by any means, because you're also trying to keep everybody motivated all the time, and often you're the one who needs to tell animators to reshoot. That's the worst part of it.

KEN: *Is there any comparison to the way you moved from animating to directing (having had prior independent filmmaking/directing experience) to the path of someone moving up the ranks for simply being a great animator?*

BRONWEN: Sure, I'd say they are actually two ways of doing the same thing. Basically it's just two different ways of getting yourself noticed in the hopes of opening the door to other opportunities. What you need to do is find a way to make yourself stand out in the crowd; play up your strengths, as it were. Some people do that by being really great animators. Other people get noticed for initiative they've taken directing their own personal projects. By the way, these two things are not mutually exclusive.

KEN: *So after four years at Cuppa Coffee, you came out to Vancouver?*

BRONWEN: Yes, I had a really fabulous time at Cuppa Coffee, but it was time for a change of scenery and a new adventure. I wasn't entirely sure what opportunities would be here for me. All kinds of opportunities opened up that I never would have thought I would be doing, like working in compositing and getting back into my own projects again. And of course, there was also the fantastic opportunity of co-directing the CG television series *Jibber Jabber* with David Bowes.

KEN: *How was the experience directing a CG series, compared to stop-motion?*

BRONWEN: It was a pretty steep learning curve for me in some ways. It was important to figure out very quickly what we could and could not do in the medium, so that we didn't write scripts that were a complete nightmare to shoot. I was actually pretty amazed at how similar the technical problems were to the issues we often faced in stop-motion. After reading the scripts for the first time, the CG supervisors would come back with comments like, "blankets are very difficult" or "can we not pour water over that character?" I thought to myself, "It's exactly the same!" Really it's just like stop-motion, but the "puppets" weigh less, and no one on the crew is running around covered in plaster.

KEN: *Did you miss stop-motion while you were on that show, or were you too busy with directing to notice?*

BRONWEN: Stop-motion will always be my favorite animation medium, but honestly, once we started production, there wasn't much time to really think about that. Besides, when someone says, "it's not going to be stop-motion, but we'd still like to hire you as the co-director," you say, "OK that sounds great!" and you just embrace it. We were still making a cartoon, and it was still really fun.

KEN: *Was it after* Jibber Jabber *that you worked on* Edison and Leo *for a while too?*

BRONWEN: Yes, the production times of *Jibber Jabber* and *Edison and Leo* overlapped quite a bit. So I just came on to *Edison and Leo* at the very end, when they needed some extra people. I think it was during reshoots, and there was really just a skeleton crew left. Many of the other animators had gone back to Toronto or elsewhere. If you ask other crew members, they probably wouldn't know that I worked on it (laughs). It was nice to get to do the bit of work on it that I did.

KEN: *What advice would you have for others working through the rigors of studio production?*

BRONWEN: Studio production is the most awesome job in the world, but it's still a job. It's important to do your best, but you must also not get too emotionally attached to it. Reshoots happen, and often the reason for it has nothing to do with the quality of your work. They just happen, whether it's because of a technical problem, or the client really hates purple, or a fly flew into your frame and is popping all over the shot. It's part of the job, and you need to be able to handle that. That said, everybody struggles with this, all the time. It helps to have your own personal projects on the side, something you love, that is completely creatively your own. It *will* save your soul. Also, because studio work is a job and not your own personal work, there are limitations to the kind of creative input you get, so find ways to enjoy what creative freedom you *are* given. The main structure of your shot—that is, what needs to happen to progress the story—will already be laid out for you, and you have to work with the framework you are given. But if you work hard and take directions well, you will earn the trust of your animation director, and in return you will get more creative input, and you will have more fun.

KEN: *So what can you tell me about your more recent and upcoming projects, now that you've put down some roots in Vancouver?*

BRONWEN: Well, I've kind of come full circle a little bit, in that I'm moving back towards puppet building. More specifically, I'm really getting into the building of ball-and-socket armatures. There are only a couple of places in Canada where you can get custom ball-and-socket armatures made. So I've teamed up with fellow animator Melanie Vachon and award-winning motorcycle designer Ian Douglas to set up that kind of service here in Vancouver. It's great because we don't need huge space to do it in and we can ship to just about anywhere. The process of puppet building can be really daunting. Let's face it, not everyone is comfortable building things, especially something as particular as an armature, and stop-motion is a medium where your animation can be really limited by how you build your puppet. So we want to be able to take the worry out of that portion of production for people and provide solid ball-and-socket armatures built by animators, for animators. We're doing that right now for a film student at Emily Carr University, Lucas Wareing. We're building two puppets for him. In this case, for Lucas, we also skinned and dressed the puppets in addition to building the armatures (Figures 8.4). I have always been a bit of a jack-of-all-trades, so it's kind of refreshing to focus in on one particular thing.

Figure 8.4

Bronwen getting Charlie ready for shooting on *Ava*.

Also earlier this year, Melanie and I ran an animation workshop for kids aged 7 to 11 during their Spring Break. This was very different from anything I had done before, trying to keep the kids engaged in animation for an entire day. Sure, kids love animation, but it's very different to try and keep them going when they realize how much work it is. We had one kid tell us she was going to take basketball next year because animation is cool, but it's *really* boring (laughs). This first time around we had eight kids doing plasticine, paper cut-outs, sand on glass, etc. for the whole week. It was great. Except for the girl who's going to take basketball, the kids had a really good time, and so did we. At least one kid even asked their mom for an animation setup at home. So I'm calling it a success. Even if they don't grow up to be animators, it's still a great experience for them to use their brains and be creative and see how animation happens. Even though we're in the TV business, I think it's important to gets the kids doing something instead of just passively watching TV all the time.

KEN: *Then when they do* watch TV, *they probably appreciate it more once they know how much work goes into it.*

BRONWEN: Yes, definitely.

KEN: *Now, I already know that one of your other passions is dance, and when I interviewed Cuppa Coffee director Dave Thomas for my last book, we talked about how some of the animators there had a knowledge of dance that influenced their animation. What would you have to say about that?*

BRONWEN: It's true; many of the animators had dance or martial arts backgrounds. Now I'm not saying that we were all ballerinas and black belts, but a lot of us seemed to gravitate towards pastimes that required a certain amount of body awareness. Stop-motion is not something that, until more recently, was taught at many animation schools, so most of the people coming into stop-motion had only done it through small workshops or figured it out on their own. I think because of that, you tend to get individuals who have a natural sense of how the body moves, whether it be from martial arts or dance. It could be that we're actually the most athletic animators out there and just don't know it (laughs).

KEN: *What connections do you see between both dance and animation as art forms?*

BRONWEN: To me, animation is essentially dancing—very slowly. I think figuring out your animation timing is very similar to choreographing dance moves and the counts that they fall on. In stop-motion you are just choreographing on a microscopic level. Where a dancer may break down a piece of choreography into individual steps, an animator needs to break down those individual steps into individual frames. There is also the additional fact that stop-motion is all done with straight-ahead animation, which is also similar to dance. You can figure out, or rehearse, a scene in smaller chunks, but when it comes time to animate, or perform it, you just have to start at the beginning and do it. It's a matter of knowing where the puppet is at one instance and where it needs to go and how to adjust it accordingly as you go to keep it on track. Of course, sometimes animation is really similar to dance because you're animating a dance scene (laughs). I've gotten to do this on a couple of shows. The most recent time was animating the famous Miser Brothers' song in the new special *A Miser Brothers' Christmas* (Figure 8.5). Animating dance is fun, but it has its own set of challenges. One of the funniest challenges is trying to resist the urge to want to make the puppets look like professional dancers. It's one of those times when a little bit of dance knowledge can sometimes work against you. You can find yourself getting caught up in the minutia of how a perfect pirouette should be done and forget that the character performing it is a fat guy with bright orange hair.

Figure 8.5

Bronwen animating on *A Miser Brothers' Christmas.* (Courtesy of Bronwen Kyffin/ Cuppa Coffee Studios.)

KEN: *What are your thoughts on the current stop-motion scene and its future potential?*

BRONWEN: What's really fantastic right now is that through platforms like YouTube, etc., filmmakers are able to connect to audiences and each other so much quicker and easier than ever before. You don't have to enter or attend film festivals and fly all over the country to be able to share your work with people. Now we can share work with each other from the comforts of home, just e-mailing each other the inspiring films that we find. Hopefully that kind of accessibility will result in more independent work being done. For TV series, I think the interest in it will always ebb and flow, depending on the appeal of the stop-motion look and how in fashion it is at the time. I think it will perhaps be more interesting to see how this new online community spreads interest in the stop-motion medium, and how that, in turn, affects the number of stop-motion shows that we see on TV.

9

Visual Effects

Stop-motion animation began as a special effect that was essentially done in the camera. Before long, other processes were invented for creating further visual effects in post-production. These effects evolved to the point that differentiation would be needed between special effects and visual effects. Today, the term "special effects" is used for practical effects that are done on set or in front of the camera during production. "Visual effects," on the other hand, are done entirely in post-production, and in some cases during the film era, the elements were simply prepared or created within the camera itself. The basic principles of many of these visual effects have remained the same, but the tools used to create them have certainly changed. What used to be done with a great sense of tedium on a single strip of film can now be done with a great sense of tedium in the computer. Today's digital tools still provide challenges and require just as much patience and skill, and they can range from very basic to much more complex.

As filmmakers become more savvy and higher-end tools become more widely available for the average person making homemade stop-motion films, the creative possibilities open up a whole new world of potential. Some in the stop-motion community even believe that today's digital compositing tools can be used to bring back the classic effects used in Ray Harryhausen's films and are moving forward to bring that genre back to the modern era. When looking at the level that stop-motion and visual effects have reached by themselves, I think the potential behind this pursuit is pretty exciting. Harryhausen's films have inspired an entire industry, so it makes sense to continue that sense of inspiration for future generations. The goal of any film should be to create inspiration, whether for a moral message, for a good story, or simply to create more films. Ultimately, the use of visual effects should not be done simply for the sake of using them, but to allow for more creative control over the performance or look of a scene. The effects should become transparent to the audience and should not draw attention to themselves, but they should always serve the story. This chapter will show some techniques that can be used to combine stop-motion animation with other elements, whether live action or digital.

Film Compositing

To better understand how visual effects are done today, it helps to understand a little bit about how they were done in the "old school," before modern digital tools were available. For stop-motion, a good number of these effects came to fruition in the original *King Kong*, which brought together several different processes for marrying animation with live-action footage. One of the most basic compositing effects that can be done on film is a split-screen matte shot. It is so basic that I used it myself many years ago on my student film, *Snot Living*, at the University of Michigan, which I shot in 16mm. For a shot where my live actor, Brandon Moses, stared at the animated clay puppet in the same shot, I simply framed up my shot and attached a glass plate to the camera lens with poster putty. In the area where I wanted the puppet, I masked out that part of the frame with black paper on the glass, creating a matte (Figure 9.1). The black matted area would not be exposed on the film, but the rest of the frame would. In the area surrounding the matte, I shot Brandon in live action. Next, I had to rewind the film to the same frame where I started, cover up the rest of the frame with black paper, and remove the previous matte, essentially reversing it (Figure 9.2). Then, in this area, I shot my animation through another pass on

Figure 9.1

For a split-screen matte, half of the frame is matted out, and live action is shot outside the matte.

Figure 9.2

The matte is reversed, and stop-motion animation is shot where the previous matte was.

the same frames in the camera. After sending the film to the lab and getting it back, both exposed elements were blended together into the same frame (Figure 9.3). The risk in using this technique was that if something went wrong with either side of the matte, the whole shot would need to be redone.

Figure 9.3
Both sides of the matted areas appear combined in the final composite.

I used the same technique for another shot in the film, where Brandon gets hit in the head and three tiny versions of the clay puppet spin around his head (like in those old cartoons where little birds or stars would spin around a character's head after a serious injury). In this case, the matted area where the animation happened was a tiny rectangular space near the top of the frame (Figures 9.4 to 9.6).

The extra trick with this shot was that because most of the frame was matted out, I was able to rig a large set in the same place that Brandon had been lying earlier. Because I wanted the puppets to look like they were spinning in mid-air, I placed them on a horizontal sheet of Plexiglas so that the background would show through. The Plexiglas was held up (precariously) by two footstools and a stack of phonebooks on each side to bring it up to the level of the matte window. This whole setup actually came crashing down in the middle of my animation, but luckily I was able to set it back up and place the puppets back where I thought they had been. Surprisingly, it worked, and I didn't have to reshoot anything, which was a complete fluke and stroke of dumb luck. (*Snot Living* can now be found on YouTube by typing the title in the Search window.)

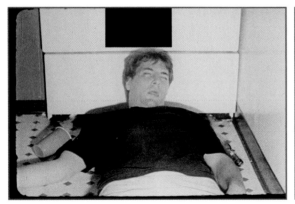

Figure 9.4

Live action of the actor is shot with the space above his head matted out.

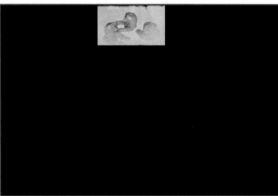

Figure 9.5

The matte is reversed, and stop-motion animation is shot where the previous matte was.

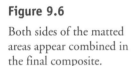

Figure 9.6

Both sides of the matted areas appear combined in the final composite.

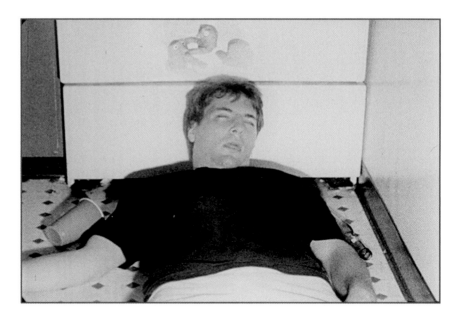

The limitation to the split-screen matte is that the live-action and animated elements in each half of the shot cannot cross the matte line. If they do, they will be cut off. For this reason, the effect can only be used for certain shots where the two elements don't need to cross over each other. For shots where a stop-motion puppet needs to move across a live-action frame or interact with it, Hollywood movies have used rear projection, a technique in which a puppet would be animated in front of a movie screen projecting previously shot live-action footage one frame at a time. The puppet would be moved to match the background, the camera took a frame, the rear projector advanced to the next frame, and the process repeated. For any moments of interaction, the puppet was simply positioned to match up to the live-action footage behind it. This was the basic premise of Ray Harryhausen's Dynamation process, which would also be combined with matting out any foreground elements in front of the puppet and matting them back in through another camera pass. When you understand how they did this, it makes watching those old Harryhausen films that much more awesome.

In other situations, a *traveling matte* can be created. This technique requires more steps and passes of the film through the camera, often done through bi-packing two strips of film together to create the various composites. One of these methods, the Williams process (named after its inventor, Frank Williams), was used for some shots on *King Kong* and other films. To illustrate this process for black-and-white film, I put together a digital re-creation of a film matte using a miniature dinosaur and a photo of Vancouver. First, the stop-motion puppet could be shot against a neutral or black background (Figure 9.7). The actual film in the camera, however, would capture a negative image of what was on set, creating a negative puppet against a white background (Figure 9.8). This strip of negative film was printed against another strip of high-contrast film stock, which created a silhouette of the puppet and left the background transparent (Figure 9.9). A live-action background would be shot separately and developed into a positive print. This positive print was reprinted behind the high-contrast silhouetted image of the puppet (Figure 9.10) and showing through the transparent negative space around it. The result was a

Figure 9.7

This is what the camera sees: a miniature puppet in front of a neutral dark background.

Figure 9.8

This negative image is what is actually captured on film inside the camera.

Figure 9.9

The negative is reprinted onto a new strip of high-contrast film, leaving the background transparent around a silhouette of the puppet.

Figure 9.10

A positive print of the live-action background is printed behind the film with the transparent background and silhouette.

new negative of the live-action background with a transparent shape of the puppet cut out of it (Figure 9.11). This negative was then combined with the original negative of the puppet, which would fit exactly into the transparent shape (Figure 9.12) and then be developed into a new positive image of both elements (Figure 9.13).

Figure 9.11

Now, there is a new negative with a transparent shape of the puppet cut out of it.

Figure 9.12

The original negative of the puppet is inserted into the transparent matte.

Figure 9.13

The negative is developed into a positive print of both elements together, and now Vancouver is under attack by dinosaurs.

With color film, this process gets much more complicated because it essentially deals with using a blue screen as the neutral background, filtering the lens with the same color blue, and running more strips of film with alternating negative and positive images repeatedly through an optical printer. An optical printer is a combined movie projector and camera that can create composites in a similar manner to the in-camera processes, which is how special effects were done up to the digital revolution of the past 15 to 20 years. The tricky thing about these methods, other than having to think about alternating positive and negative images that are backwards, is the reliance on exact alignment of every element. If one thing goes wrong, an entire composite needs to be scrapped and repeated. Although these exact methods mostly have been phased out in today's digital filmmaking era, it is fascinating to look back at how these cinema wizards brought classic images to the screen with what they had. These guys were true technical magicians, and their innovations can help us better understand and appreciate the tools available to us now. Everything we can do now comes from the logic behind these techniques.

Digital Compositing

Today, we have a lot more freedom allotted by digital tools that can create seamless composites and work around many of the errors and setbacks that would occur from using film. They are essentially a combination of the foundations laid by the old-school film techniques and other developments in video technology that bridged the gap to computers. One common tool used in digital imaging today is the alpha channel, which essentially makes any part of an image transparent and allows another image layered behind it to show through. This is very much a digital extension of the transparent negative image from a strip of film, and it can be created for the entire background around a subject or as any shape within an image where a transparent area is wanted. Many compositing software programs used today also have the capability of creating masks that will cut or matte out any part of an image to combine it with another. Also popular is the option of chroma keying out a blue- or green-screen background and replacing it with a live-action or digital background. This has been used for matte work on films and is also used in video production for weather reports, talk shows, and special effects.

Split-Screen and Masks

The split-screen and traveling matte processes have transitioned into the digital era using the same principles from film, but obviously with more flexibility and creative options for the filmmaker. To demonstrate some very simple techniques that can be done for compositing stop-motion with live action, I'm glad to present some contributions by Vancouver-based independent filmmaker Rich Johnson. I discovered Rich's films online and became a big fan of his hilarious Web series *My Friend Barry* (http://www.myfriendbarry.com), which is about a character named Frank (played by Rich) and his little blue stop-motion friend Barry. Part of the charm of the series is its simplicity, including the subtle compositing effects that bring Barry into the live-action world. Frank's dialogue is scripted but sometimes improvised, which allows for many possibilities for having the silent animated character Barry react to the action.

Many shots are done in a simple split-screen technique, where live action and stop-motion are shot as separate scenes and brought together into one shot. This can be done very easily in any nonlinear editing program by applying a mask with an alpha channel into one of the scenes and then layering them together in Premiere or After Effects. In this situation, the split-screen matte line still acts as a division where the two elements should not cross over each other (Figures 9.14 and 9.15).

Figure 9.14

Split-screen animation shot from *My Friend Barry* with half of the frame matted out. (Courtesy of Rich Johnson.)

Figure 9.15

Final composite with live-action footage matted in. (Courtesy of Rich Johnson.)

Other shots require a little more work and planning in the compositing and layering to bring Barry into interaction with the live-action world. Here, Rich himself describes the steps he takes to accomplish this:

> I start by locking the camera down and shoot the live-action video with markers so the actors know where Barry is going to be when looking at him or following him as he moves. I also make a rough note about how long things take and what new improv comes out of the shoot so that I know where I need Barry to move, react, and look. After the live-action video is done, I use a remote to capture frames of Barry moving around with a clean background behind him. I also take one or two frames of the clean backplate with no Barry or actors, in case I need it for any holes and to mask bad reflections or unwanted shadows.

For a shot in Episode 1 where Barry comes out from under the bed and rolls in front of Frank, three layers are needed to make this comp work:

1. Stop-motion layer with Barry animated and saved out as a high-res MOV file the same frame rate as my live-action plate. In this case, it was NTSC 29.97 (Figure 9.16).

2. Live-action video layer with Frank, shot using NTSC 29.97 frames per second, in standard definition (Figure 9.17).

3. Clean background plate in case it's needed (Figure 9.18).

Figure 9.16

Stop-motion layer of Barry. (Courtesy of Rich Johnson.)

Figure 9.17

Live-action video layer of Frank. (Courtesy of Rich Johnson.)

Figure 9.18

Clean background plate. (Courtesy of Rich Johnson.)

I import and/or capture the stop-motion and video layers into my editing program in this same order, with stop-motion on top. I use a temporary "garbage matte" (drawing a rough matte around the general area where Barry is) on my stop-motion layer so that I can see the video layer underneath. If you can't make a temp matte, another method is to reduce the transparency. The key is to be able to see both layers so that you can match them up for your final edit before compositing them together. This is the most important step, and you need to lock down the edit in this stage because the last thing you want to do is go back and make changes. It's too much work to do that. Each layer is edited and timed out, the temp matte is removed, and stop-motion and video layers are exported as uncompressed files to my compositing software.

Then, I import the uncompressed files into compositing software the same way, with layers arranged top to bottom. I add a 2-pop* one second before and after each clip to help ensure that they are lined up.

[*Author's note: A 2-pop is a sound tone one frame in duration that is typically placed two seconds before the exact start of a program for cueing purposes.]

Next, I mask out the stop-motion layer frame by frame as needed to reveal Frank in the video layer (Figures 9.19 and 9.20). For the mask, I only concentrate on the areas where Barry's layer passes in front of Frank's. The rest of the picture on both layers does not change from one to the other, so I don't worry about perfecting the mask in those areas. I finesse the mask by feathering the edges by two pixels or so. That softens up the edges of the mask and blends nicely with the video layer, making for a seamless composite. Now Barry passes in front of Frank (Figure 9.21). It's like magic!

Figure 9.19

Stop-motion layer being masked out.
(Courtesy of Rich Johnson.)

Figure 9.20

Masked out stop-motion layer with live-action layer behind it. (Courtesy of Rich Johnson.)

Figure 9.21

Final composite of Barry in front of Frank. (Courtesy of Rich Johnson.)

For another scene in Episode 2, where a live-action hand comes in to wipe Barry's face, the same technique is used. The only difference is that it's not Barry who is masked—it's just his eyes. One mask for each eye means all reflection and shadows are real on the rest of his body, even in his eye sockets. I put on the actor's coat and sweater and wiped Barry's face with my own hand. I made sure that Barry's eyes were closed when I did this, so in the video layer, Barry's eyes are closed (Figure 9.22), and the only animation going on is his eyeballs (Figure 9.23). Sometimes Barry's eyeballs were crooked, so I would grab the left eye, make a mask, duplicate it, flip it 180 degrees, and add it over the right eye. Now, I had two fixed eyes animating in sync. When done correctly, masks are very powerful for this type of work, and I use them for everything.

Sometimes, in production, I would choose to pose Barry in many different ways, animating his basic moves: looks right, looks left, looks up, looks down, blinks while turning, and blinks at camera. From that, I could make him do anything I wanted in the editing, and it also meant that I could improvise with Frank, which gave me tons of freedom in crafting the jokes and pacing of the show. In this case, I would only plan for his entrance or exit for the shot. Barry is made of Play Doh, which makes him tougher to animate and makes him look kind of lumpy and cracked, which is part of his charm. Sometimes, obstacles are good to have, and little mistakes can help shape the work into something new and original. As long as I stay true to that and don't get too hung up on the details, the show's overall character stays pretty consistent. Barry is an easy shape and has no mouth, so basic stop-motion with him worked perfectly for what I was trying to achieve and convey in my storytelling.

Figure 9.22

Live-action video layer with Barry's eyes closed.
(Courtesy of Rich Johnson.)

Figure 9.23

Masks added in for the animation of Barry's eyes.
(Courtesy of Rich Johnson.)

Blue/Green Screen

The technique of shooting stop-motion puppets against a neutral blue or green screen is pretty straightforward. If your intention is to combine stop-motion with a live-action shot, first shoot your live action separately (Figure 9.24), and then animate your stop-motion puppet on a miniature set with the screen behind it (Figure 9.25). In the computer, you can place the live action into another layer under the stop-motion sequence and remove (or key out) the blue or green background to reveal the live action underneath. The result will be both images composited together in the same frame (Figure 9.26).

Figure 9.24

Live-action video plate. (Courtesy of Richard Svensson.)

Figure 9.25

Puppet animation shot against a blue screen.
(Courtesy of Richard Svensson.)

Figure 9.26

Final composite of animation and live action together. (Courtesy of Richard Svensson.)

Whether you use a green or blue screen depends on several different factors. Traditionally, blue was the best color for optical matte shots on film, and green became the preferred choice for video because of the nature of the media themselves. Today, with most films being shot with video or digital cameras, there are subjective and artistic in addition to the technical considerations. One factor is the colors present in the stop-motion puppet you are shooting. If your character is designed with many shades of green, a blue screen may be a better choice (and vice versa—using a green screen for a blue character). This separation of colors helps in the compositing process and avoids any color from the actual puppet being keyed out along with the background. The lighting may also have an impact on which screen to use; a blue screen may separate from the puppet better in warm light situations, and cold lighting may be better for a green screen. The screen itself can be purchased as a precolored posterboard (Figure 9.27), a fabric sheet, or a flat screen material. You can also buy paint (Rosco or a similar brand) in the specific key color and apply it to a flat sheet of board or foam core. With either method, the background should be lit evenly or illuminated from behind to allow for a clean wash of color and no shadows, which makes it easier to key out the color later.

One of the challenges of shooting with a blue or green screen is the complete removal of the screen's color from around the animated subject. Often, there may be issues with the green reflecting onto the puppet or remaining as a thin layer around the edges. With today's digital tools, though, there are ways to deal with this. Removing the color from most of the frame around the subject

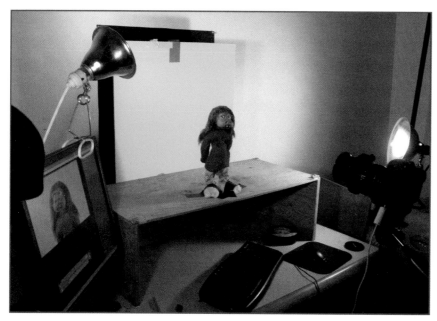

Figure 9.27
Set-up for stop-motion
against a green screen.

is the easiest part. Depending on the software, this is usually done by selecting the color (typically with an eye-dropper tool) and hitting a button or
adjusting a tolerance slider to wipe it out of the frame. In After Effects, a
plug-in called Keylight is commonly used, and Combustion uses a function
called the Diamond Keyer for the general removal of the green (Figures 9.28
and 9.29). Once most of the green is keyed out, there will often still be a thin

Figure 9.28
Selecting the Diamond Keyer in Combustion.

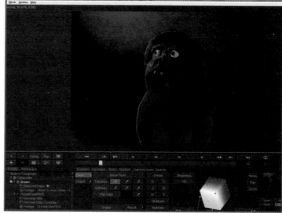

Figure 9.29
Keying out all the green color in the shot with the
Diamond Keyer.

rim of green around the edges of the subject (Figure 9.30). Some additional keying tools can be used for fine tuning the keying out of this remaining color. In Combustion, for example, these tools include the Discreet Keyer and suppressing the green color on the color map (Figure 9.31). To create further atmosphere once the background is comped in behind the puppet, a blur can be added to help create the illusion of a shallow depth of field (Figures 9.32 and 9.33). (Compositing and screen captures for Figures 9.28 to 9.33 courtesy of Shawn Tilling.)

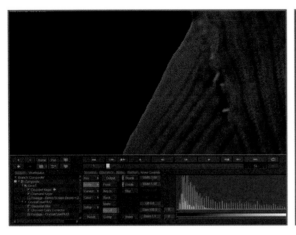

Figure 9.30

A slight green rim is left around the edge of the puppet.

Figure 9.31

The green color is suppressed (or slid down) on the color map to further erase the green.

Figure 9.32

Selecting a Gaussian blur for the comped-in background.

Figure 9.33

Final composite.

Shooting any object or stop-motion puppet with a color behind it for keying also allows for simple resizing and moving of that object into any part of the screen for compositing with other elements. The background that is composited behind the keyed-out animation frames can be a still photograph, a painting, or any type of imagery. A particularly unique use of green-screen compositing was used on a short student film called *For Sock's Sake*, made by animator Carlo Vogele at CalArts. The film uses real clothing, like pants, socks, and shirts, as a cast of characters who go on a journey to save a runaway sock. Carlo shot real clothes on a flat green screen with a digital still camera pointing down from above (Figure 9.34). To move the clothes, he placed magnets inside them and moved matching magnets underneath the green panel, which allowed

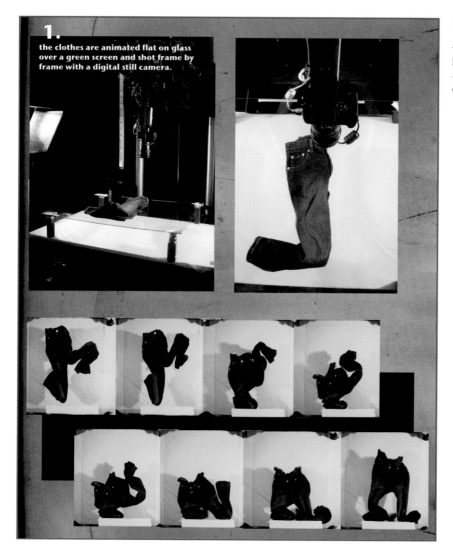

Figure 9.34

Animation shot against a green screen for the film *For Sock's Sake*. (Courtesy of Carlo Vogele.)

them to be moved without breaking the continuity of the fabric's folds and wrinkles. The backgrounds were drawn in Photoshop with photo collage and digital drawing, and the animated clothes were composited into them with After Effects (Figure 9.35). The film can be seen on Carlo's blog (http://carlovogele.blogspot.com).

Figure 9.35

Compositing effects demonstrated for the film *For Sock's Sake.* (Courtesy of Carlo Vogele.)

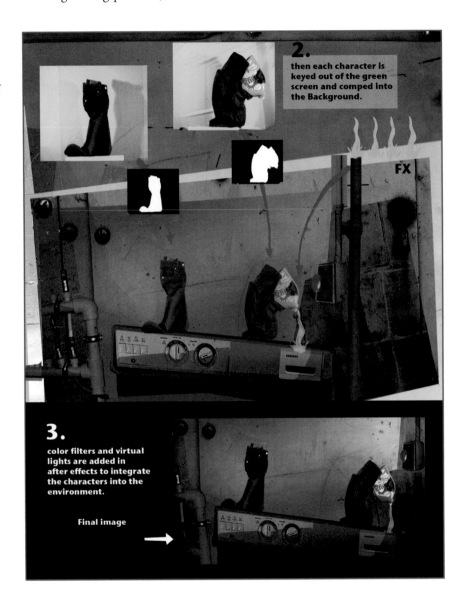

Front Light/Back Light

Another compositing method for stop-motion that harkens back to an old film technique is a checkerboard matte (or front light/back light compositing). The general idea behind it is to take a frame of the puppet against a black or neutral gray background, referred to as a "beauty shot." In this frame, the puppet is lit from the front only, with the light shielded from reflecting onto the background (Figure 9.36). Using a black card or curtain may help shield or absorb the lighting, or using "barn doors" on the light fixture. Next, the same frame is shot with a wash of light reflected onto a white card behind the puppet to create a silhouette image of it (Figure 9.37). The puppet can then be moved into the next position and the process repeated. This creates an extra step of taking each frame twice—once as a front-lit beauty shot and once as a back-lit silhouette, which serves as a transparent matte for compositing with a background. In the compositing process of layering these images together for each frame of the animation, the background is on the bottom layer. On top of the background is the back-lit silhouette matte, which provides an opaque silhouette image of the puppet over the background, and the negative space around it is transparent, so the background shows through. On top of this matte, the beauty shot image is placed over the exact silhouette, which its negative space also made transparent, resulting in a clean composite of all elements (Figure 9.38).

Figure 9.36

A beauty shot, lit from the front, for the short film *The Seventh Skol* by Nick Hilligoss. (Courtesy of Nick Hilligoss.)

Figure 9.37

Back-lit silhouette shot of the same frame. (Courtesy of Nick Hilligoss.)

Although it needs twice as many frames and an extra repetitive step to execute during shooting, this method is essentially an alternative to a green screen. It avoids the issues of the green color reflecting onto the puppet or appearing as a rim around it, and in many cases it provides a cleaner, softer

Figure 9.38

The final composite with a background. (Courtesy of Nick Hilligoss.)

edge around the puppet for compositing. Obviously, during the animation, the lighting setup for both sets of frames, as well as the camera, must be locked down tightly so that all of the images line up exactly. It is common for the back-lit silhouette images of the puppet to still have some highlights spilling into the edges and to have visible features within the silhouette. In many cases, these frames will need to have the brightness and contrast cranked up to create a crisper matte that is completely black and white. In some cases, there may also need to be the option of rig removal in the frames if your puppet is defying gravity in some way.

When this method is used on film, the single strip of film consists of alternating black-and-white images—hence, the term "checkerboard matte." It also means that the animation, when played back at speed, is twice as slow and flashes quickly with black-and-white frames. The alternate frames are separated and put back together in the optical printer. Shooting digitally with frame-grabbing software, the alternate silhouette frames can be hidden during the animation process and exported separately into another folder. Some software programs, like Dragon, can also separate the alternate frames into subfolders while you shoot the animation. Either way, at the end of the shoot, you want your beauty shot and silhouette frames separated and organized into different directories.

Many different software programs, such as Photoshop or TVPaint, can be used to composite the different layers together in each frame as long as you can create transparencies for the negative space around the puppet and adjust the contrast and brightness. Independent animator Nick Hilligoss has his own method for compositing front-lit/back-lit images together using LightWave 3D. His foreground animation elements are captured as their beauty shots

(Figure 9.39) and back-lit silhouettes (Figure 9.40). Each image sequence is separated, with the beauty shots applied to a rectangular flat object's surface in LightWave as a color image map and the back-lit sequence as a transparency map. In this environment, black is solid, white is fully transparent, and shades of gray are partly transparent, so if there are any see-through objects or motion blur in the animation, they will also show up. Directly behind this rectangular object, with the beauty shots and mattes, is another flat object with the background applied to it (Figure 9.40). Both the background and puppet screen objects are exported together from the same camera view to create the final composite (Figure 9.41).

Figure 9.39

Beauty shot from the Ray Harryhausen Tribute promo short for *Stop Motion Magazine* by Nick Hilligoss. (Courtesy of Nick Hilligoss.)

Figure 9.40

Back-lit shot of the same frame. (Courtesy of Nick Hilligoss.)

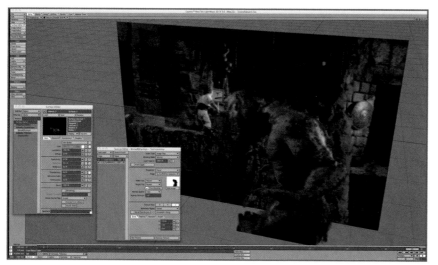

Figure 9.41

Composite in LightWave with Surface Editor and Transparency windows open, angled to show both background and foreground elements. (Courtesy of Nick Hilligoss.)

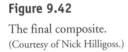

Figure 9.42

The final composite.
(Courtesy of Nick Hilligoss.)

Further tutorial details for front light and back light compositing can be found on the YouTube channels for Nick Hilligoss (http://www.youtube.com/user/StopmoNick) and Ron Cole (http://www.youtube.com/user/animatorIsomer), as well as further tips searchable through Stop Motion Animation (http://www.stopmotionanimation.com).

Advanced Compositing for *Ava*

In Chapter 4, "Digital Cinematography," I included some information that was shared with me about a moving camera shot from Lucas Wareing's student film *Ava*, made at Emily Carr University of Art + Design. The camera move itself starts by pointing up at the ceiling of the film set and then begins tilting down and moving forward through the set. The camera moves through a bunch of real foliage and eventually ends in front of the monster, Charlie, who is sleeping between two cliff facades built as part of the stop-motion set. Meanwhile, there is the effect of a moving sun being animated behind to create a real lighting change throughout the whole set. The background behind the set was a plain white backdrop instead of a green or blue screen. This was done deliberately to better match the lighting throughout the scene and to avoid worrying about blue or green reflections spilling into the set. The original footage from this particular shot in the film (Figure 9.43) went through a complex process of compositing afterward in post-production. The visual effects for this shot would involve a digitally created matte painting of a night sky from which the camera would tilt down, eventually revealing a sunrise in the far background behind the stop-motion set, including an animated sun that followed the path of the lighting change created physically on set (Figure 9.44). Lucas and his compositor, Henrique Moser, shared with me some of the steps involved to complete this shot.

Figure 9.43

Still of original footage from *Ava*, directed by Lucas Wareing. (Courtesy of Lucas Wareing.)

Figure 9.44

Still of final composited footage from *Ava*. (Courtesy of Lucas Wareing and Henrique Moser.)

The first step was to use a steadiness plug-in to minimize some of the camera shakes that resulted from the physical stop-motion camera move. Next, the camera move was tracked to create a virtual 3D version of the movement of the camera on the physical set. This was done using PFTrack, a software program used for match-moving 3D elements to live-action plates with exact precision. The shot starts with the camera's position extended past the beginning of the stop-motion camera move, pointing up at the matte painting. The virtual camera tilts downward across the sky portion of the painting and eventually merges with the tracked version of the physical camera moving through the set.

The matte painting itself, originally done in Photoshop, had its various middle-ground and background elements of mountains and clouds separated onto different layers (Figure 9.45). These split-up layers of the painting were projected onto separate cards in the 3D environment to create a parallax effect as the camera moved through the set. This basically means that there is a change of perspective in the background elements that creates more depth and simulates how it would look in a 3D space, as opposed to just one static background element that stays the same through the whole shot. In the 3D environment, there was one camera that tilted upward and moved down to match the physical camera move and another camera that was locked down and acted as a projector for the various foreground and background elements in the virtual set (Figure 9.46).

Figure 9.45

3D environment with some background elements for the sky. (Courtesy of Lucas Wareing and Henrique Moser.)

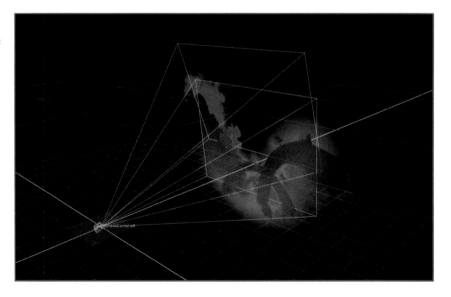

The plants and various bits of foliage were keyed out through a combination of various keying techniques to extract mattes from them. Also, in front of the virtual 3D version of the camera move, certain elements that existed in physical space on the stop-motion set were projected onto 3D cards in the exact places they appeared within the set. Certain things like the branches, plants, and cliffs would go through various stages of movement and overlap with each

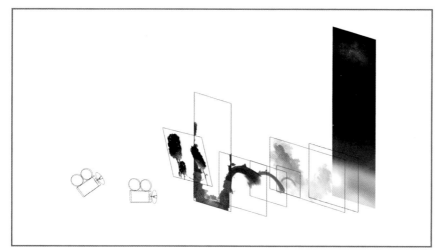

Figure 9.46

Illustration by Henrique Moser of the background and foreground elements and cameras in the 3D environment. (Courtesy of Lucas Wareing and Henrique Moser.)

other as the camera moved past them, so on certain frames, sections of these set pieces had to be matted out and projected to all match together. Many things in the set needed to be painted out, including the black disc that was animated throughout the set to line up with the moving sunlight and cover it up. The projection of mattes onto the 3D cards helped in the particular frames where the disc passed in front of the cliff, for example. To cover up the disc, a section of the cliff from another frame could be matted out and placed in the space it needed to be (Figure 9.47). The color grading would also need to be manipulated to blend in with the rest of the shot since the light changes throughout the whole scene.

Figure 9.47

Example of a matte created to mask out the passing foreground disc from the cliff, before color-correcting. (Courtesy of Lucas Wareing and Henrique Moser.)

In addition to the basic process of compositing and removing the various elements from the original footage so that the composited background could show through, other subtle effects were added to enhance the atmosphere. One example was to enhance and exaggerate the highlights created by the sunlight at the end of the shot. This was done by keying out the bright highlights in the frame itself (Figure 9.48) and then separating the foreground and background into an alpha channel matte (Figure 9.49). The highlight shapes were blurred and given a warmer color tone, which could then be layered over the original shot to exaggerate the highlights, making them brighter and softer in the rim of light along Charlie's body and next to his shadow on the ground (Figure 9.50).

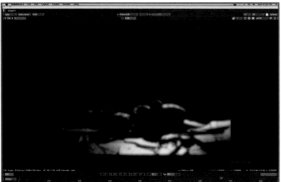

Figure 9.48

Highlights created by the lighting in the frame are keyed out. (Courtesy of Lucas Wareing and Henrique Moser.)

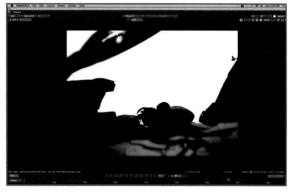

Figure 9.49

The background is separated from the foreground. (Courtesy of Lucas Wareing and Henrique Moser.)

Figure 9.50

The keyed highlights are manipulated and then layered over the original footage. (Courtesy of Lucas Wareing and Henrique Moser.)

Many other effects and subtle details were executed within the advanced production method of completing this shot, all coming together to bring to the audience a beautiful and unique approach to the art of stop-motion filmmaking. Check out the movie called Ava Footage.mov on the CD to see the original footage from the stop-motion set and breakdowns created by Henrique Moser of a few steps taken to create the final shot.

Effects

Computer software and tools allow for all kinds of live-action or CG effects to be composited into stop-motion to embellish shots or add any elements needed to tell the story. Effects such as smoke, water, fire, explosions, or gun-muzzle flashes can be downloaded or purchased as QuickTime files through various websites or service companies. These effects will typically be shot against a black background that is prekeyed with an alpha channel. This way, if you simply drag them into a timeline in Premiere or After Effects, they can easily be laid on top of any other movie file, with the background being automatically transparent. In many cases, they will then need to be repositioned and modified to line up and match with your scene.

This effect was used for my two-character dialogue scene that is featured in Chapter 7, "Character Animation," and watchable on the accompanying CD. Searching through various movie files of fireballs, I found one that was suitable to use for the effect of the monster shooting fire out of her mouth. The movie file itself had the fireball shooting upward in the middle of the frame, so it would obviously need to be rotated and repositioned to shoot diagonally off the right of the screen. This was all done in After Effects and lined up to match the monster's mouth at the proper frame in the animation. Initially, the edge of the fireball was a flat line based on the bottom frame of the movie (Figure 9.51), so the shape was modified using a mask (Figure 9.52). The mask could change shape and essentially be animated in every frame to get the proper shape for the overall effect (Figure 9.53). Two copies of the same fireball movie were ultimately mapped over each other, rotated, and blended to give all edges of the fireball some variety and texture. (Compositing and screen grabs for the fireball effect in Figures 9.51 to 9.53 courtesy of Gautam Modkar.)

Figure 9.51

The first few frames of the fireball movie file, composited and rotated to position with the puppet's mouth.

Figure 9.52

A rough mask drawn in for where the fireball will be in the frame.

Figure 9.53

Animating and manipulating the mask in the frame to shape the fireball.

Online resources where you can find effects to composite into your own stop-motion films include:

- www.stopmotionmagazine.com (under Free Stuff)
- www.videocopilot.net
- www.detonationfilms.com

In addition to compositing in live-action or CG elements that are pre-photographed, it is possible to simply draw stylized effects right over your animation frames, such as lightning bolts, laser blasts, or anything that fits your scene. This can be done easily in newer versions of stop-motion software programs or externally in Photoshop. It can also be done using TVPaint, which is a software program used primarily for drawing 2D digital animation within the program itself. It can also be used for shooting stop-motion very effectively, and all of the drawing tools that come with it can be executed right on top of the stop-motion images. You can easily add hand-drawn effects, smear your stop-motion images, paint over them, blend the edges of seams on your puppet, and do a variety of other creative tricks.

Rig and Shadow Removal

Making a puppet fly is a trick that has employed several different methods over the years. Often, the puppets would be flown on invisible strings, stuck to a plate of glass, or suspended by a rod holding them up from behind where the camera would not see it. These methods can still be used today, but in most cases, a rig is simply placed visibly into the frame to hold up the puppet and is digitally erased out of each frame of the animation afterward. This makes the animation process go much more quickly because you don't have to worry about concealing any tools that are suspending the puppet. In post-production, it can become tedious and time consuming, but this also depends on the length of the shot and how many frames need the rig removed.

One of the most straightforward ways to remove a rig from your stop-motion frames is simply to have a clean background plate prepared in addition to your animation frames. If you are shooting on any kind of set, shoot some frames of an empty set without the puppets in it and set those frames aside to use as a clean background plate in post. In the animation I did for the Thunderbean *Stop-Motion Marvels!* DVD, there were several frames of an empty stage at the beginning, and the entire scene was shot with a white limbo background. This made it pretty easy to select a background plate, and I would open this in Photoshop along with each of my animation frames (Figure 9.54). The next

Figure 9.54

Clean background plate and animation frame are both opened in Photoshop.

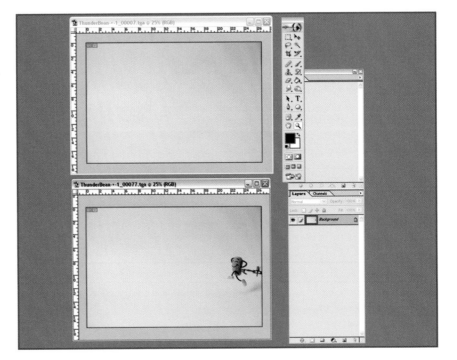

step is to paste the animation frame as a separate layer over the clean background plate (Figure 9.55). Then, with the animation layer selected, the Eraser tool is used to simply erase the rig out of the frame, and the clean background plate will show through (Figure 9.56). It is best to make the brush size smaller and to use a hard edge for delicately erasing the rig at the edge of the puppet itself. Then, you can make the brush a bit larger for quicker removal of the rest of the rig. Once it is all erased, each frame is complete, with the puppet suspended in air (Figure 9.57), and they can be flattened to go back into the animation sequence.

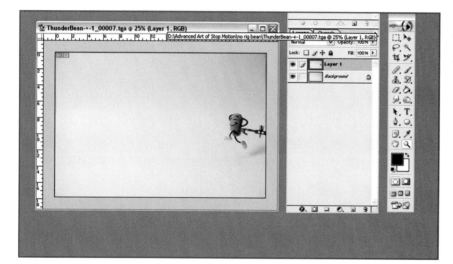

Figure 9.55

The animation frame is pasted as a layer on top of the background plate.

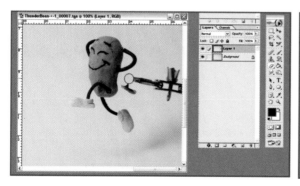

Figure 9.56

The rig is erased from the animation layer, showing the background plate underneath.

Figure 9.57

Completed frame with rig completely removed.

Some of the trickier frames to work with on the Thunderbean project were those where the shadow of the rig needed to be removed but the shadow of the bean remained in the frame. Because the shadow was a little fuzzy, it was difficult to tell exactly where the edge of the bean's shadow was. In the last few slow-in frames, it was also difficult to keep the shadow from jittering. To help soften the effect of the shadow's edge, I used a feathered Eraser tool instead of a hard-edged one and played around with the edge in the various frames until I got it to look right (Figure 9.58).

Figure 9.58

A larger feathered eraser brush is used to erase the rig's shadow.

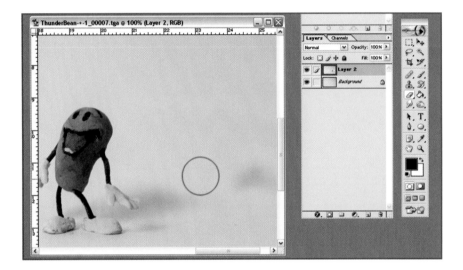

Removing a rig from a stop-motion scene is now a built-in tool in some newer versions of certain frame-grabbing software programs, which helps avoid doing it in another program like Photoshop. Alternatively, a rig can also be removed using masks and alpha channels in After Effects. Another alternative to using one still frame as a background plate for rig removal is to shoot a series of frames of the clean background plate and place them into another layer under the animation with the rig in it. The rig can be masked out, and underneath will be an actual movie sequence of the clean background plate. The advantage to this approach is that if there are any lighting changes or pixel fluctuations in the scene, there won't be any noticeable difference between the animation frames and the frozen background image under them. The background plate has a danger of standing out as a still image because of the lack of noise that would be present in the sequential animation frames.

Being able to erase or mask out parts of an image in stop-motion also comes in handy for fixing mistakes that occur on set while shooting. One mistake that can occur in the middle of a stop-motion shoot is the animator's shadow flashing into the frame. Ideally, you should be standing in exactly the same spot each time you capture a frame, with your shadow completely free of the camera frame. In the heat of the moment while animating, though, it is common to forget this and have certain frames where your shadow creeps into the shot. Unfortunately, this happened to me a few times while shooting my two-character dialogue scene. However, using After Effects, these problem frames were identified and noted as to how much of the frame had a shadow flash into it. A mask was created from some held frames that didn't have a shadow flashing into them (Figure 9.59), and this mask could be composited over the problem frames (Figure 9.60). The edges of the mask were feathered slightly to help blend them into the scene, and then all of the shadow flashes were gone. (Compositing and screen grabs for the masks in Figures 9.59 and 9.60 courtesy of Gautam Modkar.)

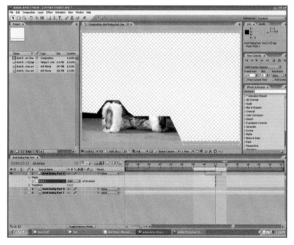

Figure 9.59

A mask is created from a clean frame with no shadows intruding into it.

Figure 9.60

The mask is composited over any frames that had a shadow intruding into them.

Motion Blur

Motion blur is a favored technique of stop-motion animators for replicating the smooth movement of live action in their work. Part of the reason that older stop-motion films always had a jerky quality to the movement was that every frame was always in focus. An even bigger part of the jerkiness, however, was the distance between frames and poor registration of the positions in relation to the speed of the movement. If the distance between two positions on a fast movement (a sword swooping through the air, for example) was too far apart, a strobing effect would occur because the eye was not able to fill in the gap between those two very clear images. If that same fast motion occurred over just a few frames captured in live action, it is likely that some of the frames would be blurred if studied frame by frame. In Chapter 4, "Digital Cinematography," I went over a few techniques for achieving motion blur on the actual stop-motion set. In this chapter, I will present a few examples of ways to get motion blur into your animation in post-production.

One really interesting method for creating an illusion of motion blur was relayed to me by Ron Cole. I noticed his work on *In the Fall of Gravity* had a very smooth, ethereal quality to it, so I asked him if he used any particular motion blur technique. He told me about a relatively simple method he used that was actually borrowed from an old film technique. The effect is one of blending the frames to suggest a kind of look that isn't really there as a blur but makes the animation feel much smoother. Ron created at least three copies of each animation scene; he then removed the first frame from the first copy, the first two frames from the second copy, and left the third as-is. These copies were layered together in QuickTime Pro, and the opacity was altered in each of the layers. That way, each frame showed three images overlapped, with the one in the center the most visible and the before-and-after frames very transparent (Figure 9.61). This gives the illusion that one frame at a time is fading in and out, and the various degrees of opacity could be adjusted, depending

Figure 9.61

Illustration of a frame-blending motion blur effect applied to a scene from *In the Fall of Gravity*. (Courtesy of Ron Cole.)

on the speed and quality of the animation. The multiple exposures of images typically shows up more on a fast movement, but for slow movements, it can create a much more subtle motion blur effect. This same effect can be done easily in After Effects, TVPaint, or any other package that allows you to layer copies of the same sequence over each other and adjust the opacity.

For a more realistic motion blur applied to certain frames or every frame of an animation sequence, there are tools and plug-ins like ReelSmart Motion Blur for After Effects, which will do the job nicely if you have the budget for it. Other simple techniques can involve using Photoshop to add an overall blur to an entire still image, using a blur effect like Gaussian blur and adjusting how extreme you want it. Another Photoshop tool that I have used for creating blurred frames is the Smudge tool, which can just be dragged by hand over any part of the puppet where you want to the motion to blur, like in a fast snappy action, for example (Figure 9.62) Whatever technique you use, the important thing to realize is that an effective blur should follow the object's path of action. If you are blurring an arm moving upward in a sharp movement, try to smear that arm so that the blur is trailing downward in the opposite direction, with a smaller amount of smearing in the direction the arm is going.

Figure 9.62

Three frames from the Thunderbean Animation logo sequence, with the middle frame blurred using Photoshop's Smudge tool.

Many of these effects for green screen, rig removal, masking, and motion blur, as well as other innovative techniques for stop-motion, are demonstrated beautifully together by Patrick Boivin in some of his YouTube videos that break down the process of his entertaining short films. Visit his YouTube page (http://www.youtube.com/user/PatrickBoivin) and, within the Stop-Motion Animation playlist, check out the "Making of" videos for *Bboy Joker*, *Jazz with a General Problem*, and *Black Ox Skateboard*. The process is described in a very entertaining way, and the shorts themselves are fantastic to watch.

Eye Compositing Effects for *Madame Tutli-Putli*

Madame Tutli-Putli (Figure 9.63) is an Academy Award–nominated short film from 2007 that was directed by Chris Lavis and Maciek Szczerbowski for the National Film Board of Canada. The film told the story of a young woman who takes a suspenseful journey aboard a train at night, using atmospheric lighting and intensely detailed puppet animation. The film amazed audiences world-wide, not only because of its cinematic resonance and story, but also because of a particular effect in the eyes of the puppets. The eyes were actually made up of video footage of real human eyes, which were painstakingly composited onto the faces of the puppets. The effect and technique for compositing the real eyes into the stop-motion frames were conceived and executed by artist Jason Walker over a period of four years from concept to the final result. The innovation behind this technique has certainly advanced the art of stop-motion animation to a whole new level in terms of performance and technical mastery.

Figure 9.63

A scene from *Madame Tutli-Putli*. Directed by Chris Lavis and Maciek Szczerbowski. Produced by Marcy Page. (© 2007 National Film Board of Canada. All rights reserved.)

I asked Jason Walker himself to share the process of his technique for *Madame Tutli-Putli* and how the project got started:

> Around the year 2000, I had started playing around with computer animation and been able to get to know the film's directors, Chris and Maciek, who were primarily doing illustration and animation at that time. I became their post-production artist on various projects, including a commercial we did for the Drive-Inn Channel in Toronto, where they had animated a stop-motion mouse. I ended up tracking and positioning a singing mouth onto the puppet, which did have eyes, but only a tracking dot where his mouth was. I tried a technique of having the puppet move only in two major positions and tracking a 2D shape onto a 3D shape, but looking like it was turning along with it. It was all set to the beat of music, and it worked really well.

Later, we found ourselves having a meeting to discuss a project for the National Film Board and what we could do. This was around the time that Peter Jackson's *Lord of the Rings* had come out, and everyone was amazed by the effects for Gollum, so we joked that we needed to create a "poor man's Gollum" for our film. I had an idea that had been in my head for a long time, since I was about 14 years old. When I was a school kid, we had a project where we had to make a papier-mâché head around a balloon and then pop the balloon to create a mask. I had the idea that instead of painting flesh tones and eyes on it, I would paste a collage of magazine clippings on it for skin and the facial features. When it came to the eyes, I found a *Vogue* magazine cover and glued the eyes onto the mask. Then, I had a thought that if I were to create an animation of this mask with these photographs stuck onto it, every time I moved the head, I would need to find a different set of eyes that were set at a different angle. This idea from my childhood came back to me at that meeting with Chris and Maciek—to shoot live-action eyes and composite them onto a puppet.

I asked Chris and Maciek to shoot some simple moves of a test puppet with blank eyes and did a test with filmed footage of actress Laurie Maher. Three basic steps were required to try to make it work: film the actress, track the puppet, and stabilize the footage of the eyes to stick onto the puppet face. Luckily, after about a month of working on it in my spare time, the test worked (Figure 9.64).

Figure 9.64

Still from an early test done for *Madame Tutli-Putli*. (Courtesy of Jason Walker.)

The directors were blown away by it, but I told them if they take this farther, they needed to make sure the puppet didn't move around very much. I went away, and they got approval from the National Film Board to make the film. Coming back a month later, I saw their footage of all this puppet movement, with flashing lights and shadows from the moving train scenes. I started thinking, "I hope my method will work for this!"

Based on the timing and movement of the puppet animation, on the live-action set, we worked together to simulate the light flashes and direct Laurie to mimic the head movements. She had make-up and tracking markers applied to her face for matching to the puppet, and she was told exactly how to move her head and directed on the acting and emotion of her eyes (Figure 9.65). I tried to keep her on track with the correct movements and orchestrated the lighting, and there was no room for error as scenes became more complicated.

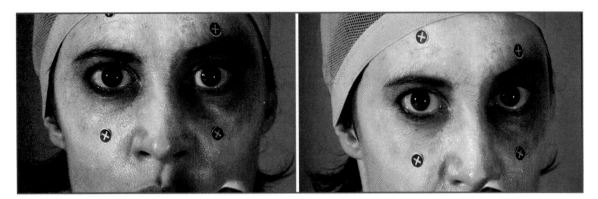

Figure 9.65

Images of Laurie Maher's eyes and head movements being filmed in live action. (Courtesy of Jason Walker.)

When I had the final eye take, I would bring it into the computer and try anything to make it work. I had created a timeline chart in After Effects and nicknamed it the "Wunderbar" (Figure 9.66). Once I had been given the puppet footage, I would analyze what was a head move and what was a camera move and indicate each on this timeline as a different color. This way, I could see a separation between what was a move and what wasn't. Also, for moments when she would encounter a light or a shadow, the Wunderbar would record what kind of light it was and how long it lasted.

On the stop-motion set, there were tracking dots for the eyes built onto the face of the puppet. You would think that would be helpful for all the stabilization, but the dots were only used to track the puppet so that I could adhere a mask layer to the face. I had the eye layer separate from a layer of masks that cut the eye out (Figure 9.67).

However, when it came time to place the eye footage onto the puppet, there was no way to do it except by hand. That was the most intricate part; the computer helps you organize your layers, cut masks, and feather the edges, but the computer has no idea what an eye is, and it has no idea of the subtlety of a human eye in the area of a human face. When it comes to visual effects, it's on one level to make it flawless, but the other level is to make your brain convinced in a way that you don't have to think about. A bad composite is when a scene seems to

Figure 9.66

Still images of *Madame Tutli-Putli*'s puppet animation, with the Wunderbar timeline. (Courtesy of Jason Walker.)

Figure 9.67

A progression of steps showing the puppet's tracking markers, masks, and composited eyes. (Courtesy of Jason Walker.)

look right, but the brain tells you it doesn't. When it comes to human eyes, there is absolutely no room for error. When placing the eye onto the puppet in After Effects, if the eye was off by even a fraction of a pixel, it wouldn't work.

So I developed a system where for every frame, I would need to zoom all the way in, use the arrow keys to move the eye up and down, and then zoom out and see if there was any independent movement. This also had to be done for scale and rotation of every frame. Often, I would zoom in, move it over one pixel, and then zoom out, and it would be too far over. Then I wondered, "How can that be, if it's only a pixel? How can I move it less than a pixel?" It started to become insanity at this point, but my solution was this: Let's say my eye was in the right place on frame 10, and I move it over one pixel for frame 11, but it was too far. What I would do is put a point there, but then drag that point over to frame 12 so that frame 11 was right in the middle. To explain this further, let's say you were on one side of a fence and you could only jump to the other side of the fence, but you wanted to be *on* the fence. You would build a wall so that when you jump over the fence, you would hit the wall before you could land on the other side, but at least you would land on the fence. That was the only way to make the eyes convincing, and the toughest part was this method of sub-pixel positioning so that it always looked like it was on the puppet.

Another point to make is that this technique has sometimes been described as simply adding live-action eyes to puppets, so people think it's not animation. This is partly correct, in that they are real eyes, but it's not merely live action. When I paint portraits of children, they don't sit still very long, so I shoot video of them, and afterward I can search until I get that one instance of the child's face that is right for the painting. The same technique applied here, where I would film the eyes and the actress going slower than the puppet, matching accuracy of the movements, but not timing of the movement. Often, I would film the actress moving at least six times, take these separate takes, and join the eyes together. I would bring in these sequences, which would add up to many hundreds of frames, but inside the scene of the puppet there might be only 100 frames.

Then, it was a matter of selectively going through each frame of the eyes, using the time-remapping feature of After Effects, and sliding through the frames one at a time until you find the one frame that works for that frame of puppet. Essentially, it's a reanimation of video stills—people may think it's not animation, but it is! I have to animate the character that's coming out of the eyes, and part of that is measuring how much she reacts to things by how many extra frames you have her looking there. You have the body language of the puppet and great performance of the actress, but there is also a third level where you can change the acting. Going back to *Lord of the Rings* again, it was noted that if the actor playing Gandalf didn't look concerned enough, for example, they would use a subtle computer mesh to change his expression that much more.

I have ideas for some similar animation techniques I want to try with the entire face, but I will only do that with the right team of people. I often get approached to help other people with these kinds of techniques, and many people ask me if there is any new technology developed in the last three years that will help, like 3D scanning. None of that really helps because you still have to manually position a human eye one frame at a time onto the head, and only your brain will know if it looks right. Your computer is not going to understand human emotion—only your brain can do that. Seeing human eyes on a stop-motion puppet in *Madame Tutli-Putli* is something we've never seen before, and the effect of the film comes down to the fact that it looks like the eyes are there. Anything beyond that is a failure because it's the eyes, and everyone in the world is an expert on this. If there is something wrong with the eyes, you know it right away. There is a quote where someone said, "If you don't believe eyes hold the human soul, then take a picture of someone you love and stab it in the eyes with a pair of scissors. I bet you can't do it." That's the power of eyes.

For more information on the film *Madame Tutli-Putli* itself, visit:
Jason Walker's website: http://www.madametutliputli.com
Official NFB site for the film: http://films.nfb.ca/madame-tutli-putli/

10

An Interview with Larry Bafia and Webster Colcord

Figure 10.1
Larry Bafia.

Figure 10.2
Webster Colcord.

Larry Bafia (Figure 10.1) and Webster Colcord (Figure 10.2) worked together as animation partners at Will Vinton Studios in the late 1980s, when the Claymation technique had peaked in popularity. Since that time, they have both branched into other aspects of stop-motion, CG animation, visual effects, and education. I have enjoyed Webster's work online and in films for many years and recently have had the privilege to work with Larry at VanArts and our local Vancouver SIGGRAPH (Special Interest Group on Graphics and Interactive Techniques) chapter. I'm glad to present their thoughts in this chapter as they talk about their respective careers and views on animation.

Larry's website: http://whoscreative.com/larry_bafia

Webster's website: http://webstercolcord.blogspot.com

KEN: *How did each of your animation careers get started?*

LARRY: The first studio I worked at straight out of school in Chicago was Crocus Productions in Evanston, Illinois, where we did some clay animation industrial videos. One was for dental hygiene, and another was about spaying your pets for the ASPCA. I also worked at Excelsior Studios, run by Gene Warren, which involved some time on *Land of the Lost*. I built some props and repaired any set damage that occurred during a shot. We also did a lot of practical effects, and that's where I learned a lot of in-camera processes. The vortex for the opening sequence of *Land of the Lost*, for example, was shot in a fish tank with a high-speed Mitchell camera whirring away like crazy, and we injected milk into swirling water to create the cloudiness. Also, at Colossal Pictures, I assisted Gary Gutierrez with commercials for San Francisco radio stations, scenes for the Grateful Dead movie, and things like that. For the most part, I was just assisting rather than animating at Colossal, but overall I had several seconds of stop-motion experience under my belt before starting at Will Vinton Studios.

WEBSTER: I was interested in animation at an early age and had done some quasi-professional work on a science-fiction film that was being shot in my hometown of Eugene, Oregon, with a USC film school graduate. I started at Will Vinton's right after high school, so that was like college for me. I like to joke that I moved straight from Super 8 to 35mm, which I really didn't because we shot on 16mm at Vinton's. They had a little Bolex mounted on these huge classic Hollywood cranes that could have held a tank! The first shot that Larry and I worked on together at Vinton's was the opening wrap-around scene for *A Claymation Christmas Celebration* in 1987.

LARRY: I had built a good portion of the main set, which was the Christmas Square (Figures 10.3 and 10.4). A few others and I had come in as apprentices on the show because Vinton had just received the contract from CBS to do three half-hour specials. Since we had been involved in building the set, we got involved in the wrap-around scenes with Herb and Rex, the dinosaur hosts. In the first shot, I got to animate Herb and Rex welcoming the audience, which was a pretty wide shot before it cut to a close-up. The only other characters on the stage at the time were a little frog band on the corner, who were supposed to be playing the opening theme music.

WEBSTER: I ended up doing armatures and sculpting the actual instruments for the frogs, along with model sculptor Kyle Bell, and then actually animating them for the shot (Figure 10.5). The way the studio operated was that everybody was a generalist, so some of us had worked on sets, we all did some of the lighting, and we loaded our own cameras most of the time. If you had the skills to do something, you ended up doing it. It was a great place to learn because we all did a little bit of everything, but Larry was a lead animator because he was one of the few who actually had lots of clay animation experience before coming to Vinton's. Claymation was a really big deal at that time since it was pre-CG, and if you wanted to do character effects that weren't cel animation, you really couldn't go any route other than stop-motion or clay animation.

Figure 10.3

Larry Bafia (left) with writer Ralph Liddle on *A Claymation Christmas Celebration*. (Courtesy of Larry Bafia/Will Vinton Productions.)

Figure 10.4

Larry Bafia working on *A Claymation Christmas Celebration*. (Courtesy of Larry Bafia/Will Vinton Productions.)

Figure 10.5

Webster Colcord working on *A Claymation Christmas Celebration*. (Courtesy of Webster Colcord/Will Vinton Productions.)

LARRY: Then somehow, as a bunch of apprentices, we ended up winning an Emmy for the first show we worked on! We were all part of a hiring wave at that time because the studio had just finished *The Adventures of Mark Twain*, commercials for Kentucky Fried Chicken, Domino's Pizza, and the first few California Raisin commercials, which quickly became very popular. That's when they were playing with the notion of starting a short-film division, and these half-hour specials were supposed to be a breeding ground for that. After the Christmas special, we continued working together on *Meet the Raisins* and lots of commercials for Tang and other clients (Figures 10.6 and 10.7).

Figure 10.6

Larry Bafia shoots a scene from *Meet the Raisins.*
(Courtesy of Larry Bafia/Will Vinton Productions.)

Figure 10.7

Webster Colcord animating on a Tang commercial.
(Courtesy of Webster Colcord/Will Vinton Productions.)

WEBSTER: There was also the "Speed Demon" sequence for Michael Jackson's feature film *Moonwalker*, plus the "Michael Raisin" commercial.

KEN: *How were animators assigned to shots on a detailed commercial like "Michael Raisin," with all of the crowd shots and multiple characters?*

WEBSTER: There were at least eight animators on the crew for that commercial, including three key animators. Jeff Mulcaster and Tony Merrithew did most of the dancing shots, and Mark Gustafson did the final shot of Michael Jackson waking up.

LARRY: I worked on one of the shots where the characters were holding their lighters up. Usually, they were carefully crafted compositions that made it feel like there were lots of characters on screen, but you may have only 15 characters to deal with at once. Most of the crowd shots didn't take more than one or two people.

WEBSTER: One exception was on the ending shot of *Claymation Christmas Celebration,* where we had four animators at once: Kyle Bell, Tom Gurney, Larry, and me. That was kind of a nightmare, actually! (Laughs.) We almost had some fights break out on set there.

LARRY: (Laughs.) Not me.

WEBSTER: No, but we found out somebody had leaned against the camera crane halfway through the shot.

LARRY: Right—that was on the second day of a shot that was supposed to take about four days.

KEN: *Did they start using CG at Vinton's while you were still there?*

LARRY: Yes. How that happened was David Daniels came into the studio and started directing, and he had a setup for a motion-control rig that he had used on a Pop-Tarts commercial. He started training some of us on it, and when he saw that I didn't mind stepping onto the computer, he brought in the video toaster with Lightwave on it, and I started trying it out. Then, when David was in New York showing tests to an agency, they showed him storyboards for a Chips Ahoy! commercial, and he began brainstorming with them on it. Upon walking out of the agency with the boards, his producer Paul Deiner told him he had just pitched a CG spot that couldn't be done in stop-motion. They called me at the studio, and I told them I had been trying to create models with the video toaster. They told me to start modeling an exclamation point for a CG test, and that's when we started combining CG with miniature sets. Then, on a sales trip to Chicago, Mark Gustafson and I gave a studio presentation of our stop-motion work along with the Chips Ahoy! commercial and another one we had done for Fanta. That's when we got asked to do a Raid commercial, which was the first one done entirely in CG, and that led to the M&M's campaign. It got to the point that there was such an influx of artists and techniques coming into the studio that if we looked at a storyboard, we had to decide which methods would suit it best.

KEN: *How did you each part ways from Vinton's into the next stage of your careers?*

LARRY: I had received an offer from Warner Bros. to work with Barry Purves on doing tests with foam latex puppets for *Mars Attacks!* When I arrived there, they only had one puppet built because the entire crew had come over from Manchester, England, and needed to build an entire stop-motion studio from scratch, including sets for the film. We also worked with a miniature company in L.A. called Brazil that built the flying saucers. I did spin tests on the saucers, designed a rig that would hold them up for motion-control shots, and continued doing tests with the Martian puppets. We actually spent lots of time developing personalities for some of the Martians, rather than just "shoot-'em-up" characters. At one point, Barry had the idea of having them use hand gestures while they made the "ack ack" sound that had been designed, as if they were pulling the sounds out of their mouths. One of my favorite tests that Barry and I animated together was of one Martian suiting up another Martian for battle. It was entirely improvised, so each of us had to keep an eye on what the other puppet was doing—it was a lot of fun. We had the advantage of being involved early enough in pre-production that we could experiment with how the characters would interact. I was also responsible for breaking down the script to determine how many stop-motion shots would be needed and how many animators we would need to build up a crew. Then, some producers from ILM (Industrial Light & Magic) came in. Since their effects for films like *Jurassic Park* and *Jumanji* had finally come of age, *Mars Attacks!* shifted there and became a CG project. I had talked with ILM about moving onto the project as well, but decided to take up another offer from PDI/DreamWorks directing CG commercials and animating on their feature film *Antz*.

WEBSTER: After my initial three years on staff at Vinton's, I continued to work for them as a freelancer, but I also travelled around and did some freelance work for David Daniels and a CBC Christmas show in Canada, as well as my own commercials. Then, I got a contract to do some work for Converse Shoes (Figure 10.8), based on some short films I made for Spike & Mike's Sick and Twisted Festival of Animation. I had my own operation going on in Portland for a while, doing stints for clients like CBS, Warner Bros. Televison, and Nickelodeon, and working on projects with animator Chel White. I also went down to San Francisco for a while and animated on *James and the Giant Peach*, along with animator Chuck Duke, but I left that production early to resume some commercial work in Portland. In 1997, I got called down to PDI/DreamWorks and started working there with Larry again. I also took a short break from PDI to work with Henry Selick again on *Monkeybone*, which was a fun but tumultuous production.

Figure 10.8

Webster Colcord working on a spot for Converse. (Courtesy of Webster Colcord.)

LARRY: I always remember you talking about how tricky the shoulder rig was on that show since the stop-motion monkey was usually on Brendan Fraser's shoulder, and you had to mimic the live-action along with the character animation.

WEBSTER: The pre-composited shots on *Monkeybone* were really interesting. They actually built a Brendan Fraser motion-control robot and match-moved the live-action movement of his body. On top of that, we animated the monkey, which was at a 1:1 scale. It was pretty awesome to see the monkey moving on this clunky robot that was rotoscoped to the live action. It was a unique technical challenge, and I don't think anyone else has done it since.

KEN: *Were there any challenges in adjusting from the animation style of television work to working on Henry Selick's feature films?*

WEBSTER: When I was doing my own commercials, I would wear several different hats and try to do the best animation I could in the end. That was a challenge, when I had my own company. Working for Henry, it was a challenge being a smaller fish in a big pond and having to learn the protocol of that kind of production. On my first day there, I was scolded in the hallway by Bonita DeCarlo in the puppet department for bringing one of the puppets up for repair. She thought I was too young to be on the animation team! (Laughs.) Later, she apologized, of course, but it was against the rules for anyone other than a fabricator or an animator to hold a puppet. It was very different from working on smaller projects, where you handled every aspect of production.

In terms of animation style, I had initially learned to animate in a rather intuitive way. There is a famous quote from a *Good Morning America* interview with Chuck Duke, when he was working on Vinton's Chips Ahoy! commercial. He was being asked about animating a chunk of chocolate and said, "You just keep a rhythm in your head, and that should get you there." There have been similar statements made by Ray Harryhausen and even by Richard Williams to the effect of finding a rhythm and thinking about where you're going as you animate straight ahead, and Tom St. Amand would always say, "A good armature should sort of animate itself." With stop-motion, whether you plan it or not, you just get your hands on the puppet and work it out as you go along. But there were animators on *James and the Giant Peach* who planned their movements more like cel animation, so that was something I had to adapt to. Even at PDI, with their early CG software, we used a spreadsheet and had to type in numbers to plan out our animation. It was the only way to do it, but it was counter-intuitive to have to analyze what you were going to animate before you even started. But I think I became a better animator between *James* and *Monkeybone* because my experience animating CG at PDI forced me to be more disciplined.

LARRY: Even if you look back at some of our old exposure sheets from Vinton's, sometimes on a commercial I would only have one track that maybe had some notes about the beats and accents in the soundtrack. But on other projects, sometimes the director would want the live-action reference analyzed on the sheet to the point where you would even plan out where you needed to animate a blink. So, it varied based on style, but also on the animator. In the beginning, we wanted to have all those notes because we had to be so precise on every frame, but after a while you learn how to get into a rhythm, especially if you have a feel for the character.

WEBSTER: Yeah, it depends on the shot, the animator, and the director. Henry Selick would block out the whole shot in editorial sessions with the animator, so you often end up doing what Henry would do if he was the one animating it. But at the same time, I had been talking recently with Richard Zimmerman and Justin Kohn about the animation from *The Nightmare Before Christmas*, and they said the animation on certain things, like Sally's hair as it blew through the wind (in the opening sequence), would typically be done straight ahead, with no surface gauges at all. Sometimes, when you're in the moment on an organic follow-through motion like that, you can just do it very quickly, and you get a better result. It's just you, the puppet, and the rhythm.

LARRY: I think that's one of the hardest things if you were trying to teach someone stop-motion—to be able to see where something is going to be three or four frames ahead of that particular pose.

KEN: *It's neat to hear you both mention how the different methods of working complement each other. Much has been said by animators about how their stop-motion experience helped them transition into CG, but it's also interesting to note how CG helps to create better stop-motion.*

LARRY: Even when we started in CG, we were arm wrestling with the tools. We didn't know to set key frames and then look at the interpolation between them since we only knew how to animate straight ahead.

WEBSTER: Plus, sometimes the only way to animate something in CG is to just animate every frame without any interpolation. That's something I learned from Harry Walton at Sony Imageworks, who animated some shots in CG that way, and Ryan Roberts at PDI told me the same thing. We were wrestling with some CG spiders for *Minority Report*, and he figured out the only way to animate it properly was on single frames—and this was coming from someone with a completely CG background. With the spiders, it was mostly because of their curvy legs. Curvy shapes are the hardest thing to animate in any medium. The snake character in *Monkeybone*, which was mostly done by Justin Kohn, had lots of labor involved to keep those curves because everything down the chain is affected. The worm in *James* was also very difficult for the same reason. I recently did some work on a commercial for Genndy Tartakovsky, and he had a CG character with snake-like rubber-hose arms. He wanted it to stretch out and snap back like cel animation, so once again the only way to do it was single frame with no interpolation, just like stop-motion but using the computer to do it.

In the end, it's all animation, but I guess the main advantage stop-motion has over CG is something that Henry Selick had said—that in stop-motion, you have everything in one place. You get your lighting interacting with the puppet when you look through the camera lens, so you know right away what the shot will look like. In CG, you don't know what the emotional resonance of that glint in the puppet's eye will be until it's lit and rendered, which is sometimes months later.

KEN: *Webster, I understand you have a strong interest in the work of stop-motion artist Wah Chang. What is your inspiration behind that?*

WEBSTER: I always knew who he was, mostly through little hints in magazine articles by people like Jim Danforth over the years. Finally, around 2000 or 2001, it was Peter Kleinow who had called me up one day asking if I'd like to help him with a short-film project he was doing with Wah Chang (Figure 10.9). So, we went down together to meet him, and I helped out by getting them equipped with a frame-grabber system. Later, the Chinese Historical Society in San Francisco had an exhibit of work by Wah and Tyrus Wong, who had both worked at Disney together on *Bambi*, *Pinocchio*, and *Fantasia*. I helped to curate the exhibit, but unfortunately Wah never made it up to see it—he had passed away around that time. For his memorial service, I wrote up a mini-biography documentary about him, and since then I've been trying between projects to get his short films together in a proper format for release. Wah's sister gave me a collection of his still photographs, so I've been passing them along to people doing articles on his work, including Jim Danforth, who is writing a memoir of his own career and had worked with Wah on a few projects. What was amazing about Wah is the range of work he did over so many years. He had worked with nearly every major figure in stop-motion, including Ray Harryhausen, George Pal, Willis O'Brien, Marcel Delgado, Gene Warren, and Gene Warren, Jr. His personal story is also amazing. He had polio in his 20s and had to wear leg braces most of his life, but despite his physical limitations he was able to produce an incredible body of work. Not enough people know about that, so I'm hoping to get more of his story out there.

Figure 10.9

Two stop-motion masters: Wah Chang (left) and Peter Kleinow (right). (Courtesy of Webster Colcord.)

KEN: *Do either of you have any other ideas for future stop-motion projects?*

LARRY: I've been knocking around an idea for a short film for quite a while and hoping to do some animation tests when I can find the time. It's also a matter of funding, if it turns out I need some extra support.

WEBSTER: For me, too, it's a matter of finding the time, money, and space. Stop-motion takes up much more physical space than just a computer station. In addition to my regular job at ImageMovers, I've been doing cel animation. I just recently animated a music video for a Portland band—the Dandy Warhols. Stop-motion is my first joy, and I'd really like to do clay animation again. Very few people do clay the way we used to. I think it's the most pure animation medium; it doesn't get any more tactile or versatile than just pure clay.

LARRY: I really used to love doing morph shots because once you started moving the clay, it took on a life of its own. It wasn't just replacement pieces used to morph into something else.

WEBSTER: I got really into liquid animation in clay when I was doing work for Converse, and I got a system down for achieving the effect. I'd like to do another short film with that technique; I still have many of the models, sets, and equipment I would need. I also have some fans online who want me to create more of my *Mad Doctors of Borneo* shorts. I have a whole storyline for that posted on my website, so someday I'd like to find the time to do that.

KEN: *What do you both think about the current and future potential of stop-motion in the animation world these days?*

LARRY: Well, to Webster's point about the purity of the clay medium, I think a lot of people are starting to see in all genres of animation that sometimes simplifying and going back to roots can really feel much more personal. Sometimes when you get more sophisticated, things can get really antiseptic. Even in CG—for example, the film *Cloudy with a Chance of Meatballs* went for that Muppet-type character design, and that helped push the animation, to make it feel very unique. Another example of unique cel animation technique is to color in the drawings with colored pencils or makers, like Bill Plympton or even Webster's 2D films. Now, it's more common to just use a program like Toon Boom to paint digitally. Things are constantly changing, and that's not necessarily a bad thing, but as long as you can be expressive with it, that's more important than where the tools are headed. You could still animate a character like Gumby and have it be more expressive than a photorealistic image. We've been through just about every style of animation out there, and at a certain point it's more about taking on a challenge rather than which medium you're working in.

WEBSTER: I think the future of stop-motion is very bright, even more than it used to be. Another thing that Ray Harryhausen said is that he knew his kind of films would never be able to compete with cel animation, but stop-motion will never die. I remember when I was in Vancouver doing motion-capture work for Electronic Arts a few years ago, they were showing the *Corpse Bride* trailer in the screening room, and somebody said those exact words—"Stop-motion will never die." I remember feeling jealous that I didn't get to work on that film, but at the same time being happy it was there. And I think *Coraline* proved that statement even further. Audiences are more sophisticated now. They used to complain about stop-motion looking jerky, but now they've seen the flawless, smooth CG alternative, so they want that handmade quality more. Their eyes have accepted it. *Coraline* has opened the door to more potential feature projects in a way that hasn't happened before. At the same time, we have a tremendous cottage industry of young people who want to learn the craft, and people like Marc Spess are feeding it with resources like his Animate Clay website. More prolific schools such as Sheridan College and Academy of Art University now have stop-motion departments and are eagerly looking for instructors. Stop-motion has always been cool, but who ever knew it would be both cool *and* popular?

11

An Interview with Marc Spess

M arc Spess (Figure 11.1), from Missouri, is an animator, sculptor, author, and educator on stop-motion. He is the author of the book *Secrets of Clay Animation Revealed* and creator of the popular website AnimateClay.com, a vast online resource for stop-motion supplies, tutorials, galleries, and much more. Marc has helped millions of people worldwide stay inspired and educated on stop-motion (and he's always been there for me when I needed armature wire), so I'm glad to present his thoughts and experience here.

Websites: www.animateclay.com; www.myspace.com/animateclay; www.youtube.com/group/animateclay; www.stopmotionmagic.com; www.zombie-pirates.com

KEN: *How did you get started with stop-motion?*

MARC: I used to sculpt a lot as a kid, and in my school art classes I would often sculpt little figures with a friend of mine. Later on I discovered the California Raisins TV commercials and specials, which really inspired me, because as a kid I was never really exposed to real sculpture. Since I liked to sculpt and realized those characters were made of clay, I would try sculpting them myself—took pictures of them and started a small portfolio (Figure 11.2). My big break came when I was introduced to Mike McKinney, an animator who had worked for Will Vinton Studios. He was going on a U.S. tour talking about Claymation, and he came to a family center in St. Louis, Missouri, called The Magic House. I was about 18 at the time, and several people had told me Mike was coming, so my sister's boyfriend drove me out there to meet him. The presentation he was doing was more geared towards little kids, but I talked to him afterwards and showed him my portfolio. He had some actual puppets from the Vinton studio with him, and answered all my questions about how they were built. From that point, I took all of this information and expanded on it. I kept in touch with Mike, and he invited me to come out and visit Will Vinton Studios in Portland. Luckily my dad worked for the airlines, so I got to fly out there for free. Mike found me a place to stay, toured me around the studio, and introduced me to another artist there named John Ashlee. John showed me around his apartment studio as well, and I got to learn all about the Claymation process. Although I never got to officially work at Vinton's, I ended up touring there at least four more times before getting to work alongside Webster Colcord at his studio (Figure 11.3). While there, I did some animation, sculpted, built puppets and sets, and got to work with other artists like John Ashlee and Mark Kendrick. So in the end I owe my big break into the world of stop-motion through that meeting with Mike McKinney.

Figure 11.2

Early sculpts by Marc Spess. (Image provided by and © Marc Spess.)

Figure 11.3

Webster Colcord (left) and Marc Spess (right). (Image courtesy of Marc Spess.)

KEN: *Then how did AnimateClay.com get started?*

MARC: AnimateClay.com started soon after I had finished working at John Lemmon Films, an animation studio in North Carolina. The Internet was still a relatively new thing, and I was part of a clay animation e-mail group on Yahoo, where someone mentioned they had created a free website through AOL. At that time, you couldn't easily create a website unless you were a huge company, but AOL had up to 2MB of free space for posting whatever you wanted. What excited me was that there were no tutorials for clay animation on the Internet, so I thought it would be great if people could visit a website to get this information rather than doing it the hard way like I did. So I started my first site through AOL around 1999 or 2000, and the business became official in August of 2001 (Figures 11.4–11.7).

Figure 11.4

AnimateClay.com home page, December 2001. (Image provided by and © Marc Spess.)

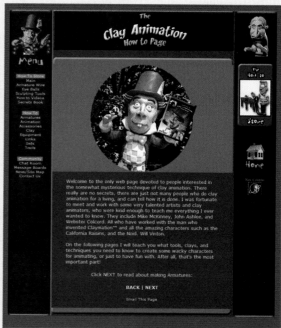

Figure 11.5

AnimateClay.com home page, March 2003. (Image provided by and © Marc Spess.)

Figure 11.6

AnimateClay.com home page, July 2004. (Image provided by and © Marc Spess.)

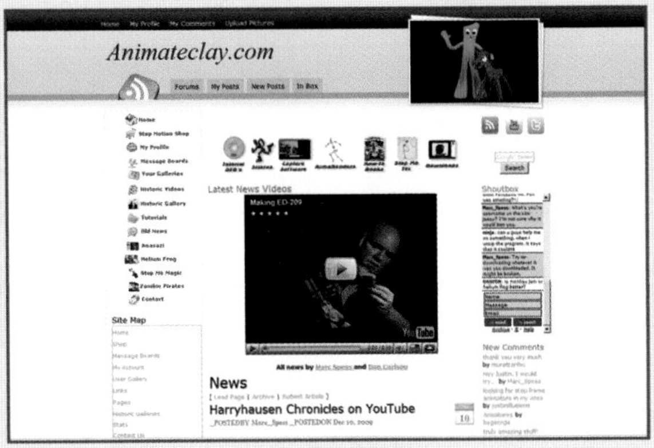

Figure 11.7

AnimateClay.com home page, December 2009. (Image provided by and © Marc Spess.)

KEN: *How did the site develop over the years?*

MARC: Basically I kept adding to it, since I like the technology, and one of my sister's friends got me into using the old Web building program called Front Page Express. I started using it to make the page more complex, adding in a news section, and when I added a counter, I realized that lots of people were visiting it. When I realized there was a growing audience on both the site and an e-mail list I had generated, I took a chance and created my first book, *Secrets of Clay Animation Revealed*, and decided to sell it. Once I had published it and the word got out, I made $600 in the first day on the site! At that time it was really hard to find steady work in animation, so at that point I decided to create my own full-time career, creating DVD tutorials and instruction on stop-motion through AnimateClay.com. My DVDs are duplicated in-house, my books plus DVDs are sold through CreateSpace.com, Amazon.com, and Lulu.com. I get puppet supplies through various warehouses. At one point I had some contacts in Pakistan for sculpting supplies, but the political climate out there is making it hard to get stuff from there now.

KEN: *Do you have any other collaborators working with you on the site?*

MARC: Independent animator Don Carlson from donmation.blogspot.com has been occasionally helping me find news items to post, although more recently he has been more focused on making his own clay animation film. I've also been getting some help from my friend Leroy Binks on another site called StopMotionMagic.com (Figure 11.8), where he is in charge of the monthly animation challenges.

Figure 11.8

The original Stop Motion Magic home page, December 2009. (Image provided by and © Marc Spess.)

KEN: *Can you tell me more about StopMotionMagic.com?*

MARC: It was started as an experimental site, to see if it would take off. If you study history of the Internet, first there were the Yahoo! e-mail groups and then message boards and forums. Now there is this new emerging technology where companies will sell you software to create a complete social network with videos, pictures, blogs, and profiles. This way, the site is essentially run by the users. Over the years, I would have a weekly picture or video posted on AnimateClay.com based on material my site visitors would send me, and it gets to be a lot of work to post material like that regularly. So when I heard about the social networking stuff, I thought I would add it to the server and see what happens. Up to this point, both AnimateClay.com and StopMotionMagic.com have served their purposes in giving stop-motion animators a way to express themselves and share what they've learned and created. The next step has been to merge features of AnimateClay.com and StopMotionMagic.com together. There are many improvements, not only to the forums where you can now post videos more easily with unique topics, but improvements where we merge social aspects with tutorials and news. One thing I'm particularly excited about is that adding embedded videos in news posts is now possible, as well as galleries. This makes the news way more fun for visitors to read and for me to write. Posting comments on news articles by members will hopefully enrich the content when others share their own stories too. So instead of going to AnimateClay.com for the updated news, and StopMotionMagic.com to upload videos or post images, AnimateClay.com will have those things combined. We are also making the live shows more visible to visitors, as well as the monthly challenges.

KEN: *That is interesting. What do you hope that will accomplish, in terms of how stop-motion is done through social networking, or perhaps video streaming?*

MARC: I think it will condense it, since right now you have YouTube, Vimeo, Flickr, StopMotionAnimation.com, AnimateClay.com, and so forth. If you have a social network where you can upload your videos and pictures, along with a message board, it will make things easier for the user to simply post all of your material in one place and just have fun instead of searching. I've had a weekly live show on StopMotionMagic.com for chatting about stop-motion in general, and there is also an emerging technology using an Adobe behind-the-scenes suite called Flash Media Server. It allows you to stream live video similar to Skype or Yahoo Messenger through any social networking website. I've been watching some of these new live streaming websites that are popular nowadays and looking for ways this could be incorporated into sharing stop-motion. I don't see a lot of use out of it yet, in terms of allowing people to collaborate easily, but I think recorded video tutorials and movies are still really useful for online sharing.

KEN: *What other ways have you seen the Internet have an impact on stop-motion animation?*

MARC: There does seem to be a larger volume of it now, and still some misunder-standings of the proper terms, like pixilation, stop-motion, or "Claymation" being applied to all kinds of different techniques. One of the things I've noticed on YouTube is, for example, a band might make a stop-motion music video that becomes viral, and then people will try to imitate it. This happened with a video called *In Her Morning Elegance*, which was a pixilation of a woman on a bed and animated elements around her to make her appear to walk, run, and fly. So people will see those things and try to understand how they work, because it piques their curiosity. More people are trying it, and it's become more accessible, so I think that will continue into the future. Twitter has especially had a big impact on helping unique stop-motion films become viral, because people keep re-tweeting them until they just take off. HD video has also blown my mind recently, and the capability of YouTube and Vimeo now to stream it. The quality is the best it's ever been, and that is something that's really impacted my belief that the Web is more important now than ever for stop-motion. The poor quality of YouTube videos used to make people afraid to post their work, so I think the HD quality changes that mentality. I think we will start to see more of a professional place for posting work online and sharing it in higher quality. Sharing your work online is also very important, because it can open doors to people who may offer you a job or collaborate with you, such as matte painters, sculptors, or other parts of your production. If I meet a great artist who doesn't have a website, I often encourage them to start one.

KEN: *What other goals or future projects do you have in mind?*

MARC: Right now my goal is to try and network with other companies that sell motion control. Some people have agreed to start working with me on that, although I'm not sure there is a big market for motion control on the Internet, as it's more suited for studio productions. I do have other ideas on ways I'd like to expand—for instance, if a stop-motion product is being sold online and I think it has some quality, I will usually approach them about marketing through the popularity of my website. Sometimes there is interest, and sometimes not, but there is only so much content or knowledge I can produce on my own. So I'm always looking for other deals I can create for myself and stop-motion partners, which is true of any business. Otherwise I am always trying to expand the site's overall content.

KEN: *Is* Zombie Pirates *still in production?*

MARC: *Zombie Pirates* (Figure 11.9) is a side project I started about five or six years ago with a friend of mine, but unfortunately there were some problems with funding and other things that occurred. I do plan on returning to it and finishing it at some point once I have more free time.

Figure 11.9

Ruble from *Zombie Pirates*. (Image provided by and © Marc Spess.)

KEN: *What do you feel has been your biggest accomplishment in providing these resources for people who want to learn stop-motion?*

MARC: I think it's been keeping stop-motion in the spotlight and helping people look at it differently than they did before. Most people think it's just for kids, and in some ways it is, because of all the family films created with it. But in my news section, for instance, I often try to mix it up by posting caricatured clay animation along with more serious genres. I see the old Harryhausen films as a more mature form of stop-motion seen in a different way by the people who grew up with them, as compared to modern films like *Coraline*. I like being able to promote all kinds of different styles of stop-motion that are done really well. Often there will be people who post their own stop-motion on YouTube that is really just junk. It's great that they're trying it, but too much of that can create an image of the medium looking only that way. With CG, many people see computers as the only viable way to make films, because everybody's doing it. But at the same time, these films are starting to make less at the box office, because the character designs and styles are beginning to blend into each other. It's hard to tell which film is which, and there is less individuality to it. Stop-motion, however, is so diverse, and every artist is so unique. I hope that is what I get across through my website, and to be able to play a part in that is a great accomplishment.

Being able to connect with people online is also a great thing. We are now in a great phase where CG is no longer seen as the cheapest, most efficient, and most entertaining form of animation. So people and studios are using them instead as a tool to create better stop-motion and connect to others in the field.

My main philosophy in starting your own stop-motion blog or site is that you should be humble and not brag about yourself, but to still put yourself out there online. This is a rather extreme example, but there was a guy who e-mailed me from Mexico on the old clay animation Yahoo! group who had seen the work I posted on my website. This was a long time ago when my site was new, and everything I learned from Mike McKinney was posted on the pages, in terms of how he taught me to make eyeballs, armatures—stuff like that. But this guy from Mexico visited my site, and he e-mailed me saying "I was going to kill myself because I felt I had nothing to live for, but seeing your work inspired me, and that's what I want to now do with my life." So you never really know who is watching or how what you put out there will impact someone.

12

An Interview with
Ryan McCulloch

Figure 12.1

Ryan McCulloch.

Ryan McCulloch (Figure 12.1) grew up in the San Francisco Bay area and now resides in Florida. He has been an independent animator for over 10 years, writing and animating his own films. We started connecting through visiting each other's blogs, and I found the sheer volume and quality of his clay animation work online to be very inspiring. Ryan's films are touching, silly, and oftentimes downright hilarious, so I thought he should be included in this volume as an artist to watch for.

Website: www.ryanmcculloch.com

Blog: http://poorclaymator.blogspot.com

KEN: *So Ryan, how did you get started with stop-motion?*

RYAN: When I was five or six, my dad showed me how to do magic tricks with our home video camera—stuff like making people disappear by stopping the camera and taking them out of the shot and restarting it. Slowly as I got older, I started learning that was basically how animation was done, so I started doing more advanced stuff. Then when I was in fifth or sixth grade, I started playing around with clay, action figures, and dolls, having fun moving them in front of the camera. Around this time I saw Nick Park's *Wallace & Gromit* for the first time, and that really opened up a whole world to me for what I could do. That's when I started making my own characters out of clay, animating stories, and really embracing the process. I had been drawing my whole life, so this was the next step for me, bringing my characters to life.

KEN: *Would you say* Wallace & Gromit *was the turning point?*

RYAN: Yeah, I think before that it was more like, 'What can I really do with this?' I was young and I had learned a little camera trick for moving characters around, but there wasn't really anywhere else to go with that except just being silly. But when I saw *The Wrong Trousers*, it just hit me that the whole world was out there for me to animate, and it was really inspiring and exciting. My dad had seen it while on a business trip and bought me the VHS, thinking it would interest me. Later I saw the "making of" special (*Inside the Wrong Trousers*) on PBS and recorded it. I'd watch the tapes over and over again.

KEN: *That's interesting, it was the exact same film and special that made me more serious about trying stop-motion, too. Had you seen much "behind the scenes" footage of professional productions before that?*

RYAN: I had a pretty good idea of how it was done. I had been to Disney World and seen animators at work there and seen the fake Hollywood versions of how animation was done, frame by frame. But I don't know that I had actually seen much behind-the-scenes for stop-motion specifically. Most of my life I was figuring it out the hard way, by myself. It wasn't until I was in high school and college that I actually had access to more documentary specials and got to meet other people who were doing the same thing. I had a few books growing up, but most of the early ones out there were mostly text with a few black-and-white images. Trying to decipher a lot of that information was really difficult for me at a young age, but the first book to come out that really helped me was Aardman's *Creating 3D Animation*. That one had big color photos and showed so much more of the process.

KEN: *So when did your animation career really take off?*

RYAN: When I was 14, I made an animated short called *Without You,* which my dad started entering into film festivals. It played in about 50 festivals worldwide and then HBO picked it up, bought it, and aired it between programs. I still get e-mails and letters from people who remember it, and that was over 10 years ago. After that I made a few more animated films that HBO Family bought, and I made some animated commercials for local companies and environmental groups. All of this work I did before I even went to college. Luckily I was getting some money for it, so I didn't need to get a real job during high school, and I had lots of people encouraging me to explore the medium. This pushed me to keep doing more and get better at it.

KEN: *It sounds like your dad was a big influence on your early work.*

RYAN: My dad is a musician and a writer and is extremely creative. For me and my sister growing up, if there was ever anything creative that we were passionate about, he and my mom were 100% behind it. During high school and college, Dad collaborated with me on many of the animations I was doing. He decided he would learn editing on the computer, which I didn't want to do, so he did all the editing. On many of the films he would write, compose music, do voices, and even build sets while I was sculpting and animating. We had a lot of fun being creative together those years. When I started making films on my own after college (Figure 12.2), it was hard for me to have to learn how to make sets and edit myself.

Figure 12.2

Ryan animating on set of *Critter Song*. (2007, Courtesy of Ryan McCulloch.)

KEN: *So how did your animation career pan out after high school?*

RYAN: When I graduated high school, I wouldn't say I was burned out, but I wasn't entirely sure if I wanted to continue animating. I entered the Academy of Art University to study illustration, and they did have two stop-motion courses, which I happily took. It wasn't a really solid education for stop-motion alone, but I also took film history and wanted to learn more about storytelling. As I kept going through college, the more I put off animating, the more I realized just how much I liked it. At the same time, I didn't think there was much money in it, in the long term, and I heavily considered being a character designer for an animation studio.

Then after graduating from the Academy of Art in 2007, I was hired to work with Tertiary Productions, a small Web entertainment company in Florida. They were doing Web series and documentaries and thought it would be great to have an animation department, and that was basically me. So having also just gotten married, my wife and I moved across the country, and I worked for Tertiary doing commercials and five episodes of an animated series called *Fox & Calf* (Figure 12.3). I also created five episodes for a new series we were going to debut, but the company didn't survive the economic recession. After that, the same people from Tertiary decided to start producing a children's book company based on some characters I had created while working there, and so I started illustrating. Hopefully we'll pick up *Fox & Calf* or some other animation projects again when the time is right, but more recently I'm having a blast illustrating, building the company website (Mutasia.com), and overseeing some computer animation as well. Stop-motion has always been just one aspect of the creative world that I love. Telling stories and designing characters is what I'm passionate about, as well as working with people who I love and respect. I'm sure I'll come back to stop-motion again in the very near future and that everything I'm learning right now will be brought into it.

Figure 12.3

Fox and Calf puppets by Ryan McCulloch. (Courtesy of Ryan McCulloch/Tertiary Productions.)

KEN: *Have you ever seen yourself working for a major Hollywood film studio or just focusing on smaller studio/independent work?*

RYAN: Right now I like being a big fish in a little pond. Especially at this stage of my life, I feel like if I worked at a big studio I would just disappear. I'm enjoying this time to just develop my own personal style, and I've been really blessed to have the opportunity to do that. On the other hand, I've learned all my lessons the hard way on my own, and learning from other brilliant animators and directors is what a studio has to offer, so that would be great for me down the road. Right now, though, I'm happy doing independent work for startup studios and having my own creative voice.

KEN: *Your stop-motion work has primarily been done in clay, as opposed to other materials. Do you have a special preference for it?*

RYAN: I definitely prefer clay. I love its workability; I love all the little imperfections like fingerprints moving on a character's face. Sometimes I feel that stop-motion puppetry with latex figures and replacement faces gets so close to computer animation in its perfection that there almost doesn't seem to be a point. What I love about clay is that it's gritty, always a little bit dirty, and always moving. When you're on a small budget, you can get more out of clay, in terms of expression, than you can with other puppets. You can move their faces and mouths much more than you could with a silicone puppet, unless you're working with a higher budget, of course. At the same time, clay puppets can be hard to work with. They can melt under the lights, they are fragile and can dent easily, but all of that adds to the charm of the look.

KEN: *I saw your film* Happiness *was just recently posted on your blog. What can you tell me about it?*

RYAN: *Happiness* (Figure 12.4) was a film I made in college as a side project for about two years. It was an interesting project because I was growing during the entire production, so I kept redesigning the main character's look throughout the film. You can see his evolution as the film progresses. It was about 15 minutes long, had lots of characters and huge sets, and I feel that making it at age 20 or so, I had bitten off way more than I could chew. When I watch it now, there are things I'm not happy with.

Figure 12.4

A scene from *Happiness.* (Courtesy of Ryan McCulloch.)

It's easy to start hating a big project like that because it becomes a burden, and you can't start anything else until you finish it. I had another film that was supposed to be 30 minutes long, and I animated five minutes that I'm very proud of, but I ended up just using those five minutes for my reel. When I finished that, I decided to keep everything short, under three minutes, so I could make each piece perfect and be proud of it. So I stuck to that. Besides, the audience gets bored after a while unless you're a master storyteller, so keep them happy at the two-minute mark and leave them wanting more.

KEN: *Another thing that's interesting about your work is the orchestral scores you've had done for them. How did that come about?*

RYAN: I happened to know a really amazing film composer who had studied at USC, named Robert Litton (Figure 12.5). We were both alumni of a scholarship group, and I had seen him conduct a score at Skywalker Ranch. I was blown away by his talent and thought he would be great to collaborate with. I showed him my rough edit of *Happiness*, and he had never scored an animated film before, but he was excited to try something new. The film would never have been half as good as it was without that score, so next I had him score the *Fox & Calf* series. The music brought so much class to the shorts, because the series itself is so silly and weird, so to have this beautiful music there legitimizes it for the audience. I'm a huge music fan and feel very strongly about music. I think every filmmaker should get out there and get to know musicians. It's a real trap to just use copyrighted material for a film or a show reel, and I have so many films I can't sell or post online for that reason. So it's best to avoid being lazy and just using a copyrighted piece of music as a soundtrack, because you never know

Figure 12.5

Ryan McCulloch and Robert Litton on set for recording the *Happiness* score. (Courtesy of Ryan McCulloch.)

when you'll want to show off your work, even if it's at a different time of your life.

KEN: *Did being around music and appreciating it your whole life have an impact on your animation, in terms of learning about timing or rhythm?*

RYAN: I think if you have rhythm, then that does make it much easier. Someone who is an actual musician would likely have an easy time with that. But it also comes down to just doing it, making mistakes, learning through trial and error, moving things too fast or too slow, until you eventually figure out how timing works.

KEN: *How does your knowledge of illustration impact your stop-motion work?*

RYAN: Having a good sense of design and being able to draw definitely help when sculpting those characters. Being able to sketch out a shot in a storyboard and having a good sense of composition are also really important. I think composition is one thing from my illustration studies I've been able to carry over into my films. When setting up my shots, I would think a lot about where my characters were and where everything in the set was, making each shot look better than just putting the camera on them (Figure 12.6). I like to add art to my scenes, so I may have portraits of the characters on the walls or even paint mural background so it looks like trees behind them. You may not necessarily need to be an illustrative artist to be a good animator, but if you're going to be an overall creative independent artist, then having a good sense of design and composition is very important. I actually cheat a lot by moving the props in the background sets around. I don't consider the background to be stuck down. If I feel like moving a fern or piano in the background, the audience isn't going to notice if it's shifted a little bit. So I'll move everything around in the frame to make

Figure 12.6

Fox & Calf set by Ryan McCulloch. (Courtesy of Ryan McCulloch/Tertiary Productions.)

every shot look its best. The set is moving all over the place, all done slightly and just to help the composition, so the audience doesn't notice.

I also try to do as many effects in camera as I can, because I feel like stop-motion should look old school. If I want smoke, I'll use cotton balls, and the audience knows it's cotton balls, but they still think, "Oooh, that's cool!" you know? To an animator it may seem like the obvious thing to do, but to 99% of your audience, they will think it's the coolest thing they've ever seen. It seems that many amateur animators just try to impress other animators instead of your average viewer. To a young animator, the walk cycle is the hardest thing to do, so logically it must be the most interesting to watch, right? Your average viewer won't think so; they take that for granted and will assume it's easy. They're looking at the face—what's the expression and emotion? So while a lot of new animators are trying to impress people with their characters walking, they're neglecting the face. That's why I have a philosophy of animating one "establishing walk shot" for the audience to see and then shoot the rest above the waist. The audience fills in the blanks without noticing. It saves a lot of time, and helps me focus on the face.

I also sometimes feel like a lot of animators only study "animation," and nothing else, and with that world view, they don't have anything new to bring to their films. Someone who has traveled, seen other cultures, studied art history, experienced things out of their comfort zone, will be influenced heavily by these things when creating a new project's story, characters, and look.

KEN: *Are there any new techniques, materials, or advanced methods you want to start trying when you return to your next stop-motion project?*

RYAN: I'd probably consider shooting with digital SLR cameras for the picture quality they provide. I've been shooting with Framethief for the past 10 years, and I've heard lots of good things about Dragon, so I might look into that as well. I still like using clay, but I might start building latex bodies, because I feel like that might give me more options for body movement.

Basically I want to keep making fun movies and telling silly stories with quirky characters. In many of the film festivals I've been to, I've noticed that people who screen work at festivals love to make dark, artsy movies, but as a whole, people like to watch upbeat funny films. If you have something that's really fun, and you get it screened at a festival, you'll have the one fun movie that's surrounded by all the dark, gross art films. It will stand out so much, and everyone's going to love it, because you didn't need to go down that road. Most other independent filmmakers seem to go anti-Hollywood and say, "I'm going to make a movie that makes everybody sad, or sick." They think they're breaking the mold, but really they're just falling into their own "indie" mold. So if you make something that makes people smile, or that can touch people, you're going to always stand out.

13

An Interview with Justin and Shel Rasch

Figure 13.1

Justin and Shel Rasch.

Justin and Shel Rasch are a husband-and-wife filmmaking team in the Los Angeles area (Figure 13.1). They have recently taken the stop-motion community by storm with their animated short *Gerald's Last Day*, the story of a dog in a pound trying to seduce someone into adopting him before he is scheduled to be terminated at 5 p.m. The entire process of making the film, over a span of three years, was documented on their blog "Stop Motion Mission" (http://justinrasch.blogspot.com), which has developed a massive following of animators and stop-motion enthusiasts, including me. Their story continues to unfold online as they move forward on another film. *Gerald's Last Day* itself is a triumph, a beautiful example of exquisite character animation where the moments of silence and stillness say just as much as the moments of expression and movement. Justin and Shel have set the bar high for what a creative family can achieve through hard work and pursuing their dreams to make entertaining films, so I'm proud to have them included in this book.

KEN: *How did this artistic journey between the two of you get started?*

JUSTIN: I attended the Art Institute of Pittsburgh back in 1993–94 and started out in industrial design because I wanted to do monsters, movie effects, and stuff like that. When *Jurassic Park* came out around that time, I was totally blown away by it and how the dinosaurs moved, so I switched to CG animation right then and there. A friend of mine who went to school with me stayed in industrial design and has been hurting job-wise ever since. But I ended up getting hired by various video-game companies, and it's been awesome, steady work the whole time.

SHEL: My background is dancing, choreographing, and performing. Justin and I met in a rock-climbing gym; we both love to move, and it was pretty much love at first sight. I hadn't done much in visual arts until Justin asked me to build some bricks for the set when we started *Gerald's Last Day*. Right away, I got sucked in, making more and more bricks, then buildings, and then cars, trucks, roads, curbs, and all the little props for the film. Then, together, we learned how to make foam latex puppets (Figure 13.2) by watching Kathi Zung's *Do-It-Yourself! Foam Latex Puppetmaking 101* DVD. By then, I was hopelessly hooked.

 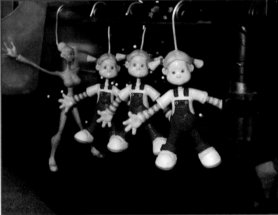

Figure 13.2

(Left) Little girl puppet sculpt in mold. (Right) Latex puppets drying after painting. (© Justin and Shel Rasch.)

JUSTIN: We knew nothing at all about the stop-motion process when we started. It was a big decision, whether to make the film in CG or try stop-motion. At the time, I was getting really frustrated with the CG films I was making since I always needed a computer in order to show my artwork. So much of the animation I had done didn't exist anymore because it was done in some outdated software or codec that could no longer be read. I decided I didn't want that situation anymore, so when I tried stop-motion, it was amazing for me. I now had something real I could put my animation knowledge into. Soon Shel and our kids got involved in making films along with me, and our whole house was just full of artwork.

SHEL: It was really seductive to be able to work together like that. It changed our whole life focus. With Justin being an animator and me being a choreographer, we have a common interest in storytelling, so we were delighted to find a medium that lets us tell stories together.

KEN: *Shel, have you tried animating as well?*

SHEL: A couple years ago, I started animating. I like it, but I got much more taken up with building sets and puppets (Figure 13.3). I'd love to pick up animation again at some point because, as a mover, the concepts are so exciting to me. I just need *time* to practice it, to get it into my body and into my experience.

Figure 13.3

Shel Rasch works on puppets for their new film *Line*. (© Justin and Shel Rasch.)

JUSTIN: We have two full-time jobs and three kids who we spend a lot of energy on, so it is a hard thing to come home after your work day and go into the second day with your family before heading into a third day's worth of filmmaking. I learned the craft of animation from the very beginning at school, and since Shel ended up doing all of the background elements, plus editing and producing, her learning animation wasn't something we could balance.

KEN: *It's rare to find animators who do CG for many years and then transition into stop-motion. Usually, it's the other way around. Do you find that the familiarity with the virtual 3D environment helped you grasp stop-motion more easily?*

JUSTIN: Absolutely! I was educated in 2D first and then applied that to CG, which is a very different thing. I've seen a lot of 2D animators who can't grasp the third dimension. The CG experience definitely helped me because I could practice that craft for years in CG very quickly without the hassle of tie-downs and wires to hold my characters up. My actual animation knowledge was well practiced, and once I got past the limitations of gravity and physical posturing in stop-motion, it was all there and completely transferable.

SHEL: There are many ways to make a living in CG but not many ways to make a living in stop-motion. Justin was making a living at a great job, getting to do what he wants, but he got to a point where he wanted to feel his art because he's a very tactile person. So, it was a natural progression for him.

JUSTIN: I went back to where I started, in a way. Industrial design is all sculpture, construction, and making...monsters! That's what I wanted to do—make monsters and animate them—so coming back to that was very natural. We're 100% into it and totally in love with the art form.

KEN: *What was the inspiration behind the idea for* Gerald's Last Day?

JUSTIN: The character at the end of the film who adopts Gerald the dog is actually named Gerald in real life. He's a good friend of mine who I've worked with for years, and he was looking for a mate. He would always come into work with these books and tapes on how to pick up women, and even took tango lessons—anything he could do to guess what women would want. And I thought, "That's a great cartoon!" It reminded me of a dog trying to get adopted. Shel and I talked about it and decided that would be our cartoon, about a dog trying to be something he's not.

SHEL: Justin has this thing where he likes to assign animals to people. Our three kids are all so different from each other. We have a bird, a bear, and a little tiger cub, and we always tell them, "Be your animal. Be who you are. Be yourself."

JUSTIN: Yeah, "Bears don't fly, so don't worry about it and don't compare yourself to a bird." We just want them to be OK with who they are.

KEN: *What did the real Gerald think of the film?*

JUSTIN: He loved it! He's got an action figure of himself now (Figure 13.4). We took pictures of him with it at our film premiere. He happened to be wearing the same shirt as the puppet that day, so it's a great shot!

SHEL: Yeah, he wanted to show the film to his church group. He loved it.

Figure 13.4

The real Gerald and his puppet counterpart. (© Justin and Shel Rasch.)

KEN: *How did your home studio setup evolve, in terms of the equipment and tools you used?*

JUSTIN: I started by shooting my very first stop-motion tests with a webcam—just got some clay puppets together with some wire and moved them around. From there we both just taught ourselves how to make molds, armatures, and foam latex, learning a lot of things through StopMotionAnimation.com and other resources. Then, we invested in a digital SLR Nikon D70 and used a spycam looking through the viewfinder for the live feed into MonkeyJam, which was the first capture program I had downloaded. And it worked great—we shot the whole film just like that, all in our garage with the sets that Shel had built (Figures 13.5).

SHEL: One thing we didn't know was that people could drill their tie-down holes as they go, so we drilled about 5,000 holes into the set floor so the dog could step anywhere.

JUSTIN: Yeah, we really didn't know what else to do, so we just made it a perforated floor and dirtied the hell out of it so it would look natural. Other than those materials, we just used Photoshop for removing wire rigs and After Effects for importing the image sequences and exporting the movie files. Then, Shel edited the film in Premiere.

Figure 13.5

Justin Rasch animates on an
exterior set built by Shel Rasch.
(© Justin and Shel Rasch.)

KEN: *How was* Gerald's Last Day *ultimately financed?*

SHEL: Credit cards! (laughs).

JUSTIN: Yes, over three years, it didn't cost as much for things like clay, wood, supplies, and a couple of cameras. That was a minor cost, but what really cost a lot was the music. We had no idea at the beginning how much it would be, but we wanted real quality music, and that cost about $8,000. That's where the credit cards came in, but it was worth every penny.

SHEL: It was two-thirds of our budget.

JUSTIN: Yes, about $5,000 for the film and another $8,000 for the music.

KEN: *How did that decision come about, to record a full orchestral score for the film?*

JUSTIN: The big dream for any filmmaker is to see your film on a big screen with live music playing along with your cartoon, just like in all the special features you see. That was all I wanted—that was the fantasy.

SHEL: Justin listens to film scores for fun or when he's animating and finds it very inspiring.

JUSTIN: Yeah, I get ideas for stories all the time from the music I listen to, so we really knew we wanted quality. We had some temp tracks we had put in along with the film as we were putting it together, so the composer and we would get a taste of what we wanted out of the film emotionally. The person who introduced us to our composer (Robert Litton) was Ryan McCulloch, who we just connected with online through our blogs. I believe he just forwarded me the link to Robert's website, and right away we thought his stuff was great. At that time, we had just started thinking about looking for a composer, so I sent him the basic idea of what the film was about, and he said, "Great—love the story! When do we meet?" We just brought some puppets and showed him what the film was going to be like, and he did the score.

SHEL: What was funny was that Ryan lives out in Florida, and for some reason we thought he was from Australia! Here was this guy who we think is halfway around the world sending us a link for a composer, who we find out lives just down the street from us, 10 minutes away. The next day, we find ourselves sitting down with Robert Litton, and we just hit it off immediately. He was awesome.

JUSTIN: Robert's like part of the family now, and we'd like to have him score all of our films from now on. It was such a great experience.

KEN: *I was talking to Ryan about that, too. It reminds me of when George Lucas was looking for a specific kind of score for* Star Wars, *Steven Spielberg introduced him to John Williams because of his work on* Jaws, *and the rest is history.*

SHEL: Yes, Robert is our John Williams.

KEN: *Through your production blog, you have developed quite a following online. How else did that affect the film before it was finally completed?*

SHEL: It definitely helped with the actual making of the film. In the beginning, a lot of the people we were meeting online were invaluable in terms of helping us and answering questions. At one point, someone had visited the blog and sent us an e-mail saying, "You know, your puppets look like they're cracking. Are you putting enough Pros-Aide in the paint?" and we were like, "What's Pros-Aide?" We just didn't know, but we learned so much through those connections online. In the end credits of our film, we thanked the online stop-motion community because we learned so much from them about how to make the film as we were going. The blog was our bridge to those people.

JUSTIN: Anybody can do it because it's all out there now, through the StopMotionAnimation.com message boards, too. Somebody in Ohio or wherever learning stop-motion on their own is not alone anymore because of all the information and people sharing online.

SHEL: We actually just went to a local screening of *Mary and Max* the other night, and a random CG animator in the audience recognized us from our blog.

JUSTIN: Yes, for the stop-motion community, our film became a known piece of work that was going to come out, and I think it was exciting for people. We think it's so cool that all the followers on our blog feed are spread out worldwide—from Africa, Australia, South America, India, all over Russia—and are seeing our site about stop-motion, this thing that we all love.

KEN: *When the film was completed, how did you organize getting it into so many festivals?*

(Justin laughs and points to Shel, who starts to blush.)

SHEL: I went a little overboard. There are a few sites online, in particular Withoutabox.com, which is used by most film festivals in America for their submissions. It's dangerously convenient because you click on a festival and it goes into your shopping cart, you collect a bunch of them, click "Buy," and it sends your submission to all those festivals in one shot. Next time around, I won't submit to quite as many because it got really expensive pretty quickly. But by going to so many of those festivals, we learned a ton. Next time around, we'll know more about which ones to enter and which ones not to bother with. We've gotten into almost 50% of the ones we've entered, but some of the festivals we got into, even if we won awards there, didn't really matter if it was a really disorganized. Another thing we learned is that if you start winning awards, then other festivals approach *you*, which means not having to pay entry fees.

JUSTIN: Basically, Shel said, "Hey, we spent three years making this film, it's our dream to see it on the big screen, and we're making another short and a feature someday, so we want exposure. Let's get it out there and put it into festivals."

SHEL: Plus, my sister lives in New York, Justin's sister is in Denver, and our family's in Washington, so we thought, "Let's get into the festivals there so we can see them and show them our film," and we've been able to do that with everyone.

JUSTIN: Another great thing that came out of this film in the festival circuit is that we got full financing for our next short film project, which is huge! The person who contacted us about the financing saw *Gerald's Last Day* on Delta Airlines. The Tribeca Film Festival had a contest where they played our film on the little airplane-seat monitors for four months. About 90,000 people got to see it, so we were getting contacted every other day by total strangers saying, "Wow, I loved it! Where can I buy it?" And one of them wanted to help us with the next film, so it was an incredible series of events that happened, and it was so exciting.

SHEL: So far, we've won our musical score budget on the film back just through contest wins, and we haven't even put it into distribution or sold a single copy yet.

JUSTIN: At the film festivals, we go to a lot of the seminars and speaker panels, and they often mention how if you want to get financing, you need to show that your film makes money, even if it's $1.

SHEL: It gave us a goal—that we have to make $13,001.

JUSTIN: Yes, just one extra dollar to show them our work is profitable. (Laughs.) It's done incredibly well. Just this past weekend, we won our 18th "best animated short" award, and it's so nice hearing from people about how much they enjoyed the film.

SHEL: Especially when we're in the middle of making another one. I've just been kicking butt making these spaceships and sets and putting in so many hours, it gets kind of desperate feeling after a while. It's like, "When is this ever going to end?" When you have a list with 5,000 things on it, it's hard to get excited about getting 50 of them done, you know? So, it's awesome to take these little film festival breaks in the middle of the deluge and get such positive feedback.

JUSTIN: Yeah, if we had known how hard *Gerald's Last Day* was going to be when we started it, we never would have done it. It was an incredibly complicated bowl of soup we were jumping into.

KEN: *Were there any mishaps or tough moments where the process of making the film caused disagreements or obstacles that were hard to get through?*

SHEL: The biggest challenge was, first of all, that Justin didn't sleep.

JUSTIN: Yeah, we have priorities in our lives towards time with each other and with our kids, so all the filming would start at midnight, which was the only way to do it. It didn't affect me physically because I was so thrilled by the magic of it. I'd be exhausted by the end of the night, but when I pressed Play, it was so rewarding that I could get a couple hours of sleep and then be OK about going to my real job. It's all in preparation for taking two years off from the industry to make our feature film. That's the goal, so it was a means to an end. I want to get more sleep on this next project, though.

SHEL: The other big challenge was that it was all new to us, and neither of us is big on reading instructions—we just dive in—so we often had to redo stuff, which was frustrating. Once, I made three full puppets with the wrong kind of wire, so they all snapped really quickly. That kind of thing is heartbreaking. Another funny thing that happened was when Justin had a scene in the film where the dog is throwing his dish around and food was flying everywhere (Figure 13.6). He used about 18 pieces of cat food, each one held up by a wire, and he got halfway through the shot, but it was 6 a.m., and he had to get some sleep.

Figure 13.6

Still image of Gerald throwing food suspended on wires. (© Justin and Shel Rasch.)

JUSTIN: Shots like that usually have to be done all in one go, but unfortunately I had to leave it. A couple nights later I went back to the set, and all the pieces were gone. Our cat had gotten in there and eaten all the food! I had to use the frame grabber to look at the action in my last few frames and pick up where I left off as best I could. Nobody noticed, so it was OK.

SHEL: Sure, we would disagree on things because we're both strong minded and a bit obsessed. But we also know each other really well and trust each other's instincts, which lets us each back off when we know we need to.

JUSTIN: One of Shel's jobs was producing the whole film, so she was there to help me get the film done and make me efficient in how I approached my work.

SHEL: Justin wanted to shoot linear—shooting the dog and then the people's reactions in the proper order—but that meant we had to keep moving the whole set around for each shot . . . major hassle. So, I told him he should do all of the dog and people shots separately and intercut them later. Most of the time, reluctantly, he would, but sometimes he really felt he needed to see the reactions together from an acting point of view.

JUSTIN: Yeah, for me, sometimes I just needed to feel the flow of it, see those three shots cut together, and feel the reward of that. If I couldn't see the shots cut together for a long time, it was disheartening.

SHEL: And Justin was living on those rewards instead of sleep. So, at those times, I would just say, "OK babe, we'll turn the set around."

JUSTIN: Many times, as well, I would work, and then Shel would critique my shot the next morning. Sometimes the shots were really hard, and I would feel like they practically killed me, but Shel would honestly feel like it should be reshot and didn't work. I'd feel deflated, but I didn't take it personally because she was right—it wasn't good enough. Other times, she would think a shot was OK, and I wouldn't think it was good enough. So, it was actually really easy working together.

SHEL: That's why we're doing it again!

JUSTIN: *Gerald's Last Day* was our first-ever experience with stop-motion, and our goal was to learn the craft, get exposure, and seek out financing for future projects through getting our work in the festival circuit. Now, our next short film is fully paid for, which is incredible for our future in this medium, so there are all kinds of things in place now going into this project that we didn't have the possibility or the knowledge of doing before. We just got back from another festival, and on the plane we were just tripping out over how professional things are getting, compared to how it used to be. We're still doing the same stuff, in our garage making a cartoon, but now we have access to equipment like better lights and cameras (Figures 13.7).

Figure 13.7

Shel Rasch touches up a spaceship for *Line*.

SHEL: A big difference is we know what that equipment is now and why we need it, whereas before, we went into it knowing very little. We decided to simplify our new film by having only two characters instead of nine, and one set, but then we totally complicated it by deciding to shoot it in stereoscopic 3D.

JUSTIN: Yeah, we finally feel like we know what we're doing, so we can take it to the next level, and then we were thinking about 3D and wondering, "Do we really want to do this?" But we decided to tackle it since 3D is a big marketable thing now, even for short films. Also, as directors, it makes us more appealing for investors that we know how to do it since we ultimately want to create a feature film next, and all new animated films seem to be in 3D.

SHEL: The 3D filming was another thing that came from the Delta Airlines screenings, where someone called us up and asked if we were considering doing our next project that way. They said they would be willing to help us and get us all set up to do it.

JUSTIN: Jason Goodman is based in Burbank at a 3D company and offered to come over and be our 3D director of photography, since he was really impressed that Shel and I basically made our entire film on our own. He hadn't seen that before.

SHEL: Yeah, he was more used to live-action films where you typically see about 500 people in the credits, and our credits were pretty much "Justin and Shel" all the way through. (Laughs.)

JUSTIN: With the 3D shooting, what I'm incredibly blown away by is that it really works! The first couple of tests we did, I was amazed seeing the results in After Effects, and that we can actually do 3D…at home! Who would have thought? I had this fantasy that Laika and these Magical Technicians of Justice were everywhere with the only capability for this, and here we are able to do it ourselves. It's mind blowing, although it is a bit more complicated in that there are more things to remember, you have twice as many images, and you need more storage space for files.

SHEL: And for setting up our shots, we're not just thinking about composition and lighting. Now, we're also thinking about depth, what should be in the foreground, what should be in the background, and what should stay right on the screen. And how intense do we want the 3D effect to be?

JUSTIN: Yeah, what you want in your face, and what you want less so. We have some moments in our new film that really pop out, but mostly we want to be tasteful about it, more like a View-Master look, which was more about 3D depth rather than being goofy in your face.

KEN: *I assume you're hoping to project it in 3D for certain screenings, too?*

JUSTIN: We have access to three different output formats in the shooting itself, all the way from IMAX to regular DVD or 3D, and the extra frames can be hidden or not on different tracks. There are about three or four 3D festivals out there right now in the world, but in a few years, most of them will have 3D showcases, so it's really great timing since we'll have this new piece to enter.

SHEL: All the TV manufacturers are also making in-home 3D TVs as well, so people are going to be looking for material. But for regular screens, it's still possible to project only the left- or right-eye view and show it as a regular film.

KEN: *I noticed on the blog that you have several interns helping you out this time.*

JUSTIN: We started getting contacted by people everywhere, through Facebook and our blog, asking if they could come by and see our studio and help us out. After about the fourth person who asked if they could intern with us, I asked Shel what she thought, and she said, "Bring them on!" Basically, she runs the shop and is going to run it on our feature as well.

SHEL: There are certainly things for them to do, but unless you have all the materials organized and designs ready, it's hard to give out tasks, so that's caused us to come up with a whole different style of working. Instead of hitting jobs here and there at a whim, I have to have up to four people's tasks prepared. It's hard to let go at times, since we're proud that *Gerald's Last Day* was only made by the two of us. This film will have so many more names on it. But we also have a lot of new, good friends now, and it helps us get things done so much faster. Of course, when we do our feature, we can't do everything ourselves, so this is good practice.

KEN: *Do your kids have any aspirations to get into animation as well?*

SHEL: Yes. Aedon, our 7-year-old, wants to be a farmer, a train driver, and a filmmaker. We figure that train driving will pay for the farm, and she can make her films in the barn. Our oldest son, Nicky, is a gifted sculptor and artist, so he wants to make films, video games, and comic books.

JUSTIN: Yes, he will definitely go into art professionally, and our other son, Shamus, grew up with video games. He wants to be a game designer and has tons of ideas.

SHEL: The ideas he comes up with are very much influenced by the games we've played at home, the physical challenges we've given to all our kids, and the problem solving we go through every day with our stop-motion antics. So, their minds are all being steeped in this art, and it's going to come out for them in different ways.

KEN: *What advice do you both have for anyone who wants to get into stop-motion professionally?*

SHEL: Pick up a camera, make a puppet, think of a story, and start shooting it. Just start, see how it comes out, and then make another one.

JUSTIN: Yeah, just do it. If you have a digital camera, just tape it down and start learning how to make things move, even before you have a story. One of our interns is a young guy who has been through art school already and now is in grad school because he wants to be a stop-motion animator. He's frustrated because he feels like he's starting from scratch learning about basic drawing and anatomy all over again, and he's anxious to get to be making films. The craft of animation is very important, in terms of getting educated in it, because otherwise you're just moving things without the principles. But you still don't have to spend thousands of dollars a year to be a stop-motion animator. You just have to have the will and discipline to dive in and make it happen. All the support you need is online these days. As an industry alone, stop-motion is tough and very difficult to keep steady work, finances, or a family—that's unacceptable to me as a husband and a parent. So, I would suggest making your animation knowledge well rounded enough that you can also find work in 2D or CG and keep going with stop-motion whenever the opportunity arises. The way we're doing it, working in CG and pursuing stop-motion as our hobby, is the best way for us.

SHEL: And that way, when it gets tough, we can look at each other and say, "Remember, we're doing this for fun."

Bibliography and Further Reading

Books, Articles, and Publications on Stop-Motion Animation

Anderson, Wes. 1999. *The Making of Fantastic Mr. Fox: A Film by Wes Anderson Based on the Book by Roald Dahl.* Rizzoli.

Brierton, Tom. 2002. *Stop-Motion Armature Machining: A Construction Manual.* McFarland & Company.

Brierton, Tom. 2004. *Stop-Motion Puppet Sculpting: A Manual of Foam Injection, Build-Up and Finishing Techniques.* McFarland & Company.

Brierton, Tom. 2006. *Stop-Motion Filming and Performance: A Guide to Cameras, Lighting and Dramatic Techniques.* McFarland & Company.

Burton, Tim. 2006. *Burton on Burton: Revised Edition.* Faber & Faber.

Cotte, Oliver. 2007. *Secrets of Oscar-Winning Animation: Behind the Scenes of 13 Classic Short Animations.* Focal Press.

Culhane, Shamus. 1998. *Talking Animals and Other People.* Da Capo Press. [Includes a section on Lou Bunin.]

Fordham, Joe. 2009. "*Coraline*: A Handmade World," *Cinefex* 117.

Frierson, Michael. 1994. *Clay Animation: American Highlights 1908 to the Present.* Twayne Publishers.

Goldschmidt, Rick. 2001. *The Enchanted World of Rankin/Bass: A Portfolio.* Miser Bros. Press.

Goldschmidt, Rick. 2001. *Rudolph the Red-Nosed Reindeer: The Making of the Rankin/Bass Holiday Classic.* Miser Bros. Press.

Harryhausen, Ray, and Tony Dalton. 2004. *Ray Harryhausen: An Animated Life.* Billboard Books.

Harryhausen, Ray, and Tony Dalton. 2006. *The Art of Ray Harryhausen.* Billboard Books.

Harryhausen, Ray, and Tony Dalton. 2008. *A Century of Stop-Motion Animation: From Melies to Aardman.* Watson-Guptill.

Holman, Bruce L. 1975. *Puppet Animation in the Cinema: History and Technique.* A.S. Barnes.

Jones, Stephen. 2009. *Coraline: A Visual Companion.* It Books.

Lane, Andy. 2003. *Creating Creature Comforts: The Award-Winning Animation Brought to Life from the Creators of Chicken Run and Wallace and Gromit.* Boxtree Ltd.

Lane, Andy, and Paul Simpson. 2005. *The Art of Wallace & Gromit: The Curse of the Were-Rabbit.* Titan Books.

Lord, Peter, and Brian Sibley. 2004. *Creating 3D Animation: The Aardman Book of Filmmaking,* Harry N Abrams.

Mandell, Paul. 1984. "Hansel and Gretel." *Cinemagic* 28.

Purves, Barry. 2007. *Stop Motion: Passion, Process and Performance.* Focal Press.

Purves, Barry. 2010. *Basics Animation: Stop-Motion.* Ava Publishing.

Salisbury, Mark. 2005. *Tim Burton's Corpse Bride: An Invitation to the Wedding.* Newmarket.

Schechter, Harold, and David Everitt. 1980. *Film Tricks: Special Effects in the Movies.* H. Quist.

Shaw, Susannah. 2008. *Stop Motion: Craft Skills for Model Animation.* Focal Press.

Sibley, Brian. 2000. *Chicken Run: Hatching the Movie.* Harry N. Abrams.

Spess, Marc. 2000. *Secrets of Clay Animation Revealed 3!* Animate Clay.

Thompson, Frank. 1994/2002. *Tim Burton's The Nightmare Before Christmas: The Film, The Art, The Vision.* Disney Editions.

Turner, George E. and Dr. Orville Goldner 2005. *Spawn of Skull Island: The Making of King Kong.* Luminary Press.

Webber, Roy P. 2004. *The Dinosaur Films of Ray Harryhausen: Features, Early 16mm Experiments and Unrealized Projects,* McFarland & Company.

Authors. 1999. "Celebrating 100 Years of Stop-Motion Pioneers." *Cinefantastique* 31 (Nos. 1 and 2).

Other Useful Books about Animation and Puppetry

Beck, Jerry, and Todd McFarlane. 2003. *Outlaw Animation: Cutting-Edge Cartoons from the Spike and Mike Festivals.* Harry N. Abrams.

Beck, Jerry. 2005. *The Animated Movie Guide.* Chicago Review Press.

Beiman, Nancy. 2007. *Prepare to Board! Creating Story and Characters for Animated Features and Shorts.* Focal Press.

Beiman, Nancy. 2010. *Animated Performance*. Ava Publishing.

Blair, Preston. 1994. *Cartoon Animation*. Walter Foster.

Curell, David. 1975. *The Complete Book of Puppetry*. Plays.

Finch, Christopher. 1993. *Jim Henson: The Works—The Art, The Magic, The Imagination*. Random House.

Goldberg, Eric. 2008. *Character Animation Crash Course!* Silman-James Press.

Hahn, Don. 2008. *The Alchemy of Animation: Making an Animated Film in the Modern Age*. Disney Editions.

Hahn, Don. 2009. *Drawn to Life: 20 Golden Years of Disney Master Classes.* Volumes 1 and 2: The Walt Stanchfield Lectures. Focal Press.

Johnston, Ollie, and Frank Thomas. 1995. *The Illusion of Life: Disney Animation*. Disney Editions.

Laybourne, Kit. 1998. *The Animation Book*. Three Rivers Press. [Includes chapters on cut-out, object, and puppet animation.]

Levy, David. 2006. *Your Career in Animation: How to Survive and Thrive*. Allworth Press.

Levy, David. 2009. *Animation Development: From Pitch to Production*. Allworth Press.

Mazurkewich, Karen. 1999. *Cartoon Capers: The History of Canadian Animators*. McArthur & Company Publishing.

Simon, Mark. 2003. *Producing Independent 2D Character Animation: Making and Selling a Short Film*. Focal Press.

Solomon, Charles. 1994. *Enchanted Drawings: The History of Animation*. Random House Value Publishing.

Taylor, Richard. 2004. *The Encyclopedia of Animation Techniques*. Booksales. [Includes chapters on stop-motion puppets and sets.]

Whitaker, Harold, and John Halas. 2009. *Timing for Animation*. Focal Press.

White, Tony. 1988. *The Animator's Workbook: Step-by-Step Techniques of Drawn Animation*. Watson-Guptill.

White, Tony. 2006. *Animation from Pencils to Pixels: Classical Techniques for the Digital Animator*. Focal Press.

White, Tony. 2009. *How to Make Animated Films: Tony White's Complete Masterclass on the Traditional Principles of Animation*. Focal Press.

Williams, Richard. 2009. *The Animator's Survival Kit: A Manual of Methods, Principles and Formulas for Classical, Computer, Games, Stop Motion and Internet Animators*. Faber & Faber.

Online Resources Cited for the History of Stop-Motion Animation

Anthony Scott's StopMotionAnimation.com: http://www.stopmotionanimation.com

Caprino's World of Adventure: http://www.caprino.no

Cartoon Brew: http://www.cartoonbrew.com

The Crab with the Golden Claws: http://www.tintinologist.org/guides/screen/crab1947.html

Gumby: The Movie: http://www.premavision.com/studio/1990.htm

Internet Movie Database: http://www.imdb.com

Michael Sporn's Splog: Puppet Animation Category: http://www.michaelspornanimation.com/splog/?cat=20

Resource for British animation and comics: http://www.toonhound.com

Rick Goldschmidt's Enchanted World of Rankin/Bass: http://www.rankinbass.com

Website for Ladislas Starewitch by his own granddaughter, L.B. Martin-Starewitch: http://perso.wanadoo.fr/ls/tsommair

Wikipedia list of stop-motion films: http://en.wikipedia.org/wiki/List_of_stop_motion_films

Will Vinton's studio history and current projects: http://www.willvinton.net

Index

License Agreement/Notice of Limited Warranty

By opening the sealed disc container in this book, you agree to the following terms and conditions. If, upon reading the following license agreement and notice of limited warranty, you cannot agree to the terms and conditions set forth, return the unused book with unopened disc to the place where you purchased it for a refund.

License:

The enclosed software is copyrighted by the copyright holder(s) indicated on the software disc. You are licensed to copy the software onto a single computer for use by a single user and to a backup disc. You may not reproduce, make copies, or distribute copies or rent or lease the software in whole or in part, except with written permission of the copyright holder(s). You may transfer the enclosed disc only together with this license, and only if you destroy all other copies of the software and the transferee agrees to the terms of the license. You may not decompile, reverse assemble, or reverse engineer the software.

Notice of Limited Warranty:

The enclosed disc is warranted by Course Technology to be free of physical defects in materials and workmanship for a period of sixty (60) days from end user's purchase of the book/disc combination. During the sixty-day term of the limited warranty, Course Technology will provide a replacement disc upon the return of a defective disc.

Limited Liability:

THE SOLE REMEDY FOR BREACH OF THIS LIMITED WARRANTY SHALL CONSIST ENTIRELY OF REPLACEMENT OF THE DEFECTIVE DISC. IN NO EVENT SHALL COURSE TECHNOLOGY OR THE AUTHOR BE LIABLE FOR ANY OTHER DAMAGES, INCLUDING LOSS OR CORRUPTION OF DATA, CHANGES IN THE FUNCTIONAL CHARACTERISTICS OF THE HARDWARE OR OPERATING SYSTEM, DELETERIOUS INTERACTION WITH OTHER SOFTWARE, OR ANY OTHER SPECIAL, INCIDENTAL, OR CONSEQUENTIAL DAMAGES THAT MAY ARISE, EVEN IF COURSE TECHNOLOGY AND/OR THE AUTHOR HAS PREVIOUSLY BEEN NOTIFIED THAT THE POSSIBILITY OF SUCH DAMAGES EXISTS.

Disclaimer of Warranties:

COURSE TECHNOLOGY AND THE AUTHOR SPECIFICALLY DISCLAIM ANY AND ALL OTHER WARRANTIES, EITHER EXPRESS OR IMPLIED, INCLUDING WARRANTIES OF MERCHANT-ABILITY, SUITABILITY TO A PARTICULAR TASK OR PURPOSE, OR FREEDOM FROM ERRORS. SOME STATES DO NOT ALLOW FOR EXCLUSION OF IMPLIED WARRANTIES OR LIMITATION OF INCIDENTAL OR CONSEQUENTIAL DAMAGES, SO THESE LIMITATIONS MIGHT NOT APPLY TO YOU.

Other:

This Agreement is governed by the laws of the State of Massachusetts without regard to choice of law principles. The United Convention of Contracts for the International Sale of Goods is specifically disclaimed. This Agreement constitutes the entire agreement between you and Course Technology regarding use of the software.